SCIENCE
OBSERVED

SCIENCE OBSERVED

Perspectives on the Social Study of Science

editors

KARIN D KNORR-CETINA
& MICHAEL MULKAY

SAGE Publications ● London ● Beverly Hills ● New Delhi

For information address

SAGE Publications Ltd
28 Banner Street
London EC1Y 8QE

 SAGE Publications India Pvt Ltd
C-236 Defence Colony
New Delhi 110 024
India

SAGE Publications Inc
275 South Beverly Drive
Beverly Hills, California 90212

British Library Cataloguing in Publication Data

Science observed.
    1. Science—social aspects
    I. Knorr-Cetina, Karin D.
    II. Mulkay, Michael
    306'.45   P175.5   82-042701

    ISBN 0-8039-9782-5
    ISBN 0-8039-9783-3 Pbk

Printed in Great Britain by
J. W. Arrowsmith Ltd., Bristol

Contents

Preface

Preface

Our aim in this book is to bring together within one volume a series of statements presenting systematically the most recent developments within the sociology of science. What one identifies as an interesting new development depends partly, of course, on one's own interests and analytical inclinations. In addition, it is not always possible to persuade those involved in such developments to spare the time to write the kind of general, programmatic formulation required for the present book. Thus we cannot claim that our coverage is completely comprehensive. Nevertheless, we do claim that readers of this book will find in the chapters below a useful survey of much of the recent work in social studies of science that is exploring new analytical possibilities.

A book along the lines of this volume is urgently needed, not only by students but also by established researchers in the area and in related fields, because the last few years have seen a dramatic increase in the range of analytical positions used in studying science as a social phenomenon. During the 1960s, the sociology of science owed its impetus to the influential writings of Robert Merton and, to a lesser extent, to the quantitative work of Derek Price. During the 1970s, considerable effort was given to applying and refining various ideas proposed by Thomas Kuhn. Although there was much critical debate between those adhering to these two major research programmes, we can now see in retrospect that both programmes were traditional in their conception of sociological research and in their own research practices.

Since the late 1970s, the situation has changed rapidly. On the one hand, we have distinctive research programmes which began some years earlier now coming to maturity. Examples of these are to be found in what has come to be called the Edinburgh School of interest theory (see chapter 2 by Barnes) and the relativist programme (see chapter 4 by Collins). At the same time, these perspectives are already generating critiques and modifications (see, for example, the weak programme of Chubin and Restivo in chapter 3). Furthermore, there are radically new approaches which grow partly out of the application to science of new analytical perspectives and research methodologies appearing in the wider realm of social analysis; for example, the ethnomethodological study of science (see chapter 8 by Lynch, Livingston and Garfinkel, and chapter 9 by Woolgar), the discourse analysis programme (see chapter 7 by Mulkay, Potter and Yearley), and the constructivist/ethnographic study of scientific work (see chapter 5 by Knorr-Cetina and chapter 6 by Latour).

Such a rush of new analytical perspectives on social studies of science can easily lead to confusion; and confusion can lead, in turn, to misunderstanding and ill-informed rejection. We hope this book will help to reduce the confusion, whilst at the same time encouraging critical, yet sympathetic, debate and a lively exchange of views. In each chapter below, one or more scholars provide an exposition of and a justification for their particular approach to the analysis of science as a social phenomenon. The references accompanying each chapter furnish a basic introduction to the research literature for each specific approach. We hope that the text as a whole offers a helpful guide through some of the complexities of recent developments in the sociology of science. As such it should be useful for sociology students, for students of social studies of science, for sociologists of science who are unfamiliar with one or more of these developments, and for those friendly historians and philosophers who take notice of empirical investigations of the social world of science. Moreover, because so many recent analytical innovations in sociology at large are being put seriously to work in the study of science, we believe that sociologists in general can benefit greatly by dipping into this collection of interpretative explorations and by comparing the achievements of the perspectives here on view.

We are much obliged to our contributors for the effort they have made to present and summarize their own work and that of relevant colleagues. We wish to thank the Center for the Study of Science in Society, Virginia Polytechnic Institute and State University, and the Department of Sociology, University of York, for helping with the preparation of the manuscript.

Karin Knorr-Cetina
Michael Mulkay

1

Introduction:
Emerging Principles in Social
Studies of Science

Karin D. Knorr-Cetina
Wesleyan University, USA
Michael Mulkay
University of York, UK

Several times in recent years we have witnessed the appearance of new analytical perspectives in social studies of science. Inspired by wider developments in philosophy and sociology, these perspectives have redefined traditional concerns in the study of science and reformulated problems of current interest and relevance. All of these perspectives are sustained by a programme of detailed empirical research which substantiates and elaborates their theoretical concerns. Those included in this volume are as follows: the ethnomethodological study of scientific practice (chapters 8 and 9); the discourse analysis of scientists' talk, writing and pictures (chapter 7); the ethnography of scientific work (chapters 5 and 6); the relativist programme in science studies (chapter 4); and the sociology of knowledge perspective in 'strong' and 'weak' versions (chapters 2 and 3). It is impossible to identify a single set of characteristics shared by all of these analytical positions. Nevertheless, there are certain broad themes which link them together through a series of family resemblances. In these introductory remarks, we will focus on four themes which are common to most of the following chapters. These themes are, first, a concern to include the technical content of science within the scope of sociological analysis; second, whether to adopt an internalist or an externalist methodology in the study of science; third, the 'linguistic turn' underlying several of these perspectives; and fourth, their rejection of traditional distinctions such as that between the social and the scientific. In sketching these characteristics, we pass over some of the major divides which separate the above perspectives from each other. Without fail, the attention of the reader will be drawn to these differences in subsequent chapters.

The rise of the sociology of scientific knowledge

Perhaps the most significant event in the social study of science since the emergence of the sociology of science pioneered by Robert Merton in the 1930s is the rise of a genuine sociology of scientific knowledge in the 1970s. For the first time in the history of sociological thought there was a vigorous and systematic effort to subject natural and technological scientific knowledge to the same scrutiny which has long been brought to bear on other systems of beliefs, such as religious and philosophical knowledge or political thought. The sociology of knowledge has been broadly defined as a theory of the social or existential conditioning of thought (Mannheim, 1954). Its roots are found in the writings of Marx and Durkheim, its development as an autonomous discipline is commonly credited to Max Scheler (1926) and Karl Mannheim (1954). Several authors have recently traced the long and varied history of the sociology of knowledge, and commented upon its virtual disappearance from view after the second world war (e.g., Barnes, 1974, 1977; Barber, 1975; Bloor, 1976; Mulkay, 1979a; Stehr, 1981; Stehr and Meja, 1982; Gieryn, 1982).

However, it appears that far from dying a premature death, the issues raised by the classical sociology of knowledge gained much potential and appeal during their slumber. As a result of subsequent developments in the philosophy and historiography of science, these problems were vigorously revived in a number of fresh approaches to the sociology of knowledge, including those spelled out in the works mentioned above (see in addition Collins, 1974, 1975; Restivo, 1975, 1978, 1982; Mulkay, 1979b; Latour and Woolgar, 1979; Krohn, 1980; Knorr-Cetina, 1981; the studies collected in Barnes and Shapin, 1979; Knorr, et al., 1980: 88–193; Collins, 1981; as well as virtually all contributions to this volume). These studies suggest that not only are we in a position to ask sociology of knowledge questions on the basis of a new empirical foundation, but that we are now able to address these questions with some hope of success to the most authoritative and esoteric system of knowledge in modern societies, that of the natural sciences. There are several lines of argument which are commonly cited in support of a new sociology of scientific knowledge (e.g., Bloor, 1976; Mulkay, 1979a; Hesse, 1980). These are best summarized as the thesis of the underdetermination of scientific theories by the evidence; and the thesis of the theory-ladenness of observation.

The notion that scientific theories are underdetermined by the data derives from a line of argument promoted by Duhem, Poincaré, Einstein and Quine.[1] In a nutshell, the thesis says that any theory can be maintained in face of any evidence, provided that we make sufficiently radical adjustments elsewhere in our beliefs. This follows from the fact that no one single theory or theoretical hypothesis can ever be extricated from 'the ever present web of collateral assumptions' so as to be open to conclusive refutation.[2] Rather, if certain observational consequences are entailed by a Theory in connection with a set of auxiliary hypotheses and these consequences do not materialize, we can only draw the weaker conclusion that the Theory and the auxiliary assumptions cannot both be true. It follows that a theory whose predictions do not materialize can always in principle be retained by making appropriate adjustments in the auxiliary hypotheses, if so desired. Conversely, it follows that there are in principle always alternative theories which are equally consistent with the evidence and which might reasonably be adopted by scientists.

As Laudan (1982) has recently reminded us, from the logical thesis of underdetermination it does not follow that social factors will have to be invoked to explain why scientists adopt a particular theory.[3] After all, there could be all kinds of factors which influence scientific choice in face of inconclusive evidence. Furthermore, the evidence need not *appear* inconclusive in practice even though it might be from a strictly logical point of view. Nevertheless, if the thesis that scientific theories are logically underdetermined by the evidence is correct, it removes one important constraint on theory acceptance which opens the way for social science investigation. Consider the opposite case, namely that only one out of many theoretical interpretations would ever be fully consistent with the evidence. If the proponents of this hypothesis could demonstrate that a set of data uniquely and conclusively supported their interpretation (which would have to be possible if logical determination existed), they ought to be able to gain acceptance of their interpretation even against the will of their opponents. To deny a demonstrably conclusive relationship of logical entailment would be like denying, in any non-contrived context, some of the most entrenched conventions of our language game. For example, it would be like denying that a bachelor is an unmarried man.

Thus, while the Duhem-Quine thesis of underdetermination does not prove that social factors structure scientists' theory choices, it does make it more likely that some kinds of non-logical factors play a role. Hence, it can be held *against* any attempt to continue to exempt natural scientific knowledge from social science investigation. If it is true that earlier sociologists of knowledge were prevented from subjecting natural and technological science to sociological analysis by the conviction that nature alone decides (entails) scientific theory choices, then sociology today should no longer be so prevented.

The thesis of the 'theory-ladenness' of observation supports the case for a sociology of scientific knowledge from a slightly different angle. The version of the thesis attributed to Kuhn and Feyerabend and supported by the arguments of Bohm, Hanson, and Toulmin appears to make two major points:[4] (1) observations are theory-impregnated in the sense that they involve auxiliary assumptions in the form of measurement theories, theories of the psychology of observation, theories of linguistic classification, etc.; and (2) observations are theory-impregnated in the sense that what counts as relevant and proper evidence is partly determined by the theoretical paradigm which the evidence is supposed to test. The first point comes down to the thesis of underdetermination, if the auxiliary assumptions on which observation depends are included among those mentioned above in connection with scientific theories. The implications we think are clear. If scientific observations are ridden with theoretical assumptions, then scientists can in principle always doubt a particular observation by challenging the auxiliary assumptions upon which it is based. As some historians and sociologists of science have documented, what counts as a proper and competent observation is indeed at stake in many scientific arguments (e.g., Collins, 1975; see the summary in Shapin, 1982). What bearing the evidence is thought to have on a theory depends on its being accepted as valid information, which in turn depends on the unproblematic acceptance of the background assumptions which are constitutive of the observations.

The second point made by the thesis of the theory-ladenness of observation has implications for the role of observations in theory choice. Observations cannot serve as independent arbiters in questions of theory choice if their relevance, their descriptive identification and their proper measurement depend on the theories involved. This part of the thesis denies that 'observations' remain stable and relevant under a specific description across competing or successive theories, thus

leading to the notion of incommensurable paradigms (Kuhn, 1970).
This idea has been challenged for portraying scientific change as a
succession of all-encompassing and mutually incomprehensible world-
views which leave no room for the diversity, multiple coherence and
flexibility of paradigm components observed in scientific practice
(cf., Mulkay, 1979a: 48). Yet even if the thesis of incommensurability
is relaxed to allow for the fact that proponents of different theories
can, in practice, often agree on a 'crucial' observation, it is plausible
to assume that scientists' theoretical preferences will inform their
appraisal of the experiment and the resources they mobilize for or
against the observation. The claims made in connection with the thesis
of the theory-ladenness of observation direct our attention to the
possible existence of such differential preferences. Sociologists have
concluded that it is open to them to study their form and their consequences in actual scientific practice.

In sum, the thesis of underdetermination of scientific theories by
the evidence and the thesis of the theory-ladenness of observation
support the case of those studies of science which do not exempt
knowledge production in the natural sciences from social science
investigation. These theses have helped to get the sociology of scientific knowledge off the ground. Yet they have also reopened the debate
on relativism in a form that is rife with polemics and misunderstandings. Since the earliest days of the sociology of knowledge, the charge
against relativism continues to be that it is an 'ideology of helpless
surrender' (Lucacs, 1974: 89) which cannot discriminate among different forms of knowledge (such as those of science and fascism).
Furthermore, it is claimed that any insistence on the universal social
conditioning of knowledge is self-refuting, since there is no reason to
accept the claims of a sociology of knowledge which must themselves
be seen as socially conditioned. To assess these charges, let us briefly
consider a distinction between epistemic relativism and judgmental
relativism.[5]

Epistemic relativism asserts that knowledge is rooted in a particular
time and culture. It holds that knowledge does not just mimic nature,
and insofar as scientific realism wishes to make such a claim, epistemic
relativism is anti-realist. On the other hand, judgmental relativism
appears to make the additional claims that all forms of knowledge are
'equally valid', and that we cannot compare different forms of knowledge and discriminate among them. If this were to mean that all
forms of knowledge are equally good for a particular agreed-upon
purpose it would lead to the consequences spelled out above and

to the traditional criticism levelled against relativism.

It should be clear, however, that judgmental relativism manifestly does not follow from epistemic relativism. The belief that scientific knowledge does not merely replicate nature *in no way* commits the epistemic relativist to the view that therefore all forms of knowledge will be equally successful in solving a practical problem, equally adequate in explaining a puzzling phenomenon or, in general, equally acceptable to all participants. Nor does it follow that we cannot discriminate between different forms of knowledge with a view to their relevance or adequacy in regard to a specific goal. Of course, some analysts may wish to argue for the assumptions of judgmental relativism.[6] But the study of the relationship between scientific knowledge and social life in no way entails these assumptions. To claim that judgmental relativism logically follows from epistemic relativism presupposes among other things that we know exactly what we mean by the assertion that knowledge is 'socially or existentially conditioned'. Yet it is precisely the project of the sociology of scientific knowledge to work out *in what sense* and *to what degree* we can speak coherently of knowledge as being rooted in social life. Conceivably, the results of this project may turn out to be perfectly consistent with an instrumentalist interpretation of knowledge or with other epistemological positions which contrast with judgmental relativism.

Methodological internalism

To talk about the emergence of a new sociology of scientific knowledge is not to suggest that there exists a single and clearly defined research programme which circumscribes the area. Rather, we are talking about an upsurge of studies relevant to sociology of knowledge questions.[7] Their common characteristic is that social scientists are for the first time engaged in a systematic investigation of the technical activities, judgments and interpretations of natural and technological scientists from a broadly sociological perspective. Several of the perspectives in which this goal is paramount adopt what can be described as a form of *methodological internalism*: the 'internal' practices of the scientific enterprise constitute the focus of inquiry. Methodological internalism should not be confused with the attempt to explain scientific belief exclusively in terms of technical-rational considerations imputed to scientists, a tendency evident in much traditional historiography and philosophy of science. Explanatory internalism, as the latter could be called, is unsympathetic to the idea that scientific knowledge may have other than 'scientific' explanations. In contrast, methodological internalists tend actively to entertain the possibility of social explanations, whatever these may be. As we shall see, some perspectives ignore questions of explanation, but still maintain their focus on the internal practices of science.

The methodological internalism found in recent social studies of science can be further characterized in terms of the following tendencies: (1) a preference for the microscopic study of scientific practice; (2) a tendency to give priority to the question HOW scientists go about talking and doing science over the question WHY they act as they do; and (3) a tendency to adopt what can loosely be described as a constructivist perspective in addition to the received perspective of the sociology of knowledge. Note that we are talking about tendencies; not all research programmes in the area necessarily subscribe to all three characterizations.

(1) The tendency to analyze scientists' practices in microscopic detail is not new. Historians of science have often preferred the detailed study of a particular period of scientific work or of a particular scientist's life to the study of collective social action. However, both sociology in general and social studies of science have until recently shown the opposite preference. For example, Mannheim's sociology of knowledge was in its classical period marked 'by a tendency to set up grandiose hypothetical schemes' (Coser, 1968: 433) which it sought to verify only on a very general level. Similarly, Durkheim analyzed the social origin of 'collective representations' such as systems of values or systems of classification and advocated a macro- rather than a microscopic methodology. Functionalist sociology of science and scientometrics also prefer the institutional level of analysis and the use of aggregate data. Some current internalist studies of science employ microscopic methods in conjunction with generalizations that refer to social collectivities (e.g., Young, 1977; MacKenzie, 1977; Barnes and Shapin, 1979; Restivo, 1982; see also Barnes, and Chubin and Restivo, this volume). The microscopism of recent science studies is a methodological principle rather than a principle of social explanation and is closely associated with sociologists' growing interest in the production of scientific knowledge.[8]

(2) Like the preference for a microscopic methodology, the tendency to give priority to the question HOW rather than to the question WHY is not limited to recent science studies. Microsociology in general in the last two decades has shown a marked inclination to refrain from

traditional forms of sociological theorizing. Some proponents of microsociology profess to be uninterested in furnishing sociological explanation and concentrate on providing a systematic description of *participants'* interpretative (explanatory) practices (Garfinkel, 1967). Others reject the notion that theories ought to be stated in terms of formal propositions sustained by unambiguous definitions and specified initial conditions. They substitute instead a version of theorizing which seeks to elaborate analytical frames of meaning capable of opening up new research questions and yielding a fresh stream of defensible interpretations in response to these questions (Geertz, 1973). The latter form of theorizing is imbued with what Gilbert Ryle called 'thick description' (1971). In both forms of inquiry, the question HOW rather than WHY receives most attention from the analyst.

Several perspectives in social studies of science have moved in this direction. Ethnographic studies of scientific work tend to advance theoretical frameworks in conjunction with thick description (cf., Latour and Woolgar, 1979; Knorr-Cetina, 1981; Traweek, 1982; see also Latour, and Knorr-Cetina, this volume). Ethnomethodological studies of scientific practice display no interest in theoretical explanation (e.g., Woolgar, 1981; Lynch, 1982; Lynch et al., and Woolgar, this volume). This commitment is shared by the programme of discourse analysis in science studies which rejects traditional forms of explanation on methodological grounds (e.g., Mulkay and Gilbert, 1982a; Mulkay, Potter and Yearley, this volume). Within these research traditions, the question HOW receives primary consideration. On the other hand, the relativist programme and research in the Edinburgh tradition continue to promote the development of explanatory hypotheses (e.g., Collins, 1981: 3ff.; and Collins, this volume; Bloor, 1976; Barnes, 1977; and Barnes, this volume). With the 'weak' programme and the Marxist tradition, the distinctive characteristic is an interest in critique (e.g., Restivo and Zenzen, 1978; Chubin and Restivo, this volume). Thus, these two latter perspectives treat sociological explanation as important only insofar as it leads to and makes possible effective practical action. Their concern with HOW questions, therefore, is dominant in the sense that the ultimate justification for their analysis lies in the practical realm. Analysis is valid when it tells us *how to change the world.*

(3) The inclination to adopt what can loosely be described as a constructivist perspective is characterized by a concern for the processes by which outcomes are brought about through the mundane transactions of participants. It entails the assumption that outcomes

are the result of participants' interactive and interpretative work. Within this perspective, the sociology of knowledge question of the 'social or existential conditioning of thought' is analyzed with a view to the (social) processes which are constitutive of the production and acceptance of knowledge claims. This constructivist approach to the production of scientific culture and action is closely allied to, and dependent on, the detailed microsociological study of scientists' routine practices and discourse. However, although this kind of microsociological approach dominates much recent academic analysis, there are clear signs of an opposing trend in which the interpenetration of science and wider social processes is emphasized (see Chubin and Restivo, this volume).

The 'linguistic turn' in social studies of science

The study of communication among scientists has a history that can be traced back almost to the very beginning of the sociology of science (cf., Edge, 1979). Until very recently, communication in science was conceived primarily in terms of the exchange of scientific products for some form of scientific credit and measured by means of citation and publication counts. This conception of communication treats language as a neutral medium for the transmission of information or as a mere channel through which social transactions take place. In contrast, some recent social studies of science have adopted the view that linguistic utterances are basically speech *actions* (Searle, 1969). Since human interaction to a significant extent consists of such speech actions, they must in themselves become a focus, and for some analysts *the* focus, of investigation.

As a consequence, a series of new questions has been raised about scientific communication. What are the persuasive functions of scientific speech acts and how do speech acts further participants' goals? How do speech acts become organized into orderly sequences of discourse? How are they turned into patterns of argument which appear 'rational' and 'coherent' to participants? Prompted to some extent by developments in literary criticism and by the emergence of a semiotic method of text analysis (Greimas), similar questions have been asked about scientific texts. Several distinctive, yet overlapping, approaches to the discourse of scientists can at present be differentiated: (1) the model of 'literary inscription' formulated by Latour and Woolgar (1979); (2) the analysis of the practical reasoning of scientists outlined below;

and (3) the 'discourse analysis' of Mulkay and Gilbert (1982b; see also Mulkay, Potter and Yearley, this volume).

(1) Latour and Woolgar's conception of scientific work as essentially a form of writing comes closest to the semiotic approach to discourse. These authors portray scientific activities as 'the organization of persuasion through literary inscription' (1979: 88). The process is depicted as a struggle for the transformation of conjectural statements which are linguistically qualified into statements of 'fact' formulated without linguistic qualification. Within this approach, the notion of 'writing' or of 'literary inscription' is a central part of the theoretical framework which guides the analysis. It is used to explicate scientists' preoccupations and to account for the scientific laboratory as an instrument of persuasion.

(2) The second approach distinguished above shares with the former an interest in the analysis of scientific writings. However, it equally emphasizes that scientists' informal practical reasoning is a process within which writing is embedded and through which meaning and significance is attributed to scientists' literary inscriptions. The organizational properties of scientists' talk and texts, the negotiation of meaning in scientific conversations, and the strategies of persuasion employed in scientific discourse are topics of investigation. Most analysts draw upon the practical reasoning of scientists both as a topic of analysis and as a resource in describing and accounting for scientific practice (e.g., Lynch, 1982; Woolgar, 1980; Knorr-Cetina, 1981; Law and Williams, 1982).

(3) The third approach mentioned above is perhaps the most radical in that it attributes absolute priority to the study of the organization of meaning in scientific discourse (e.g., Mulkay and Gilbert, 1982a and 1982b; Mulkay, Potter and Yearley, this volume). It treats the discourse of scientists as a topic of analysis, but objects to its use by the analyst as a resource to describe and explain action and belief. This concern with discourse rather than action is said to follow from the interpretative flexibility of scientists' accounts, from the variation of accounts between social contexts, and from the difficulties facing the analyst in his attempts to extract a coherent version of participants' actions and beliefs from the diverse interpretations generated by these same participants. Clearly, generalizations about scientific practice derived from scientists' accounts are only as dependable, as precise and as valid as the accounting practices on which they are based. The authors conclude that instead of relying on scientists' accounts as indicators of scientific practice, we first have to improve our understanding of these accounting

practices. The claim is made that, not only is discourse analysis a methodological priority, but also that it makes most traditional forms of analysis redundant.

Systematic inquiries into the properties of scientists' talk and writing partly overlap with ethnographic studies of scientific work (cf., Latour and Woolgar, 1979, Knorr-Cetina, 1981; Law and Williams 1982; Lynch, 1982). Though a wealth of material has already been accumulated (see Mulkay, Potter and Yearley, this volume), both perspectives are among the most recent developments in social studies of science. The linguistic turn in science studies reflects an awakening to the role of language which sociology in general has only recently experienced. Since the production of discourse which purports to have a systematic relationship to scientific work is such a crucial part of the scientific enterprise, its study promises to be particularly critical to the study of science as a social phenomenon.

The breakdown of received distinctions

Traditional sociology of knowledge and the received sociology of science have tended to consider the social side of science as something that exists apart from and in addition to the technical core of science. In keeping with everyday usage of the terms 'social' and 'scientific', some perspectives have implicitly *defined* the social element in science by contrasting it with the technical component. In general, it appears that the more recent studies of science have looked closely at the 'technical' work of science, the more thoroughly social an accomplishment it has turned out to be. The social has come increasingly to appear to be integral to the cognitive and technical, and the latter has come to seem to display those characteristics which have traditionally been attributed to social phenomena.

Studies of scientific 'reasoning' in the laboratory, during controversies, and generally on occasions when scientists communicate with each other, tend to document the negotiated or socially accomplished character of technical outcomes. Whether it is the nature of the things one 'sees' in scientific observation, the proper conduct of an experiment, or the adequacy of a theoretical interpretation, scientific agreement appears to be open to contestation and modification, a process often referred to as 'negotiation'. Through contestation and modification, the meaning of scientific observations as well as of theoretical interpretations tends to get selectively constructed and reconstructed in scientific practice.

The negotiability of scientific outcomes is seen as arising from the underdetermination of theoretical interpretations by the evidence which has been discussed above. Recent studies of scientific practice have therefore considered the negotiation of technical outcomes as a social process. This assumes that the negotiation of scientific outcomes cannot be fully understood as merely a necessary step in the process of dispelling initial uncertainties about the validity of results. It entails that scientific outcomes may depend on the argumentative skills, the prestige or other symbolic and material resources which participants mobilize to convince each other. If there exists an unavoidable indeterminacy in principle in relation to scientific decisions, then it may be that the rhetorical brilliance of those advocating a particular outcome, the political saliency of the findings, or the support proponents can draw on, etc., may tip the balance in favour of a specific choice. The negotiation of scientific reality documented in internalist studies of science is presented as a process of persuasion which involves, among other things, subtle linguistic strategies of argumentation. Persuasion can be considered to be a basically social phenomenon. If agreement in science is founded upon processes of persuasion and dissuasion, as several of the perspectives outlined below maintain, both the attainment and the dissolution of technical consensus in science can be taken to be social accomplishments.

A related sense in which the core of technical scientific inquiry is held to be 'social' refers to the contextual contingencies manifest in scientific work. Internalist studies of science describe scientific inquiry as a process in which decisions are occasioned in part by the local circumstances of the work. They have pointed out the logic of circumstances according to which scientists' decision criteria vary with the situation, and they have documented the idiosyncrasies of the local interpretations on which scientists draw to give meaning to seemingly universal conclusions. Contextual conditions nearly always involve 'social' factors and may have social explanations.

Reasoned decisions, then, are treated as decisions in which the variables selected for consideration and the values attributed to these variables depend on the specific situation. They are rooted in definitions of the situation which are partly constituted by the perceptions and beliefs of other participants in the situation, and which take into account the crystallized outcome of previous social action. Situational variables, of course, often originate in the larger social context or have other social explanations. A scientific decision itself may at the same time be a social strategy. There are a multitude of ways in which what has traditionally been called the 'social' appears to be part of the contextually contingent logic of technical inquiry.

At the same time, there is a sense in which the very distinction between 'social' and 'technical' is produced through scientists' own interpretative practices. It has been argued that practitioners (as well as social scientists) make reference to social factors in connection with scientific results which have not yet been fully established, but tend to exempt these results from social explanation when they have become generally accepted (Bloor, 1976; Latour and Woolgar, 1979). The transition from a scientist's knowledge *claim* to a taken-for-granted *object* in the real world is accompanied by a break in participants' use of social explanations (Mulkay and Gilbert, 1982b). For participants, established scientific results become part of an independent, technical realm, in relation to which 'social' factors have no explanatory relevance. As a result, as scientists continually revise their conceptions of the natural world, so they reinterpret the nature of their own and their colleagues' past and present actions (Gilbert and Mulkay, forthcoming). In the past, sociologists have tended to be dependent for their own conclusions on interpretative work of this kind, carried out by scientists. Only recently have sociologists begun to examine empirically practitioners' use of the distinction between the social and the scientific. However, one of the central tendencies in recent work has been to try to avoid adopting participants' folk sociology and to try to concentrate analytically instead on describing how participants construct and deconstruct the technical substance of the natural world along with their own social world of science.

Conclusion

Social studies of science today reflect tendencies in sociology in general, such as the increasing awareness of the relevance of language to sociological investigation, the move towards a sensitive methodology which can cope with the concrete course of human conduct, and the rejection of theorizing which is detached from close empirical study of the complexities of social action. In the most general sense, we can perhaps speak of an influx of the concerns of microsocial theory and methodology into science studies. This is accompanied in some cases by a pronounced concern to link the detailed study of scientists' actions and culture to an understanding of the overall structure of modern societies, and by a growing concern with the practical implications of our own knowledge.

These concerns have far-reaching consequences for the study of science. They have helped to revive and revitalize the daring questions posed by the classical sociology of knowledge, for which they promise to provide a new empirical foundation, as well as to generate questions and findings which have no precedents in prior sociological study of science. In the view of some authors, they have opened up the prospect of an epistemologically relevant sociology of science (Campbell, 1977).

On the preceding pages we have drawn attention to some of the pertinent characteristics of these new developments in the sociology of science. But we have hardly done them justice. Readers are now invited to sample them for themselves.

Notes

1. See Grunbaum (1960) for a summary and critical discussion of the arguments made by these authors.
2. Ibid., p. 76.
3. These claims have been made most forcefully by Bloor (1976: 12ff.) and Hesse (1980: 32ff.).
4. See Suppe (1974, particularly the introduction) for a summary and critical philosophical discussion of the arguments of these authors.
5. See Bhaskar (1979) for a more detailed elaboration of the distinction between epistemic and judgmental relativism.
6. Few authors have actually made these assumptions, as becomes clear upon closer reading of Mannheim (1954) or Feyerabend (1975).
7. This development owes much to 'cognitive' sociology of science which has, for some time, been interested in the relation between and interaction of social and cognitive factors in science (e.g., Whitley, 1972; Weingart, 1976). Present perspectives tend to reject the distinction between social and cognitive factors.
8. Some authors have attempted a mixture of the use of aggregate data and the use of a qualitative methodology oriented towards processes internal to a scientific specialty (see Studer and Chubin, 1980).

References

Barber, B. (1975) 'Toward a New View of the Sociology of Knowledge', pp. 102–16 in L. Coser (ed.), *The Idea of Social Structure*, New York: Harcourt, Brace, Jovanovich.

Barnes, B. (1974) *Scientific Knowledge and Sociological Theory*, London: Routledge & Kegan Paul.

Barnes, B. (1977) *Interests and the Growth of Knowledge*, London: Routledge & Kegan Paul.

Barnes, B. and S. Shapin (eds) (1979) *Natural Order*, London and Beverly Hills: Sage.

Bhaskar, R. (1979) *The Possibility of Naturalism: A Critique of the Contemporary Human Sciences*, Brighton, Sussex: Harvester Press.

Bloor, D. (1976) *Knowledge and Social Imagery*, London: Routledge & Kegan Paul.

Campbell, D. (1977) 'Descriptive Epistemology: Psychological, Sociological and Evolutionary', William James Lectures, Harvard University (Spring).

Collins, H. (1974) 'The TEA Set: Tacit Knowledge and Scientific Networks', *Science Studies*, 4: 165–85.

Collins, H. (1975) 'The Seven Sexes: A Study in the Sociology of a Phenomenon, or the Replication of Experiments in Physics', *Sociology*, 9: 206–24.

Collins, H. (ed.) (1981) 'Knowledge and Controversy: Studies of Modern Natural Science', *Social Studies of Science*, 11 (1), special issue.

Coser, L. (1968) 'Sociology of Knowledge', pp. 428–35 in D. Sills (ed.), *International Encyclopedia of the Social Sciences*, vol. 8, New York: Macmillan/Free Press.

Edge, D. (1979) 'Quantitative Measures of Communication in Science: A Critical Review', *History of Science*, 17: 102–34.

Feyerabend, P. (1975) *Against Method*, London: New Left Books.

Garfinkel, H. (1967) *Studies in Ethnomethodology*, Englewood Cliffs, NJ: Prentice-Hall.

Geertz, C. (1973) 'Thick Description: Towards an Interpretative Theory of Culture', pp. 3–20 in *The Interpretation of Cultures*, New York: Basic Books.

Gieryn, T. (1982) 'Durkheim's Sociology of Scientific Knowledge', *Journal of the History of the Behavioral Sciences*, 18: 107–29.

Gilbert, G. N. and Mulkay, M. (forthcoming) *Opening Pandora's Box: A Sociological Analysis of Scientists' Discourse*, Cambridge and New York: Cambridge University Press.

Grunbaum, A. (1960) 'The Duhemian Argument', *Philosophy of Science*, 27 (1): 75–87.

Hesse, M. (1980) *Revolutions and Reconstructions in the Philosophy of Science*, Brighton, Sussex: Harvester Press.

Knorr-Cetina, K. D. (1981) *The Manufacture of Knowledge: An Essay on the Constructivist and Contextual Nature of Science*, Oxford: Pergamon Press.

Knorr, K., Krohn, R. and Whitley, R. (eds) (1980) *The Social Process of Scientific Investigation*, Sociology of the Sciences Yearbook, vol. 4, Boston and Dordrecht: D. Reidel.

Krohn, R. (1980) 'Toward the Empirical Study of Scientific Practice, introduction', pp. vii–xxv in K. Knorr, R. Krohn and R. Whitley (eds), *The Social Process of Scientific Investigation, Sociology of the Sciences Yearbook*, vol. 4, Boston and Dordrecht: D. Reidel.

Kuhn, T. (1970) *The Structure of Scientific Revolutions*, Chicago: University of Chicago Press (second enlarged edition).

Latour, B. and Woolgar, S. (1979) *Laboratory Life. The Social Construction of Scientific Facts*, London and Beverly Hills: Sage.

Laudan, L. (1982) 'Overestimating Underdetermination', paper presented at the Philosophy Colloquium, Virginia Polytechnic Institute and State University, Blacksburg, Va. (April).

Law, J. and Williams, R. (1982) 'Putting Facts Together: A Study of Scientific Persuasion', *Social Studies of Science*, 12 (4): 535–58.

Lucacs, G. (1974) *Die Zerstörung der Vernunft*, Bd. 3, Neuwied: Luchterhand.

Lynch, M. (1982) *Art and Artifacts in Laboratory Science*, London: Routledge & Kegan Paul.

MacKenzie, D. (1977) 'The Development of Statistical Theory in Britain, 1865–1923: A Historical and Sociological Perspective', PhD dissertation, Edinburgh: University of Edinburgh.

Mannheim, K. (1954) *Ideology and Utopia: An Introduction to the Sociology of Knowledge*, New York: Harcourt Brace and World. (First published in German, 1929–31.)

Mulkay, M. (1979a) *Science and the Sociology of Knowledge*, London: George Allen and Unwin.

Mulkay, M. (1979b) 'Knowledge and Utility: Implications for the Sociology of Knowledge', *Social Studies of Science*, 9: 63–80.

Mulkay, M. and Gilbert, G. N. (1982a) 'What is the Ultimate Question? Some Remarks in Defence of the Analysis of Scientific Discourse', *Social Studies of Science*, 12 (1): 309–19.

Mulkay, M. and Gilbert, G. N. (1982b) 'Accounting for Error: How scientists construct their social world when they account for correct and incorrect belief', *Sociology*, 16 (2): 165–83.

Restivo, S. (1975) 'Toward a Sociology of Objectivity', *Sociological Analysis and Theory*, 5 (2): 155–83.

Restivo, S. (1982) 'The Epistemological Relevance of the Sociology of Science', in D. Campbell and A. Rosenberg (eds), *Proceedings of the Conference on Epistemologically Relevant Internalist Sociology of Science*.

Restivo, S. and Zenzen, M. (1978) 'A Humanistic Perspective on Science and Society', *Humanity and Society*, 2 (4): 211–36.

Ryle, G. (1971) 'Thinking and Reflecting', pp. 465–79 in *Collected Papers*, London: Hutchinson.

Scheler, M. (1926) *Die Wissensformen und die Gesellschaft*, Bern: Francke.

Searle, J. (1969) *Speech Acts*, London: Cambridge University Press.

Shapin, S. (1982) 'History of Science and its Sociological Reconstructions', *History of Science*, 20.

Stehr, N. (1981) 'The Magic Triangle: in Defense of a General Sociology of Knowledge', *Philosophy of the Social Sciences*, 11: 225–9.

Stehr, N. and Meja, V. (1982) 'Zur gegenwärtigen Lage wissenssoziologischer Konzeptionen', pp. 893–946 in V. Meja and N. Stehr (eds), *Streit um die*

Wissenssoziologie, Frankfurt am Main: Suhrkamp.

Studer, K. and Chubin, D. (1980) *The Cancer Mission, Social Contexts of Biomedical Research*, London and Beverly Hills: Sage.

Suppe, F. (1974) *The Structure of Scientific Theories*, Urbana, Ill.: University of Illinois Press.

Traweek, S. (1982) 'Uptime, Downtime, Spacetime and Power: An Ethnography of the Particle Physics Community in Japan and the US', PhD dissertation, Santa Cruz: University of California.

Weingart, P. (1976) *Wissensproduktion und Soziale Struktur*, Frankfurt am Main: Suhrkamp.

Whitley, R. (1972) 'Black Boxism and the Sociology of Science', pp. 61–92 in P. Halmos (ed.), *The Sociology of Science*, Sociological Review Monograph 18, Keele: University of Keele.

Woolgar, S. (1980) 'Discovery: Logic and Sequence in a Scientific Text', pp. 239–68 in K. Knorr, R. Krohn and R. Whitley (eds), *The Social Process of Scientific Investigation, Sociology of the Sciences Yearbook*, vol. 4, Boston and Dordrecht: D. Reidel.

Woolgar, S. (1981) 'Interests and Explanation in the Social Study of Science', *Social Studies of Science*, 11: 365–94.

Young, R. (1977) 'Science *is* Social Relations', *Radical Science Journal*, 5: 65–129.

2

On the Conventional Character of Knowledge and Cognition

Barry Barnes
University of Edinburgh

Introduction

The sociology of knowledge has had a chequered history. At one point, soon after the second world war, it appeared about to expire completely, and sociologists and epistemologists, concurring in the Pelagian misconceptions of the time, were tempted into premature obsequies. How premature is now all too clearly apparent. Over the last decade the subject has enjoyed a widespread and vigorous revival, so that its continuing existence and significance is no longer in doubt. Its problems are favoured foci for empirical investigation and theoretical analysis. Its practice is at last satisfactorily woven into the overall texture of sociological research.

In its current form, the sociology of knowledge is less restrictively conceived than before. It no longer attempts to study the content of cognition without any reference to cognitive processes and the contexts of activity wherein they are situated. Nor does it heed any evaluative distinction between knowledge and accepted belief. Traditional scruples about addressing what is true or valid, or rationally justified, have been overcome. Knowledge in general is held to be constitutively social in character, and hence an appropriate subject for sociological enquiry. Indeed our own natural science is a prominent focus for research — empirical research upon the generation, evaluation and employment of scientific culture, which recognizes no a priori constraints upon the form of its results. Whereas earlier work in the sociology of knowledge was (paradoxically) inspired

by the need to account for erroneous or distorted cognition, today
the basis of our own routine, 'rational' cognitive processes is the predominant concern: we have grown more authentically curious about
ourselves.

Now that it is again a firmly established field, the main developments in the sociology of knowledge will arise from its empirical
projects, and from comparable investigations in such diverse yet closely
related fields as cultural anthropology and the history of science. None
the less, at a lower level, there is still point in continuing to address
general problems, and in seeking clearer formulations of the overall
theoretical perspective of the field. Among academics generally, for
example, the constitutively social character of knowledge is not everywhere recognized. And even within the sociology of knowledge itself,
where the social character of knowledge may be routinely acknowledged, the *precise* implication of the assertion is often far from clear,
and remnants of earlier modes of thought abound. The social character
of knowledge is still portrayed as an optional extra, or, alternatively,
as something which stands in opposition to the character of knowledge
as a representation of reality.

There is a need to set out as precisely as possible what it is about
knowledge generally, including scientific knowledge, which gives it
its inalienable social, collective dimension. And having achieved such
an analysis, there is a need to illustrate and exemplify it until it becomes
obvious, or even platitudinous. Only in this way will there be laid down
a routine basis for further work unhampered by the remnants of earlier,
unduly individualistic, habits of thought. It is as a contribution to the
achievement of these two objectives that the present paper is designed.

There are obvious difficulties involved in any attempt to consider
knowledge as a whole, and delineate its general characteristics. In
particular it is difficult to establish the unrestricted scope of any such
account; and to find grounds for holding that it must apply, say, to
theoretical physics or dialectical materialism, or any other specific body
of doctrine not actually considered in detail at the outset. Fortunately,
the severity of this problem has been much alleviated by the demonstration that no absolute distinction can be drawn between theoretical and
observational concepts and statements. This is a finding which has been
examined in detail many times over the last few years, and is now
routinely accepted; it has been particularly carefully considered and
justified by Mary Hesse in her recent study of *The Structure of Scientific Inference*. Hesse's work indicates a general analogy between a
great range of concepts and forms of knowledge, including empirical

common sense and esoteric scientific theory. This implies that conclusions of very general significance can be derived from the study of specific, everyday, readily intelligible concepts. The abolition of the fact/theory distinction gives the study of simple examples of concept learning and use a greatly enhanced importance. In what follows, animal kinds and their properties form the basis for discussion. They serve well to illustrate many of the points to be made, and their ready intelligibility is plentiful compensation in those instances where esoteric and technical concepts might otherwise have made more vivid and impressive examples. The conclusions to be derived will, however, be offered as conjectures concerning concepts and beliefs generally, and those who would restrict their scope, or make exceptions, should accept that the need for justification lies upon their side, even though the argument for full generality is only touched upon briefly in this chapter.

The context of learning

The sociology of knowledge is an empirical discipline; insofar as its focus is verbally articulated knowledge its concern must be with the verbal utterances of various communities. As a starting point, such utterances can be addressed as instances of concept application, or as beliefs and assertions. The former will be the favoured approach here, although, as will be seen, it is immaterial in the long term which method of organizing the material is initially selected.

The present concern, then, is to obtain some understanding of concept application. And the obvious way is to consider how people learn to apply concepts — that is, how they learn to classify. Let us, accordingly, postulate some basic features of any context of learning. First, people learn as they move around in an indefinitely complex physical environment of which they are aware; learning takes place in the course of the reception of complex inputs of information from 'experience' or 'the world' or 'reality' or whatever term one favours. Secondly, learning always initially occurs within a social context; to learn to classify is to learn to employ the classifications of some community or culture, and this involves interaction with competent members of the culture.

These two postulates are of such importance to the argument that it is worthwhile to incorporate them into a rudimentary image or symbol of the learning context. Imagine, therefore, a neophyte concerned solely to master the ways of classifying the physical environment currently accepted by his culture. Let us characterize him as an incompetent learner, L, interacting with a competent member or teacher, T, in a particular environment. Our concern must be with the processes whereby the learner acquires and the teacher transmits competence in the employment of concepts. Two types of processes can be employed: ostension and generalization.

Ostension

Any attempt to make a direct association between a term, and an object, event, or process evident in the environment, I shall treat as an act of ostension. Since I shall be discussing animal kinds, the image of pointing and saying is the best symbol for such an act in the present context. Imagine T conveying the usage of term 'x' by repeatedly pointing to some particular and simultaneously saying 'x'. As a result, L acquires a series of memories of particulars, all associated with 'x': in practice, he remembers so many particular x's. For example, T might point to a succession of particular birds, and on each occasion say 'bird'. As a result, L would become familiar with a number of accepted instances of 'bird', and would himself take those instances simply as birds.[1]

Ostension is an essential element in all verbally mediated learning. It is the ingredient which knots terms to the environment itself. It shows directly the things to which terms properly apply. No account of language learning can omit ostension; for if the conditions of application of a term or concept are specified purely by verbal rules, new problems concerning the proper application of terms are generated by the rules themselves. A potentially infinite series of questions is generated, concerning the proper application of terms. Such a series terminates in actual situations only because ostensibly given indications of usage lead out of the morass.

Generalization

Generalizations connect terms together, and indicate associations between their instances. Thus, the generalizations attested by T provide L with standard expectations as to whether an instance of one term is also, or may become, or is in some way related to, an instance of another: 'birds are egg-layers', 'birds can fly', 'birds have feathers' are obvious examples. Like ostension, generalization is an essential ingredient in all verbally mediated learning. Generalizations provide expectations of experience. They are what make us regard a form of culture as a body of knowledge rather than a mere taxonomy. The form of a generalization is variable, and can be used to convey the manner or intensity of the association of the instances of its terms. With animal-kind terms, indications of probability are typically an important component of generalizations. The frequency of a relation may be indicated: 'birds can usually fly'; or its reliability: 'we think all birds have beaks'; or its analyticity, where an assertion is simply not allowed to be other than certain: 'birds just are feathered bipeds'. (In what follows the specific forms taken by generalizations are not of great importance; and although indications of probability are of some interest, their detailed character is not. Accordingly, although a symbol *p* will be attached to generalizations *G*, as an indicator of the probability [in whatever sense] associated with *G*, most of the arguments which ensue will be made assuming very highly probable or certain generalizations, or even analyticity. These arguments would only be strengthened by considering generalizations of lower probability.)

The Hesse net

In describing verbally mediated learning, it is not only necessary to refer to ostension and generalization; it is probably also sufficient. To convey the use of a term, *T* can make direct reference to the environment, which is just ostension broadly conceived as above; or he can use other words, which is just to present generalizations similarly broadly conceived. It is hard to imagine what further strategies are open to *T*; and here I shall assume that there are none. If this is so, then *L* acquires all his information about the concepts of his community via these two processes. And, since any *T* was once an *L*, it follows that all competent members of a community have built up their knowledge via such processes. This suggests that the knowledge of a competent member can be modelled by the scheme in Figure 1, which I shall call a *Hesse net* (cf. Hesse, 1974).

In Figure 1 a number of concepts, *C*, are shown, tied together by generalizations, *G*, each *G* with an associated 'probability', *p*. The net should be imagined extending out of the figure, involving more

FIGURE 1
Detail of the Hesse net

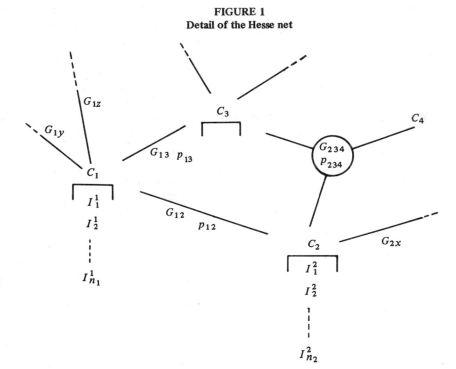

and more terms, until the entire conceptual resources possessed by the individual are included within it to comprise a connected whole. (Many of the concepts in a net will accordingly not be natural-kind terms, but will stand for processes or for properties. But no additional problems are thereby created. Such concepts function in generalizations as readily as do kind terms. And to associate a term with a behaviour or a property by ostension is no more difficult than to associate it with an object.) Finally, it will be seen that under every concept stands a number of specific instances thereof. These instances I shall call the *tension* of the associated concept.[2] A tension may be constructed entirely by acts of ostension. But it may also be synthesized verbally, using particularly strong forms of generalization. For example, the tension of 'animal' can be constructed, via statements like 'cows are animals' or 'pigs are animals', from the tensions of 'cow', 'pig' and the like. Note, however, that it remains possible at any time to point out animals *directly*, and thus to add to the tension of 'animal' by ostension. There are no inherently different kinds of term, some with tensions given by ostension, and some by verbal methods. Rather there are different preferences for the extent of the use of ostension and of verbal teaching strategies — preferences which will vary from context to context. Moreover, such preferences do not lie between reliance upon ostension *or* upon verbal strategies of definition; they lie between direct and indirect reliance upon ostension. Some tensions in any network must be constructed by ostension; and any other tensions, built up from these by verbal means, will as it were incorporate into themselves the results of previous ostensive activity. Thus the tensions of a net stand in a formal equivalence to each other: they are all fundamentally of one kind. One at each junction, the tensions provide the connections which attach the net to the physical environment.

The Hesse net is, in the last analysis, only a reification, a crude image derived from acts of linguistic usage. None the less, the structure of the net, once under the control of the imagination, is an invaluable tool in understanding the character of concept application. (My argument throughout requires that the reader be thoroughly conversant with this structure, although it can be readily memorized in a concrete manifestation, as in Figure 3; and there is no particular need to dwell upon the completely abstract representation in Figure 1.)

Concept application

The net has been presented as a model of the conceptual resources acquired by an individual as he becomes a competent member of his community. It summarizes everything that can be taught concerning proper usage of a term. The important thing now is to see that the acquisition of all that the culture can provide still leaves future concept application underdetermined and open-ended. Concepts are invariably applied to successions of particulars which differ in detail the one from the other. Proper competence is displayed by their use in ways which go beyond what is initially taught; for example, L shows that he knows what a dog is by correctly identifying dogs generally in his environment, and not just the particular instances of 'dog' given by T. How then does L accomplish such feats of identification?

As a first step in considering this problem imagine that a new particular, O, has to be labelled as C or not C purely by reference to the tension of the concept C. In this case everything rests upon the degree of resemblance between O and the particular instances in the tension of C. But the notion of 'degree of resemblance' is problematic. Any

functioning perceptual and cognitive apparatus will be able to make
out many patterns of similarity and of difference between O and
existing instances of C. Even after cognition and perception has been
structured by the social process of learning this will still be true. O
will always be discernibly similar to, yet different from, what has
gone before.

An assertion of resemblance therefore, which is what the application of a concept amounts to in this case, involves asserting that
similarities outweigh differences. But there is no scale for the weighting
of similarity against difference given in the nature of external reality,
or inherent in the nature of the mind. An agent could as well assert
insufficient resemblance and withhold application of the concept as far
as reality or reason is concerned. It follows that the tension of a term
such as 'dog' is an insufficient determinant of its subsequent usage.
All applications of 'dog' involve the contingent *judgment* that similarity outweighs difference in that case. This is true even where the
agent experiences the overwhelming psychological conviction that
resemblance is extremely strong. Such conviction does not arise from
the 'meaning' of a concept, but from the routine operation of the
agent's own perception and cognition — something which is contingent and revisable.

Thus, if concept application depends only upon the tension of a
term it is sociologically interesting in a profound sense. Not only is
it the case that the instances within the tension are part of received
culture,[3] the very processes whereby instances are one by one added
to the tension are processes involving socially situated judgment. To
put it another way: concept application is not a social activity in the
sense that it is determined by a culturally given classification of reality,
but a social activity which gives rise to and develops the pattern of that
very classification. The pattern does not account for the activity;
rather the activity accounts for the pattern.

It is true that a concept is always a part of a net, and that its application involves more than reference to the particular instances known
to fall into its tension. But when allowance is made for this it trans-
pires that the conclusion of the simple analysis above remains intact.
As part of a net, a concept will not normally be applied on the basis
of a single resemblance relation. If O is held to be a dog it will be
thought to resemble existing instances of 'dog' more than it resembles
instances of 'wolf' or any comparable term. It will be the greatest
perceived resemblance in a series of comparisons which is crucial. But
this merely increases the extent to which weightings of similarity and

difference have to be made, and thus it merely serves to reinforce the impact of what has already been said.

What, however, of the network of verbal generalizations (including perhaps definitions) in which a concept is included? Certainly such generalizations may have an important bearing upon how a concept is applied, but they do not in any circumstances solve the difficulty of the underdetermination of concept application. All that they can do at best is to effect a sideways shift in the location of the problem of resemblance. For example, the generalization 'dogs always have hair', can only take us across to another term, 'hair', where the problem of resemblance recurs. Whatever in the appearance of *O* is taken as a candidate for being hair will be perceptibly similar and different to the instances in the tension of 'hair'. Analogously, with any number of generalizations, even if they are explicitly presented as necessary conditions of the applicability of a term, the basic problem remains. 'Defining one's terms' is not a strategy which can provide a sufficient basis for their subsequent use.

Our inclination to apply a term in a given instance may be strengthened by taking heed of the verbal generalizations in which it appears, and the tensions of the terms to which it is thereby linked. But no strategy of definition can replace a problematic overall resemblance with an unproblematic 'actual' measure of resemblance in some particular defined respect. Definition strategies fail here because they lead only to some cluster of instances under a term, i.e. to a tension, wherein the difficulties of the resemblance relation recur. Tensions are the sources of similarity and difference, perceived and as yet unperceived, verbalized and unverbalized, in terms of which concept application must be legitimated.

The past usage of a term could only provide a sufficient basis for future usage if the relation of resemblance were replaced with one of perfect identity. This implies the existence of terms which are applicable only to identical instances, between which no discrimination is possible. The application of such terms would be unproblematic, and their involvement in verbal generalizations could be used to render the application of other terms unproblematic. 'All dogs and only dogs manifest dogginess' it might be held, whereupon the application of 'dog' would become unproblematic, given the existence of a tension of 'dogginess' containing only perfectly identical instances. (In such a case, of course, the tension need only contain one instance, which would embody or indeed *be* the very idea of dogginess.) Such an *essentialist* account of concept application would, if established, amount to a refutation of the claims of this paper. Fortunately, however, there is no empirical evidence which supports such an account, despite the attraction of an essentialist ontology to many philosophers. Essences appear not to act as magnets for our concepts. Actual processes of concept application do not involve identity: we get by without it. The open-ended use of natural-kind terms proceeds on the basis of nothing stronger than the resemblance of instances, and there is no way of avoiding the consequences of this with respect to these terms.

The outlines of the required account of concept application have now been set out. The key points are few in number: that concepts are learned from authoritative sources within particular physical environments; that the learning processes, ostension and generalization, build up a pattern of associations that can be imaged as a Hesse net; and finally, and very importantly, that the development of the pattern proceeds upon the basis of resemblance and not identity. Some implications of the account can now be examined; or more precisely, some of the themes already touched upon can be developed in more detail. It is surprising how much can be derived from such a simple starting point.

Implication A: delocalization

Consider a case where T and L are concerned to classify what is for both of them a new particular, O. L, being L, has not yet acquired all the terms current in his community. This can be conveniently symbolized in terms of a three-term culture available to T, but with one term remaining to be acquired by L (see Figure 2). L, deciding that O resembles the instances of C_2 more than those of C_1 calls O a C_2. However, T, who might well agree with L's assessment of resemblance, finds a still greater resemblance between O and the instances of C_3. Accordingly, L is informed that O is actually a C_3, and finds himself learning a new term through a process of ostension. Because and only because of ignorance of C_3, L is less competent than T in the use of C_2.

In this simple episode the correct application of terms is established by a process of social control operating in conjunction with the indications of experience. Very often a contrast is made between learning by observation and direct confrontation with the environment, and learning by the acceptance of authority and tradition. But the contrast is a false one: to understand the learning process is to understand the interdependent operation of both the contrasted factors. This interdependence, as symbolized above, runs through the whole range of learning processes. Indeed the particular scheme set out in the preceding paragraph can itself provide a passable model of actual processes of concept acquisition.

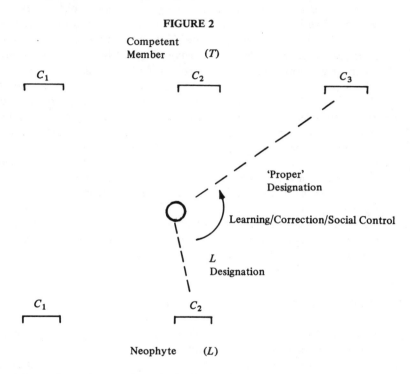

FIGURE 2

A hypothetical example with the form of Figure 2 has been discussed by T. S. Kuhn (1977). A boy, familiar with the terms 'duck' and 'goose' and appropriate instances, calls a large white bird a goose, only to be corrected by his father, who offers the proper designation 'swan'. As the boy's experience of swans increases, so his use of the term 'goose' becomes more competent. Moreover, it is difficult to see how this increase in competence could have been brought about either purely verbally, or through further ostensive indications of accepted instances of 'goose'. Evidently, knowing what a goose is involves knowing what a swan is. Proper application of the term 'goose' involves familiarity with accepted instances of 'swan'. By generalizing this point, we arrive at the interesting conclusion that competent usage of a term ideally

requires command of all the terms in the associated net. Atomistic
theories of concept application (and hence of 'meaning'), which consider solely the relationship between a single isolated concept and that
to which it applies, are inadequate. Delocalized accounts, which deal
with connected sets of concepts as organized wholes, are required.

Such accounts are sometimes thought to apply only to specific
sectors of verbal culture, namely those sectors related to communica-
tive interaction and properly studied by hermeneutic and interpretative
methods. A contrast is drawn between scientific or common-sense
descriptive terms and the concepts employed in history, literature,
philosophy or even everyday face-to-face interaction. The meaning of
the former, it is said, can be understood atomistically, in terms of
a correspondence with what they describe; but the latter constitute
connected systems of meaning, with holistic properties needing elucidation by hermeneutic techniques. In fact, however, atomistic conceptions
of 'meaning' have no relevance to any part of verbal culture; 'hermeneutic' methods are everywhere appropriate, whether to deal with 'being
is becoming' or 'the cat sat on the mat'. (Needless to say, 'hermeneutic'
methods point up the culturally specific forms in which concepts
are coherently organized and interrelated, and it is doubtless because
they thereby expose the conventional character of knowledge that they
have been little used in the analysis of science.)

Implication B: the application of a term is a judgment

When an individual refers to previous usage in order to ascertain what
a new particular should properly be called, he is confronted by a
complex array of similarities and differences. Even if he acts in good
faith, and as a normal 'reasonable' agent, he cannot find therein a
sufficient basis for selecting one term rather than another, or even
for asserting '*C*' rather than 'not *C*'. There are grounds to be found
in previous usage for *any* selection: whatever the new particular is
called can be made out as in accordance with previous usage. Therefore,
what the particular is *actually* called must be understood formally as
a contingent judgment of the agent or agents involved.

Concepts do not come with labels attached, carrying instructions
which tell us how they are to be used. We ourselves determine usage,
taking previous usage as precedent. Moreover, such precedent is corrig-
ible, since it is itself the product of judgments. It can always be said
that previous usage was wrong, that it weighed similarity and difference

incorrectly, and that it must be revised. Kinds of thing can be reclassified so that even previously paradigmatic examples of the proper usage of one term come to fall under another.

Thus, usage develops as a sequence of on the spot judgments each of which adds a particular to the tension of a term (or, where previous usage is revised, removes one). Accordingly, it is false to assume that usage is determined in advance, by meanings, rules, norms, logic or similar entities. Usage requires detailed empirical study at every point: agents develop usage in ways which at all times relate to their full complexity as social actors and as biological organisms. To understand concept application we must understand ourselves.

A convenient metaphor which preserves these points takes concepts as resources, to be applied as agents find point or purpose (Barnes, 1977). The tension of a term represents a conventional relationship of sameness between the instances within it. When agents apply the term to the next instance, one must ask what is the point in their developing the pattern of sameness in that particular way. It might be thought that such an image of concept application does not fit well with instances of unthinking, heavily routinized usage. But formally it remains appropriate, just as it can be appropriate to say that people decide to get dressed in the morning, and see the point of it, even though this is typically done routinely and without thought. The metaphor serves as a reminder that there is nothing inherently incorrect in alternative behaviour, and that the actual behaviour found, routinized as it is, must be understood in terms of its point, i.e. by the use of such notions as 'goal' or 'interest'.

Implication C: proper usage is agreed usage

Most of the time individuals apply classifications without hesitation, confident that their designations are correct and will be verified as correct by fellow members of their community. And, for the most part, such designations are so verified. Suppose, however, that two individuals in a community were to differ over what they took to be a routine act of concept application. For the first, a creature was obviously and indubitably a dog; for the second, it was a cat. No amount of discussion altered matters. What sounded like growling to the one, sounded like purring to the other. And although both agreed in attributing feline characteristics to the feet and canine aspects to the head, for the one it was clear that the latter outweighed the former, whereas the other was unable to understand how any reasonable man could neglect the really significant appearance of the feet and stress trivial features of the face and skull. Perhaps the two individuals were developing notions of sameness for different ends; or perhaps they possessed radically different inherent capabilities for perception and cognition.

Consider now the question of which of the two individuals had correctly labelled the creature. There is no absolute criterion available here. However, if, in their particular community, all other competent members happened to agree with the ascription 'dog', then that would be, as far as they were concerned, the correct ascription; and their communal behaviour would doubtless reflect this shared judgment. This judgment of correctness would, moreover, be the only shared judgment with any empirical consequences in the actual context in question. Hence, it would be the only such judgment of interest from a sociological point of view. For the most part, therefore, from a sociological viewpoint, proper usage is what is agreed to be proper usage; it is made evident by the practice of the relevant community (Wittgenstein, 1953). External evaluations of proper usage, such as, for example, an epistemologist might be tempted to apply to the discourse of an alien culture, have no sociological significance.

It is, of course, an empirical matter whether, and how far, a sense of proper concept application can be sustained in a collectivity. There is never any guarantee that consensus will continue unproblematically, or that disputes over usage will always be resolved by straightforward appeal to communal authority. Where members of a community differ on the proper application of a term and communal authority offers no resolution, then a consensus, if one is to be achieved at all, must be brought about by active negotiation. Members must seek to come to an agreement about usage in that particular case, perhaps hoping that, following from that precedent, future open-ended usage will be rendered less problematic. For example, parties may agree, as a matter of convention or nomenclature, that a certain, particular, problematic specimen be called 'moth' rather than 'butterfly'; and they may expect that as a result of such agreement the future labelling of 'similar' specimens will proceed without problems of consensus. Cases such as this are sometimes thought to result from an inadequate knowledge of the 'real meanings' of terms themselves; and occasionally the achievement of consensus in these cases is conceived of as 'discovery' of the 'real meaning'. But such consensus merely marks the successful negotiation of an extension of usage.

Implication D: equivalence

To the extent that a classification, or a body of knowledge, can be modelled by a Hesse net, an equivalence is implied with all others that can be so modelled. Thus, an equivalence is implied between our system of animal kinds and those in other cultures or subcultures, sustained by ancestors, aliens, deviants and experts. More generally, I have conjectured that *all* systems of verbal culture can be modelled as Hesse nets which, if correct, makes the nature of the implied equivalence of even greater interest.

There are two crucially significant ways in which different Hesse nets are always equivalent. Consider first the different tensions in any two nets. These represent different ways of clustering particulars together. But the clustering is something which we do to the particulars, not something which is already done in 'reality'. 'Reality' does not mind how we cluster it; 'reality' is simply the massively complex array of unverbalized information which we cluster. This suggests that *different nets stand equivalently in relation to 'reality' or to the physical environment.* Consider next the cognitive processes involved in acquiring, developing and revising networks. These reasoning processes are involved whichever network is considered, so they do not provide a basis for choosing between networks. This strongly suggests that *different nets stand equivalently as far as the possibility of 'rational justification' is concerned.* All systems of verbal culture are equally rationally-held: any sociological enquiry into the rationality of communities sustaining different, even conflicting, networks, should result in the same outcome in every case. These two equivalences (which will be more decisively established below) indicate that alternative classifications are *conventions* between which neither 'reality' nor 'pure reason' can discriminate. Accepted systems of classification are *institutions* which are socially sustained.

That accepted classifications of natural kinds invariably have the character of institutions is an eminently plausible hypothesis, and one which is perfectly clear and straightforward. Yet, not only is it ignored or denied in many academic fields, it is even, on occasion, found unintelligible. People are unable to understand how 'good' classifications, or 'rationally held' beliefs couched in terms of such classifications, can have anything of the social about them. Instead, socially sustained beliefs and classifications are *contrasted* with those arising from rational appraisal of experience or reality. If something is analyzed as a convention or an institution it is conceived of as some sort of fantasy, with no connection with the real world (or perhaps an inverted or spurious connection). But it is not that classifications are conventions *as opposed to* good representations of the world. Rather they are precisely conventional representations *of* the world.

The false contrast between the rational and the social, or between nature and culture, dies hard. Indeed, it even lingers in the writings of those who have made major contributions to the emergence of a properly impartial sociology of knowledge. Therefore, I shall reinforce the preceding arguments by use of a concrete example. It is taken from social anthropology, where a number of admirable studies of animal classification exist, and where the movement to a properly relativist treatment of knowledge and culture is well under way. It should be emphasized that in pointing to a certain residual ethnocentrism in the work to be cited, and to its tendency to treat our own natural kind classifications as special, no general criticism of its empirical merits or theoretical significance is intended.

Consider then Bulmer's (1967) discussion of Karam animal taxonomy. This work attempts to explain why, for the Karam, the cassowary occupies a 'special taxonomic status', being placed in the 'special' taxon *kobtiy*, set apart from the taxon *yakt* of birds and bats. As Bulmer formulates the problem, 'Why, to the Karam, is the cassowary not a bird?' The answer is allegedly that cassowaries perform a special role in Karam culture as representations of cross-cousins. Men's relations with cassowaries are structured in isomorphism to their relations with cross-cousins; and the special activities which thereby become appropriate with regard to the cassowary justify its being given a 'special taxonomic status'.

For the moment, the details of this explanation can be set aside. Let us accept it as plausible, and assume that the fieldwork upon which it is based is reliable. What is of immediate interest is the framework within which the explanation is set. It is assumed that *nature* and *culture* have separate effects upon Karam knowledge. Hence, the extent to which their knowledge properly reflects nature is first discussed as a method of setting limits on the role of culture. It is only because nature cannot account for the taxonomic status of the cassowary that culture is given the opportunity to do so. Culture can explain only what nature does not explain.

But how does Bulmer ascertain the extent to which Karam taxonomy actually corresponds with what exists in nature? This is done by comparing their taxonomy with our own, or, more precisely, with the taxonomy of our specialists in zoology and natural history. Our natural kinds, it is assumed, are the ones which correspond to real divisions in the nature of things. Hence, to the extent that Karam taxonomy corresponds to ours it is intelligible by reference to nature, and to the extent that it does not it is intelligible by reference to culture. This general explanatory scheme is clearly evident in the following:

at [the level of terminal taxa] Karam show an enormous, detailed and on the whole highly accurate knowledge of natural history, and...though, even with vertebrate animals, their terminal taxa only correspond well in about 60 per cent of cases with the species recognised by the scientific zoologist, they are nevertheless in general well aware of species differences among larger and more familiar creatures.

At the upper level of Karam taxonomy, however, objective biological facts no longer dominate the scene. They are still important, but they allow a far greater, almost infinitely varied, set of possibilities to the taxonomist. This is the level at which culture takes over and determines the selection of taxonomically significant characters. (Bulmer, 1967: 6)

A similar contrast between nature and culture is apparent in the work of Mary Douglas, for all that it has been so significant in stimulating a relativist approach to classification. Reviewing a range of work on the classification of physical nature, including Bulmer's 1967 paper, Douglas writes: 'Physical nature is masticated and driven through the cognitive meshes to satisfy social demands for clarity which *compete* with logical demands for consistency' (Douglas, 1973: 113, my italics).

This idea of competition between what is logical and natural on the one hand, and what derives from culture and society on the other, is deeply entrenched. Classifications may conform to the objective facts of nature *or* to cultural requirements. They may be logical or social. But this is the very opposite of what a careful examination reveals: we need to think in terms of *symbiosis*, not competition.

Bulmer's work indicates that the alternative zoological taxonomies of the Karam and ourselves can be modelled as alternative Hesse nets (see Figure 3). Both nets can be satisfactorily read on to reality (in the sense of the physical environment). It is not that one net distorts reality more or less than the other. How can the pattern of either net distort reality? Rather, reality provides the information incorporated in both nets: it has no preference for the one or the other. Thus, reality confers no privilege upon our methods of classification; they have no special anthropological significance. And as for reality, so too for logic. The equivalence of the alternative nets indicates a lack of any formal differences in the two related patterns of cognition, their

FIGURE 3

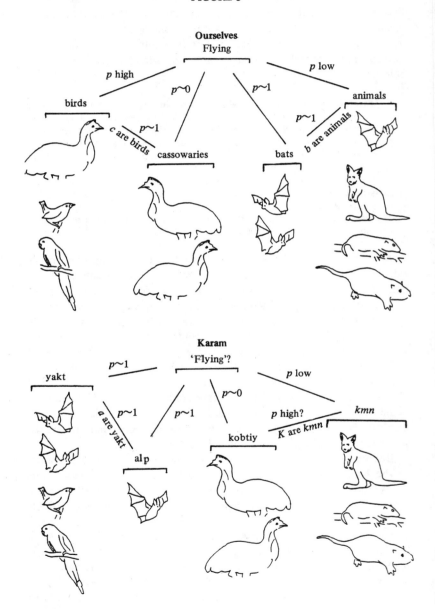

and ours. Again the alternatives stand equivalently. There are no differences in logical consistency to be found.

By assuming a privileged status for our own taxonomy Bulmer was led into organizing his admirable paper around the wrong question. It is misleading to enquire why, in Karam taxonomy, the cassowary is not a bird. This is analogous to asking: 'why to the British are kobtiy yakt?', which could readily lead on to pseudo-problems concerning the logical incompetence of the western mind. The real problems, with important questions being raised by both, are 'why, to the Karam, are kobtiy not yakt?' and 'why, to the British, are cassowaries birds?'[4]

Induction

So far the various generalizations on a network and the associated probabilities have scarcely been considered. Yet they constitute what is actually believed of the world. To talk of the equivalence of networks without proper consideration of generalizations and probabilities was premature, and requires immediate remedy. It will transpire, however, that nothing already asserted needs to be modified as a consequence.

The probabilities of generalizations were initially introduced as givens, transmitted on the basis of authority to new members of a community. But direct awareness and ongoing investigation of a particular environment must surely have some bearing on how probable this or that generalization is taken to be; so the problem arises of how the probabilities supplied by the ancestors relate to the information supplied by the world.

Universally, the processes of inference involved here are associative or ind ictive in style. People derive or legitimate expected future associations by reference to the strength of such associations in the past: the more strongly particulars are thought to have been associated in the past, the more are they expected to be associated together in the future. This inductive or associative characteristic of cognition is evident at many levels. General associative tendencies underlie simple, unconscious, non-verbal learning, such as we continually automatically engage in as organisms moving through a physical environment. Similarly, there is experimental evidence of basic inductive propensities operative in conscious, but primarily non-verbal problem-solving situations (Bruner et al., 1956). With regard to verbal culture, it has often been pointed out that messages can only transmit information if their component terms retain some of the associations acquired in earlier usage; an inductive presupposition is built into the way such messages are decoded. More generally, an inductive idiom is presumed whenever we engage in verbal discourse. Counter-inductive assertions are unintelligible just as they stand, for instance, 'I no longer believe that ducks have webbed feet, since all the ducks I have seen recently have had webbed feet.' In all the many existing styles of discourse and inference, accepted instances of a generalization tend to increase its p, and accepted counter-instances to decrease it. The opposite style produces bafflement, so that, for example, the 'since' in the quote above is likely to generate fundamental problems in most contexts of use.

Given all this, it is difficult to argue that basic inductive propensities are learned, or conventional or optional in character. Induction is a propensity we possess prior to learning, which is necessary for learning. Even the most heavily socialized kinds of learning depend upon prior inductive propensities, which structure the form of the operations whereby verbal messages are decoded and their information extracted. We should not shrink from admitting that cognitively we operate as inductive learning machines (Hesse, 1974). This crude formulation stresses that basic inductive propensities are inherent in our characteristics as organisms. They are the form of our cognitive apparatus, not conventions learned by that apparatus. We are congenitally inductive.

How then do our inductive propensities relate to the given probabilities of our accepted generalizations? It is plausible but none the less misconceived to set the two factors in opposition, and make induction from experience a continuing threat to the prior probabilities given by authority. Just as with concept application there is no inherent conflict between external nature and culture, so with the probability of generalizations there is no inherent conflict between our inner nature and culture. Indeed, the argument in each case is the same: the way we apply terms and the degree to which we accept generalizations are different sides of the same coin. It is true that when we accept something as confirming or disconfirming a generalization we tend to modify its probability appropriately. But, just as classifying something as this or that is, in the last analysis, a contingent judgment, so, as a consequence, is taking something as a confirmation of a particular generalization. And just as the application of a term involves consideration of all the terms in a network, so confirmation of a generalization involves, as a consequence, consideration of all the generalizations and associated probabilities. Thus, simply by reminding ourselves of the open-ended character of concept application, we can see at once that a given system of generalizations and prior probabilities can never be unproblematically revealed as incompatible with experience. In this sense, the different generalizations, and/or different associated probabilities, maintained in different cultures all stand on a par with each other. For example, if we hark back again to Figure 3, and then consider Bulmer's description of Karam life and the generalizations in which their animal-kind terms function, we find, insofar as we can tell, a perfectly adequate system of instrumentally applicable knowledge. Karam generalizations about kobtiy appear as reliable, and compatible with inductive propensities, as our generalizations about cassowaries. Neither external nor internal nature threatens either system.

It is important to note the limits of this form of argument, lest it be taken as an assertion that beliefs and convictions can be voluntarily, even whimsically, picked up and set down again. The argument does indeed show that an object can be *asserted* to be anything at all, and thus a confirmation of anything at all, without *formal* difficulties of any kind arising. But this is not to say that a given agent, in a given situation, is capable of *believing* anything at all. To assert something is one thing; to believe it another. A belief may formally have the character of a judgment, but judgments may be determined by circumstances: it may be out of the question to call a hawk a handsaw, in just the way that it may be out of the question to embark upon a suicidal course of action.

The point of the argument is not to show that agents can believe any random thing they wish of experience, but to indicate that the generalizations and associated probabilities on actual, existing networks never in themselves stand opposed to experience. In actual situations, the application of terms and the confirmation of generalizations are alternative abstractions from the same cognitive processes, which are themselves a part of an ongoing overall pattern of activity. In stable situations, the linguistic acts which place particulars under the tensions of concepts thereby sustain the probabilities of the generalizations wherein the concepts are employed. In a network model of the verbal component of the culture of a stable collectivity, the probabilities on the network are what the cognitive operations of the collectivity bring them to. The probabilities are compatible with some mode of interaction with and experience of the environment, since they are sustained by a community with that mode of interaction and experience. In a stable culture, the preferred modes of concept application and inductive inference, carried out in the given environment of the culture, both utilize and sustain the probabilities on the Hesse net. Conversely, in a changing culture, any clash between present inductive inferences and previously given probabilities is merely a clash between present inductive strategy and that of the ancestors.

It might be accepted that, in stable environments, inductive propensities, far from threatening a particular, communally accepted scheme of things, actually become organized into the very pattern which is the scheme; but questions might still be raised concerning a changing environment. If physical surroundings change, does this not force inductive inferences into conflict with accepted authority? An immediate 'no' can be given to this question simply by referring back to the earlier discussion of resemblances: any 'new' particular will have similarities and differences with the instances in the tensions of a net, and will thus not differ fundamentally from a routinely expected particular. No additional insights into the general properties of networks, or rather of the processes which networks represent, can be produced by consideration of oddities or unexpected events.

A well-worn example will serve to illustrate this point, as well as earlier themes about the relationship of concept application and confirmation. Imagine a community wherein animal kinds are ordered much as we informally order them, but which has something less than our range of familiarity with such kinds. And imagine that members of the culture encounter, for the first time as we would say, a creature which we would label with the term 'whale'. It is worth citing some of the simplest options among the innumerable ways in which the encounter might cognitively be dealt with.

One possibility is to take the visible appearance of the creature as grounds for calling it a 'fish'. However, if it were also routinely classified as 'live-bearing' and 'air-breathing', it would then disconfirm any accepted generalizations to the effect that 'fish are egg-laying' or 'fish cannot breathe air'. Alternatively the label 'animal' could be applied. This would remove pressure from all generalizations about fish, but perhaps at the cost of threatening others − 'all animals are land-based', for example, or 'animals are not finned'. In addition, routine visual identification of animals and fish based upon unverbalized intuitions of similarity and difference could become inadequate after such a designation. Another possibility, which is of particular importance to the present argument, involves insistence upon the completely 'new' character of the creature. It is neither fish nor animal, it might be said, but a new kind altogether − say, a 'whale'. With this strategy no existing generalizations need be disturbed. And, since the strategy is always possible, it follows, as was claimed earlier, that no threat to an existing scheme of things ever necessarily arises from a changing physical environment. Decisions between alternative strategies of this kind are continually made in the course of communal life, but they are not always explicitly recognized. Sometimes we blame our knowledge for what we ourselves have brought it to, or we praise its immunity to what we ourselves have cured it of. Thus, having invented the new kind 'whale', a community might note that all its previously existing knowledge was perfectly satisfactory within its appropriate scope, and that the knowledge had never covered whales. In a more iconoclastic mood, the same community might envisage replacing the old inadequate notion of fish (including whales) with a satisfactory notion of fish plus a new notion 'whale'. As conceived by such ex post facto analyses, the previous term 'fish' either did not cover instances properly called whales, and was thus adequate, or it did so cover them and was inadequate. Terms, however, do not cover future instances ahead of use. Ex post facto analysis of the allegedly predetermined domains of application of terms themselves, merely provides the occasion for stressing continuity with the ancestors or asserting superiority to them, according to taste.

Coherence

At any point in the history of a culture, however stable, there are innumerable ways of assimilating information from the environment along inductive lines. If such developments were the consequence of totally independent individual decisions, involving even just a part of the range of associative possibilities, then it would soon be impossible any longer to talk of a shared verbal culture; a massive breakdown of communication would soon ensue, and exchange of information would become impossible. There is, of course, no a priori reason why this should not happen, but there are known cases where in fact it does not; among them can be counted the Karam and ourselves, as well as practically anything we are inclined to call a culture. Clearly, in all existing cultures inferences show pattern, and hence are in some way restricted. The restrictions, however, are required neither by reality nor by our basic individual inductive propensities. They stand, just as the accepted forms of concept application stand, as the practices of some community, as institutions. Just as concept application is institutionalized, so is inductive inference: indeed, it has been shown that these are little more than alternative ways of talking of the same processes. Such processes, within a stable culture, display a coherent pattern.

One way of talking of such a pattern is to say that the members of a culture share a *theory*. For example, it can be said that we ourselves have accepted from the ancestors a 'species' theory. This is a convenient and economical way of referring to the pattern in our modes of inference concerning animal kinds: our strong inclination to make out all the instances we encounter as belonging to a fixed list of kinds; our organization of instances in life cycles; our assertions of between-species relationships; our references to sports, hybrids, teratogens and the like.

There can be no objection to presenting an economical description of our beliefs and inferences involving animal kinds as an account of our theory of species. Yet it is but a little way from here to the major error of idealist explanation, so frequently encountered in sociology, history and philosophy. The error consists in citing the theory imputed to agents as the *explanation* of the details of their belief and cognition. For example, in the present context, it consists in accounting for our beliefs and inferences about animal kinds as derived from and determined by our theory of species.

Such a position, given what has already been said, is clearly absurd. It has been held that no inherent restrictions bear upon the use of a concept or upon the particular conclusions which may be drawn from a generalization. But a theory is itself commonly understood to be a set of concepts and generalizations. Since there are no inherent restrictions upon concept application and modes of inference, and hence upon what a theory can be taken to imply, any attempt to invoke a theory as an explanation must accordingly be spurious. Yet there is no denying the popularity of this idealist mode of explanation, nor the temptation to explain cognition, in actual situations, as the consequence of holding to a theory.

A theory is not the explanation of restricted cognition in a culture; it simply *is* that restricted cognition. To *describe* the coherent character of a mode of cognition in terms of restrictions in the range of observed cognitive strategies is a tolerable idiom of representation, but then to make out the restrictions as the *explanations* of coherence is to complete a vicious circle. Coherent, restricted communal cognitions are institutions. To describe the specific characteristics of our representations of natural kinds, in contrast say to those of the Karam, is to describe alternative institutions. The explanatory problem is one standard throughout sociology, 'why this institution, in this context?' And, just as elsewhere in sociology it is absurd to explain a given pattern of action as determined by the very pattern which it displays, so too with a given pattern of cognition. (Or, to be more precise, so as a consequence with a given pattern of cognition; for cognition is not independent of action but a feature of it.)

Networks, goals and interests

Insofar as the argument in the foregoing is sound, it shows that knowledge is institutionalized cognition. Insofar as the exposition is clear, it reveals something of how cognition is institutionalized, and thus of the precise ways in which knowledge is a social phenomenon. These were the explicit objectives of the paper. The further question, 'why this institution, in this context?', is a general problem in sociological theory; this is the point where the sociology of knowledge has to proceed in step with the overall research front in sociology. None the less I shall continue a little further, and sketch the beginnings of an answer to the question.

In looking at the linguistic routines of a stable culture we are looking at institutions sustained by authority and an apparatus of control. Such institutions will have specific advantages for the culture, or for some sector of it; they will serve interests or further goals. There is, in addition, a diffuse collective advantage which derives from any form of co-ordination and routinization of behaviour, and which discourages any massive breakdown in it, once established. Any institution, in coming into being, creates a vested interest in its own continuation. For example, any system of animal kinds may serve as a basis for communication, the transmission of information, and thus prediction, contingent only upon the general maintenance of routines of usage. If someone shouts to us 'cassowaries are coming', or, among the Karam, if someone shouts something like 'kobtiy are coming', predictions can be made on the basis of transmitted information. But, in both cases, information is only successfully transmitted if both sender and receiver operate in terms of routinized, habituated, cognitive processes. Message encoding and decoding in stable contexts operate on a principle of maximum cognitive laziness. In any context where information is flowing there must be some tendency to make routine habituated cognitive operations the initial basis for decoding messages. Without some such tendency to cognitive laziness, innumerable alternative treatments of similarity/difference would be equally plausible.

In the idealized case of a fully stable culture, linguistic routines are sustained by some combination of specific interests or objectives, and diffused vested interests. Changes in such a set of routines arise, analogously, from changes in associated interests, or in the ability of some subsection of a community to further its interests at the expense of another. In general, the dynamics of institutions must be understood by reference to interests, and this is as true of linguistic routines as of routine activities. Tensions and probabilities on a Hesse net are modified over time so that shared interests are better served. The process whereby knowledge is evaluated, changed and re-evaluated involves continuing reference to shared goals and interests. But among such goals are specific, socially situated, predictive and technical requirements: it is not that agents operate by reference to goals and interests instead of considerations of technical and empirical adequacy; rather it is that their sense of technical and empirical adequacy is itself intelligible only in terms of contingent goals and interests.

Although this is not a new or startling hypothesis it is one that has received little attention. Invocation of interests is thought appropriate in relation to 'ideology' but not to natural knowledge, which is more commonly understood in terms of an image of disinterested contemplation. Only the pragmatists, and more recently Habermas and his school, have attempted to identify an essential connection between interests and the evaluation of knowledge. Accordingly, all current views of the connection are highly tentative and will indubitably require considerable modification as the subject is given more detailed consideration.

All that I shall attempt to do here is to present a simple example where the development of knowledge can be seen to be conditioned by goals and interests, and where specific technical and predictive goals figure prominently. Although appropriate examples do exist involving straightforward natural-kind terms (Dean, 1979), they do require a more extended and involved presentation than is appropriate here. Accordingly, I shall use a hypothetical example involving the human gender terms 'male' and 'female'; the reader will, I hope, already be familiar with some of the problems involved in identifying these kinds.

Imagine, then, a stable subculture wherein 'male' and 'female' are used of humans much as we ourselves use them. Instances of both kinds are routinely recognized and agreed upon; generalizations about both kinds can be said to occupy typical positions in a net, with tensions lying under them, and generalizations radiating from them. And since the subculture is stable, the institution of gender thus represented can be assumed to be, as it were, in equilibrium with the existing interests and goals running through the subculture. Now let us introduce a new interest or goal into the system. Imagine that the subculture becomes concerned to use generalizations about males as effectively as possible for predicting internal conditions in the human body, or future tendencies in a person's behaviour. (This can be symbolized by conceiving of our subculture as a scientific one, and imagining a grant being passed to it, tied to the project in question.) Present knowledge of males, routinely and unthinkingly interpreted, leads to successful predictions about males only some of the time in the context in question: the requirement is to obtain successful predictions more frequently. (Note that this project has nothing at all to do with increasing the truth content, so called, of a body of belief. The discussion concerns the utility of a conventional system, conventionally evaluated in a restricted context.) The new goal would no doubt lead to the empirical investigation of the characteristics of males, to attempts to perceive as yet unperceived similarities among them, and to verbalize as yet unverbalized similarities. And it would lead also to tentative reorderings of particulars, to revisions of the tension of 'male', made with a mind to increasing predictive power. There are any number of ways in which such changes might proceed: let us follow just one possibility.

Imagine then that in the course of this activity the *XY* chromosome complement is recognized and labelled. And imagine also that several generalizations are found to be more predictively useful, better to guess with as it were, when routinely applied to persons with the *XY* complement. Since nearly all persons with this complement are in the tension of male, a revision of this tension is favoured. By inserting *XY*'s and ejecting non-*XY*'s, many generalizations, like 'males secrete testosterone' or 'males grow beards', acquire an increased predictive utility.

Thus, a development in the tension of the term 'male' is made intelligible by reference to specific, newly-introduced predictive goals. Note, however, that the entire pre-existing constellation of goals and interests in the context are necessary conditions of the particular development, and also affect the way in which it is conceptualized. At one extreme, the revision of a tension can be effected by processes which are seen as completely routine acts of concept application: 'meaning change' can go unnoticed as a result, and only become evident when agents look back upon their usage of many years previously.[5] At the other extreme, revisions can be carried out explicitly, employing the language of realism. It can be said that males have been discovered to be 'really' individuals with the XY characteristic: errors in past usage can now be corrected; those individuals in the tension of 'male' who are not 'real' males, and therefore never were, can be removed. In using the language of realism, a community typically adjusts the tensions of terms, but denies that meaning-change has occurred: the community claims finally to have found out what a term has always 'really' meant. Yet another way of proceeding is to adjust a tension and refer to what is produced as a new concept. Thus, the revised tension of 'male' could be held to belong to a new concept 'XY' or 'XY-male', usable alongside the initial unmodified original 'male'. 'XY' would enter those generalizations where the replacement of 'male' proved predictively profitable, but otherwise the old concept would continue in use. (Of course, this would involve a change in the sense of 'male', which could in itself be commemorated as a change of concept, and symbolized by a new verbal sign, for example 'male-actor' or 'common-sense-male'.)

The precise way in which a community assimilates a cultural change into its own self-understanding depends upon the overall system of goals and interests within it, and upon the distribution of power. To claim that males really are XY's is usually to invite conflict with other subcultures with other interests, and also to claim priority over common-sense knowledge in a society such as ours. The claim challenges others who might hold 'male-personality' or 'male-status' to be revisions of 'male' with every bit as much predictive utility. And, likewise, in implying that the common-sense term 'male' is ontologically inadequate, it sets the expertise of a subculture above the common-sense knowledge available to the lay person. Conversely, peaceful coexistence of 'XY-male' and 'male' usually implies peaceful coexistence between a subculture and the wider community, with the former either having no wish to, or no power to challenge the latter. Although there is no necessary connection here, realism does tend to be the language of cognitive colonialism and instrumentalism the language of compromise and toleration. Finally, in these cases where cultural change goes entirely unnoticed, and is effected by the drift of routine usage, it is likely that the adjustment which accommodates to some new goal or interest puts no others under threat, and thus never provokes explicit attention.

In the above example a specific *predictive* goal was taken to condition the initial processes of learning and the reconstruction of knowledge. But there is no reason why other kinds of goal or interest should not set off such processes and be taken as evaluative points of reference as knowledge and culture are modified. It is clear enough historically that socio-political goals and interests are frequently the initial stimuli to modifications in systems of natural knowledge; although for many reasons the role of such goals and interests is rarely explicitly acknowledged by the actors involved (Barnes and Shapin, 1979).

As a scheme of things changes over time, it is in response to whatever goals and interests people bring to bear upon its evaluation, and refer to in its development. At any point of time it is the basis of usage and the product of usage. Such indeed is the present state of our own knowledge and classification, and of any other. We can now abandon the expedient assumption of stability with which the discussion started. Stability is a special case of the normal dynamic character of culture, wherein an ongoing usage advancing a diversity of shared goals and interests tends to reconstitute and reproduce the pattern of associations from which it initially develops.

Conclusion

The previous section took the natural step of developing a sociological, conventionalist account of knowledge and classification into a thoroughly instrumentalist one. It is difficult to see how a move of this kind is to be avoided. It is, however, worth summarizing some particular features of the instrumentalism which is being put forward.

First, the goals and interests referred to are those sustained in the public domain, and they account for changes to a public phenomenon. There can be no private language; communication in any culture requires shared routines which have point only in as far as they are shared. Trying to employ a private language is like trying to spend money where nobody uses and nobody believes in money. Changes in linguistic usage, and associated changes in knowledge, are collective decisions which must relate to collective goals and interests. Even technical, predictive goals and interests vary from one context to another and are socially sustained. Insofar as a particular predictive goal structures the evaluation of knowledge, its very particularity must be understood by relating it to its social context, the existing knowledge therein, and the whole associated system of goals and interests.

This leads directly to a second point. In saying that specific, context-bound, interests or goals feedback into and structure the evaluation of knowledge, the emphasis is upon the terms 'specific' and 'context-bound'. It is not meaningful to talk, as Habermas (1972) for example has done, of evaluation in terms of 'transcendental' interests; and to conceive of knowledge being judged in relation to every possible kind of prediction and control. This would require the simultaneous management of every probability on an entire network, and the simultaneous evaluation of innumerable cognitive strategies. There is no method for such management, and no criterion for such evaluation. Contingent restrictions in cognition are essential to coherent learning, and anything one might be inclined to call the growth of knowledge.

Thirdly, it must be emphasized that in no sense are classifications or beliefs 'for' this or that. Still less are there different kinds of knowledge: 'science' 'for' technical-predictive interests; 'ideology' 'for' social-political interests. Goals and interests help to account for institutional dynamics. They help us to understand why, at such a time, in such a context, classifications were changed or developed in the way that they were. We can hope to understand why concepts and beliefs are as they are only in the very limited sense of understanding something of why they differ (or do not differ) from what was the case at some earlier point in time.

Nor should it even be thought that technical and social interests are, of necessity, conflicting influences on the growth of culture, so that, for instance, there is a 'scientifically appropriate' and a 'socially expedient' strategy to decide between at any point. Karam animal taxonomy, for example, gives no sign of having been developed as a symbolic representation of an aspect of the social order *rather than* as an instrumentally applicable set of terms and generalizations. Bulmer's paper makes clear the instrumental adequacy of Karam knowledge. Karam possess practical knowledge of kobtiy, their appearance, habits, behaviour, and so on. Nor are there grounds for assuming that they have lost technical information, or been encumbered with misleading or unreliable generalizations, by making a contrast between 'yakt' and 'kobtiy'. Karam culture, we might loosely say, is multifunctional, as a consequence of its development in a long historical process wherein many interests have borne upon its users.

Indeed, consideration of the network model shows immediately that this is generally the case, and that conflicts over classification and belief are 'chosen', rather than 'forced' by the opposition of different kinds of goal. Imagine, for example, that the structure of terms and generalizations takes on a particular form at a point in time through judgments and negotiations moved by some instrumental objective, so that what is regarded as a satisfactory structure and set of probabilities emerges. It is then always possible for the information in that pattern to be preserved, and additional cultural change to occur, simply by means of a differentiation of terminology. For example, valued generalizations might be established concerning the natural kind 'man' and might appear in a network of some community. Imagine then that the term is replaced with 'noble'/'commoner' or 'saved'/ 'damned' or any number of analogous terms reflecting further communal concerns. In such cases, all existing generalizations could be run to both new terms separately.

Concepts cannot determine their next instance of use. They lack inherent properties. Nor do they mind how they are used: only people mind. Failure to recognize these points is a recurrent source of difficulty in the social sciences, where the idealist tendency to refer directly to concepts as 'scientific', 'symbolic', 'ideological', and so on, attributes to them what should be attributed to their users.

It is true that agents themselves impute inherent properties to terms. The inherent properties of key concepts and classifications are often the subjects of social conflict. People have argued about what definitions of human nature, sanity, death, gender, species, matter, force, space and time are really correct. It is tempting to imagine here that ideas grind against each other in destructive confrontation. But, of course, the confrontation in such cases is between people, who oppose each other through the usages they adopt. If compromise or coexistence is acceptable in life then it is always possible at the level of ideas. Anything is possible at the level of ideas. This indeed is why there is always a role for the sociology of knowledge.

Notes

The original version of this chapter appeared in *Philosophy of the Social Sciences*, 11: 303–33. Most of the notes included in the original version have been omitted here.

1. The actual process of ostension is, of course, complex, and an endless
source of problems. The simple account above assumes that particulars can be
identified in the environment, that we perceive the environment as differentiated or lumpy, and that an interaction can, as it were, be brought to focus
on some lump or particular. And it assumes, further, that the association of a
particular with a term results in the particular being taken as an instance of
the term. These are far-reaching assumptions; but they are needed as a way of
allowing for the fact that we possess an incompletely understood perceptual
and cognitive apparatus with at least some rudimentary inherent properties
which make learning possible. Possession by L of such an apparatus makes it
possible for T to provide instances of terms like 'bird' for him (or, for that matter
terms like 'red' and 'flying' and 'up' and so on). For an extended discussion of
the difficulty of understanding ostensive learning see Campbell, 1979.
2. I use the term 'tension' in deliberate allusion to 'extension' as used in
philosophical semantics. In the extension of a term are thought to be included
all the entities to which it properly applies, or of which it is true. In the tension
of a term are included only past instances of use – a finite number of instances.
To talk merely of the tension of a term is to accept that its future proper usage
is indeterminate. To talk of an extension is to imply that future proper usage is
determined already. The position in this paper is thus in clear opposition to the
extensional semantics advocated by many philosophers.
3. Because concepts are employed *open-endedly* to successive instances
which differ in detail from each other, any state of identity between the nets
of individuals would be unstable, and would immediately deteriorate as those
individuals cited different specific instances of concepts in using or passing on
their knowledge. Hence, even in cultures wherein communication appears unproblematic, and knowledge homogeneous, the nets of different individuals differ
in detail in their tensions. Only the overall morphology of a net is capable of
becoming the common property of all the individuals of a community. This
implies that 'the culture' of a community is a highly problematic notion, and
that even the most routine interpersonal communication is a very complex
process, demanding extended empirical study if its accomplishment is to be
understood. (However, for the arguments to follow, the hardest case is generally
the unlikely and unstable state of affairs where all individuals possess identical
nets. Accordingly, this unrealistic assumption will occasionally be made to sim-
plify the presentation: I shall allow myself to talk of 'the culture' of a community
as though it is there as an identical resource for every member.)
4. The discussion implies that the languages of the Karam and ourselves are
not directly inter-translatable in these instances. The emptiness of the notion of
perfect translation is a general implication of the network model of concept
application as developed here.
5. The possibilities of 'meaning change' by the drift of routine usage are
limitless. Nor is even the slightest deviation from routine required. Consider
two colours, say green and yellow. Now generate a hundred intermediate colours
in a series from one to the other. If two colours next to each other in the series
are discernibly different, construct a hundred intermediate shades between the
two. Proceed in this way again and again until all shades in the series are indistinguishable from their immediate neighbours. Routine application of the term
'green' can now begin at one end of the series and end at the other. Stretch the

series of applications of 'green' over a period of years, and assume that earlier applications are forgotten, and that the tension of 'green' at any point is effectively constituted by only the more recent instances. Now the routine usage of a culture can move from one point on the spectrum to another without any individual being aware of any change of meaning – indeed, in a sense, without any 'change' having occurred.

References

Barnes, B. (1974) *Scientific Knowledge and Sociological Theory*, London: Routledge & Kegan Paul.

Barnes, B. (1977) *Interests and the Growth of Knowledge*, London: Routledge & Kegan Paul.

Barnes, B. and S. Shapin (1979) *Natural Order*, London and Beverly Hills: Sage.

Bloor, D. (1976) *Knowledge and Social Imagery*, London: Routledge & Kegan Paul.

Bruner, J. S., Goodnow, J. J., and Austin, G. A. (1956) *A Study of Thinking*, New York: Wiley.

Bulmer, R. (1967) 'Why is the Cassowary not a Bird?', *Man*, 2: 5–25.

Campbell, D. (1979) *Descriptive Epistemology*, Cambridge, Mass.: Harvard University Press.

Collins, H. M. (1975) 'The Seven Sexes', *Sociology*, 9: 205–24.

Dean, J. (1979) 'Controversy over Classification', in B. Barnes and S. Shapin (eds), *Natural Order*, London and Beverly Hills: Sage.

Douglas, M. (ed.) (1973) *Rules and Meanings*, Harmondsworth: Penguin.

Garfinkel, H. (1967) *Studies in Ethnomethodology*, Englewood Cliffs, NJ: Prentice-Hall.

Habermas, J. (1972) *Knowledge and Human Interests*, London: Heinemann.

Hesse, M. (1974) *The Structure of Scientific Inference*, London: Macmillan.

Kuhn, T. S. (1977) 'Second Thoughts on Paradigms', in *The Essential Tension*, Chicago: Chicago University Press.

Latour, B. and Woolgar, S. (1979) *Laboratory Life*, London and Beverly Hills: Sage.

Quine, W. V. O. (1953) *From a Logical Point of View*, Cambridge, Mass.: Harvard University Press.

Wittgenstein, L. (1953) *Philosophical Investigations*, Oxford: Blackwell.

3

The 'Mooting' of Science Studies: Research Programmes and Science Policy

Daryl E. Chubin
Georgia Institute of Technology, USA
Sal Restivo
Rensselaer Polytechnic Institute, USA

If science studies were a legal proceeding, one lawyer might focus on the inadmissability of evidence, another on the form of argument, and a third on the credibility of the proceeding as the appropriate forum to resolve the dispute. Science studies is not a court, it is a scholarly community; but it is a community with deep divisions and split loyalties. As a result, the community often operates as a court and scholars behave like lawyers. There are 'legalistic' debates about the origins of science studies, its disciplinary components, epistemological assumptions, theories, methods, and ultimate purposes (Chubin, 1982a). In what sense, then, is science studies a community? To what extent do its divisions 'cleave' interests and along what lines? At what points, if any, are there ontological and epistemological convergences?

This chapter approaches such questions as would a moot court:

Authors' note: Our thanks go to Karin Knorr-Cetina for her thoughtful commentary on an earlier draft. Support for part of the discussion on cancer controversies was provided to D.E.C. by The Hastings Center's project, Principles of Closure in Ethical and Scientific Disputes (Spring 1980). Parts of the chapter are also based on S.R.'s presentation at the International Colloquy on Epistemologically Relevant Internalist Sociology of Science, held at Lake Cazenovia, NY (June 1981), organized by D. T. Campbell and A. Rosenberg.

why, it asks, should the reader care that science studies now resembles a three-ring circus, each ring forming its own arena for discourse and seeking pre-eminence as an explanatory programme? Since we have advocated elsewhere (Restivo, 1981a, 1981b; Chubin, 1981a, 1981b) spotlighting the separate arenas as a means for comparing their programmatic components, we propose here to focus on our own programme, a 'synthetic' fourth ring emerging from the shadows in the science studies circus. Our programme is part of an heuristic for illuminating the other rings as 'world views' for producing, interpreting, and utilizing knowledge claims.

The three rings as arenas for science studies discourse

Because our fourth ring and *its* agenda derive primarily from three others, it behooves us to characterize them first. Our characterizations are not comprehensive; rather, they indicate programmatic strengths that should be retained in the fourth ring. Our selective characterizations thus reflect a point of view on the current science studies literature, its analytical foci, and its respective contributions to 'another' world view — one constructed inductively and with science policy considerations in mind.

The strong programme

The most prolific and perhaps coherent arena of empirical science studies has been the 'strong programme' in the sociology of scientific knowledge. Anchored by the programme statements of Barnes (1974, 1977) and Bloor (1976), the Edinburgh branch of this arena has produced a set of tenets for the social analysis of scientific content, and a set of case studies that putatively demonstrate the fulfilment of the programme's promise (Barnes and Shapin, 1979; MacKenzie, 1978). For at least one critic, however, the Edinburgh strong programme (SP) is still a pretender (Woolgar, 1981b). We share Woolgar's reservations insofar as Barnes's 'interests model' explains everything and nothing — and does so retrospectively. That is, this SP is built exclusively on historical case studies and the re-examination of textual accounts. In the process, the twin tenets of 'impartiality' and 'symmetry' (as regards 'true' and 'false' knowledge) are observed at the expense of charging that *others* act in accordance with their interests. Meanwhile, the

SP'er claims 'reflexivity' as his/her code of conduct.

A second branch of the strong programme has sought to extend and contemporize the relativism that Edinburgh operationalized. The 'Bath school' has focused on modern episodes of discovery and replication in the physical sciences (Collins, 1975, 1981; Pinch, 1977). In an effort to show that controversy is normal in mainstream as well as in marginal sciences, the Bath SP has investigated the debates over psi phenomena (parapsychology) (Collins and Pinch, 1982), solar neutrinos (Pinch, 1980), and learning among planaria (Travis, 1980) – do they exist? Here too, however, fascinating cases have failed to convince realists (Gieryn, 1982) or satisfy other qualified relativists (Knorr, 1982; Chubin, 1982b) that the SP has been programmatically faithful to its own tenets. Intriguing episodes often resist generalization. Further, the cases share the deficiencies of internalist history; rank-and-file scientists, non-scientists and the 'external' culture seldom command attention. These issues may be of small concern to SP'ers, but are of great significance to the less doctrinaire. We of the fourth ring are potential users, not product champions of the extant strong programme.

Epistemologically, the strong programmes tend to link sociological and scientific rationality, and so link the standards of what constitutes 'correct' sociological work with the standards of natural sciences (e.g. Whitley, 1974). This is one way of formulating Bloor's notion that if sociologists study science using the methods of science, 'all will be well'. The sociology of science can also focus attention on the social structural requirements of scientific practice and progress. This is the goal of Donald Campbell's (1974) work on descriptive and evolutionary epistemology. Campbell's programme shares a demarcationist perspective with the strong programme, but is based on a more dynamic conception of scientific change. Campbell (1979: 198), for example, refers to the 'iterative oscillations of theoretical emphases', and a 'continual dialectic that never achieves a stable synthesis'. Thus Restivo (1981b) has labelled this 'the mild programme'; however, it can be considered a fringe form of strong programme. We will outline a 'weak programme' below which is guided by a different set of epistemological assumptions from the strong and mild programmes and the other arenas we discuss in the following pages.

Laboratory studies

A second arena that has flourished in science studies falls under the rubric of 'lab studies'. Spurred by Latour and Woolgar's (1979) study of the Salk Institute, the laboratory as a site for 'science in the making' has become a research focus for biography (Goodfield, 1981), discourse analysis (Woolgar, 1980), organizational analysis (Traweek, 1981), and the social construction of knowledge (Knorr, 1981a; Zenzen and Restivo, 1982). All of these variants, however, claim an anthropological perspective on the process of negotiating, or socially constructing, scientific reality.

The clearest programmatic statement of what this 'constructivist' approach entails is contained in Knorr (1977 and this volume). In attempting to distinguish constructivism from Bath School relativism and recast the micro-macro distinction, Knorr (1982) has sought nothing less than a redefinition of the scientific community, one that refines the economic metaphor on which it rests (Bourdieu, 1975) and, at the same time, relates the creativity of the 'tinkerer' to the world beyond the laboratory bench. Knorr's bold theorizing thus bridges the concerns of the ethnomethodologist (e.g. Woolgar, 1981a) and the preoccupations of the policy analyst who must consider communication and evaluation for the sake of knowledge-utilization and decision-making.[1]

Thus, the disparate traditions found in the lab-studies arena render it sufficiently diffuse to attract labels and charges (e.g. Cozzens, 1980) that suggest basic epistemological differences. Such differences help imbue the few lab studies now completed or still in progress with a mystery that arouses suspicions from other arenas. For example, what are appropriate units of analysis? – a seven-minute excerpt of a conversation taped during the operation of experimental apparatus? A content analysis of successive drafts of a paper produced over several months through a four-person inter-lab collaboration?

Clearly, ethnographies of scientists in their natural habitat provide insights into processes that other methodologies cannot equal (Chubin, 1981a). But a reliance on single sites, more or less direct observation, and a lack of comparability in analytical focus hampers the use of lab studies by those enamoured of conventional social science inquiry. To view a lab study as merely a case study of the context and process of doing scientific craftwork – before the professional trappings of rhetoric and scholarly convention set in – is to sustain the mystery and the sacrosanct privileges that scientists themselves seek to protect (Latour, 1980). Criticisms of the 'subjectivism' of knowledge claims and the bumbling irrationality of scientists that lab studies inevitably disclose is reminiscent of the knee-jerk defences of orthodox positivistic philosophy of science mounted in the face of challenges by Popper, Kuhn, Habermas, Feyerabend and others. Whenever orthodoxy is permitted to escape, or new variables bearing the force of another reality are welcomed, some recoil. The lab-studies arena is no exception; it has been repudiated for committing, nay, promoting, a multitude of epistemological and empirical sins. Such a reaction, emanating from arenas that usually remain aloof from the in-fighting among those of an 'alien' programme, is itself telling.

Scientometrics

The third and final arena considered here is a catch-all of quantitative analyses that rely mainly on archival sources, without direct observation, and are devoted to the products or outcomes of the processes that other arenas exalt. For some (Hargens, 1978) scientometrics *is* the sociology of science: it includes bibliometrics (citation and productivity studies), science manpower and career histories, and science-indicators compilations. The epistemology underlying scientometrics differs radically from that subscribed to by practitioners of the strong programme and the lab study. For the scientometrician the world exists *sui generis*; it can be sampled, measured, captured, and revealed according to 'objective inquirers'. Those inquirers 'make estimates' and 'test hypotheses' rather than 'make knowledge claims' and 'construct realities'.[2] Such differences in perspective and *modus operandi* constitute a formidable wedge that divides scientometrics from other arenas.

The division, however, is significant for another reason as well: the time frame. Whereas the present to the distant past circumscribes the cases alluded to in the first two arenas, the present to the immediate future occupies those practising scientometrics. Making predictions about forthcoming trends, patterns, and relationships is, after all, what 'science' is all about. The control and evaluation of science for policy-making and application, as well as understanding, are implicit in the National Science Foundation's (NSF) *Science Indicators* reports (e.g. National Science Board, 1979), and commentaries on such reports (Elkana et al., 1977; Zuckerman and Miller, 1980). The same could be said, to a lesser degree, of more basic bibliometric analyses of the behaviour of journals (Narin, 1976), authors (Mullins et al., 1977; Lindsey, 1978), and whole disciplines and specialty areas within them (reviewed in Chubin, 1982a).

This work is united by an interventionist presumption: to know something about a relationship raises the prospect of manipulating and changing it. Such optimism over future mastery requires assertions of certainty — even in the absence of compelling data. That is, in contrast to the SP's pledge to explain true and false beliefs in the *same* way, the scientometricians must declare what they believe to be true and seek to explain only those truths. Of course, the tone of such declarations and explanations must be as agnostic, objective, value- and interest-free as possible. That is the credo of the realist, the sieve through which reality passes. Such a revelatory, burning-bush quality may not be decisive in science policy-making, but can it hurt? (One can imagine why discourse analysts would want to dissect the rhetoric of scientometricians, or those who have learned, and avowedly emulate, the forked-tongue idioms of the scientific journal article.)

One programmatic curiosity here is the contradiction among the slavish realists. In admitting 'cultural context' as a variable, they deny or subordinate its effects to the collective wisdom of a sovereign 'scientific community' which knows best when it comes to self-governance and matters of accountability and even reform.[3] Mertonians who have, until recently, offered unqualified endorsements of federal peer-review systems (e.g. Cole et al., 1978) and justified inequities in the allocation of incentives and rewards (Zuckerman, 1970; Cole and Cole, 1973; Gaston, 1978) as systematically (read *functionally*) necessary and efficient are now issuing apologies for flaws in the community's rationality. Luck has finally been recognized as a component of peer-review decisions (Cole et al., 1981), instead of elitism, particularism, and all those other aberrations in the normative framework that binds the scientific community. If fraud, whimsy, and error have infiltrated science, then its stratification as well may be aberrant (Turner and Chubin, 1979), its rational decision-making authority diminished (Dolby, 1979), and its omniscient certainty about future outcomes severely impaired (Chubin, 1980, 1981a).

This third arena, in sum, can be reproached for its pretensions — its forms and not its substance. Its invocation of number, method, and truth enchant only the like-minded. Scientometricians are not backward-looking; their professional future hangs on the ability to draw 'reality' closer, finer, and more certain than it is. Those are seductive characteristics for people trained to celebrate science by practising its cherished routines. Celebration may prevail in the scientometric arena and others may sneer at the illusion, at the like-minded acting in single- (if not close-) minded ways. Whose reality dare we ignore? Those in the fourth ring, hovering over the three arenas, cannot be so smug. Our own programmatic concerns prohibit it.

The fourth ring: between strong programmes and meta-inquiry

The social trappings that spur the development of institutional centres, intellectual leaders, and signal works have materialized in the three dominant arenas of science studies that we have reviewed. Such social supports are essential for bringing visibility, legitimacy, and resiliency to research programmes (Mullins, 1973; Mulkay, 1980). For the trappings of success insulate programmes from external criticism. Indeed, they defuse overt challenges to the programmatic core and 'buy time' for programme development to occur. During that time, core problems gain clarity, literature accumulates, favoured theories and methods are installed through repeated use and debate. A separate sphere of discourse — pet concepts, turns of phrase, research procedures, and interpretive modes — is constructed. Research is no longer mere hypothesis-testing; it is incrementally and self-consciously performed as part of a 'research tradition' (Radnitzky, 1970; Laudan, 1977). Those working within it develop an identity; simultaneously, an amorphous out-group is defined. The tradition becomes epistemologically self-sufficient — responsive to the 'constructive' dialogue of those who share assumptions and work within it (the 'true believers'), immune from the assaults of 'uninformed', uninitiated alien researchers.

Traditions thus come to define researchers in science studies in (arguably) mutually exclusive ways. Exchange across traditions, and between arenas (as we have called them) declines. As the boundaries that separate them become opaque (e.g. through non-citation patterns), we realize that arenas are not merely separated by subject or content; they are reflections of distinctive, though not mutually exclusive, 'world views'. Each arena has its own world to study in specified ways for specified purposes. Commitment defines *what* one sees, *how* one studies it, and *why* its importance is 'self-evident' to those of like commitment and 'dubious' or 'irrelevant' to others. For example, while SP'ers and lab analysts seem to agree that there is no such thing as a 'definitive account' of a discovery or some episode wherein the meaning of a finding is negotiated, they assert this with the authority that they assail in others. In Woolgar's (1981b: 375) terms, SP'ers portray *others* as 'rationality-dopes', explaining scientists' actions as hewing out a rational course. Meanwhile, the SP'ers, alleges Woolgar, can be seen as 'interest-dopes', explaining scientists' actions as guided by whatever promotes their self-interest or intellectual commitment. But *both* of these views carry a moral imperative, for instance the scientist as rational man is wrong, the scientist as self-interested actor is also wrong.

If there is no definitive account, as relativists would contend, then the arena of discourse in which the claim is made must provide rules for judging alternative accounts, for deciding the resiliency of the world view, and for evaluating value implications. We perceive that the three programmes we have characterized, each forming an arena of discourse and a research tradition, lack the internal consistency and intellectual integrity that they claim. Nevertheless, each is a strong research programme with the social trappings and critical mass of practitioners to perpetuate it as a coherent world view within science studies.

In contrast to these research programmes, the fourth ring of inquiry constitutes a 'weak programme'. This weak programme is not based on a *belief* in or *commitment* to modern science. While it shares the mild programme's enthusiasm for wild speculation, it does not share that programme's 'strong' dimension. As Campbell expresses it: '...of all the analytically coherent epistemologies possible, we are interested in those (or that one) compatible with the description of man, and of the world provided by contemporary science' (1974: 413). In the strong programme, it is assumed that we know something important about the way science works. The mild programme makes this assumption problematic to some extent: it is guided by the basic query: 'In what kind of world would what kind of procedures lead a knowing community to improve the validity of its model of the world?' (Campbell, 1977: 2). In the weak programme this query is translated as follows: In what kind of world would what kind of epistemic activities lead an epistemic community to conclude that it was (according to its own definition) improving its model of the world *and what are the implications for those inside and outside of the epistemic community* (in terms of quality of life, the distribution of power, and so on)? The weak programme entails a world-view approach to science and, more generally, inquiry.

There are numerous hidden and uncritically accepted assumptions that guide the selection of problems, research methods, explanatory modes, and legitimating logics and rationalities in the sociology of science. Research advances clandestinely supported by assumptions about the nature of reality, ways to study reality, and ways of experiencing reality. Methods and theories are developed, utilized, and changed with scarce regard for what they imply about how one comes to know about reality, what one does with such knowledge, the nature of the research, the social relations of research (in the critical, introspective sense), and the values and ethics of research. It is a small, though not necessarily intuitively obvious, step from the idea of hidden or taken-for-granted assumptions to the idea that methods and modes of explanation, problem-selection criteria, and rationalities and logics are embedded in world views. This insight is implied in one of the various interpretations Kuhn gives to paradigm, and in other works in the post-Mertonian sociology of science, but it has taken root outside of the sociology of science proper.

The 'sequence of widening perspectives' sketched in Radnitzky's (1970) call for meta-science studies carries us toward a world-view analysis. Hooker (1975) is more explicit in construing philosophies of science such as empiricism and realism as world views. Metaphilosophy is the process of making the world view associated with any given philosophy of science explicit. In Bohm's book, *Fragmentation and Wholeness* (1976), theories are seen as world views. World views are concerned with all aspects of our lives – nature, ourselves, our relations to others and to external nature. The function of metaphysics, Bohm notes, is to make the implicit world views of theories explicit. Feyerabend's (1978) Galilean studies and critique of method are yet another affirmation and exemplar of the meta-analysis of science as world view.

The weak programme is based in part on the nature and implications of meta-science studies. It changes the focus of the sociology of science from 'science' to the broader epistemic activity, 'inquiry'. And it replaces such terms as 'objective statement' and 'truth' with the term 'insight'. It operates under three assumptions: (1) no insight (more broadly, 'world view', more narrowly, 'objective statement' or 'truth') can ever be final or absolute; (2) no system for arriving at insights can ever be universally valid and unchanging in its foundations; and (3) there is always a broader context, or higher level for establishing an insight than that of any given system of inquiry. There are no paradoxes here at least insofar as paradoxes would emerge if these assumptions were proposed as truths.

As we shall see, the research agenda of the weak programme encompasses both traditional and new themes in the arenas we have surveyed. Its overriding concern is for ethical and value issues in the translation of knowledge claims into policies designed to change the world and not

simply understand it. Put another way, the weak programme casts
the meta-inquirer as social critic and activist, one who must surmount
the advocacy of world views and the politics of self-interested inquiry.
Few are inclined to play this role and so the fourth ring is virtually
empty. But the weak programme seeks not to compete with the science
studies trinity. Science is not a moot court; science studies should not
be one either.

The weak programme: issues and cases

Prescriptive methodology and the issue of policy

What we have argued thus far is that arenas of science-studies discourse
house centripetal research traditions. They direct practitioners towards
one another and a restricted set of problems, variables, and techniques
that refine their common world view. Such intra-arena negotiation
precludes self-conscious inquiry. Accordingly, practitioners need not
confront their own rationality or be held accountable — collectively or
otherwise — for their advocacy of certain knowledge. But the weak
programme seeks to change all that.

   Through meta-inquiry, the weak programme mounts an 'assault'
from outside all arenas. It seeks to sample world views in the service
of its own agenda. That agenda features its own methodology as well
— 'prescriptive' methodology that is self-conscious and committed to
introducing the claims derived from social studies of science to the
policy process. The agenda, in short, emanates from a political, and
not a research, programme. It comes from outside science altogether.[4]
For policy is neither made nor executed by scientists alone. Indeed,
typically sociologists of science are ignored or used only as credentialed
ornaments for those in power.

   Prescriptive methodology represents a change in status and tactic.
In Laudan's (1977: 57) words,

> It is one of the central functions of any philosophy or methodology of science
> to specify...goals and to indicate the most effective *means* for achieving them.
> The whole point of a methodological rule...is to offer a norm for scientific
> behavior, to tell us what we should, or should not, do.

The weak programme specifies new goals for the meta-analyst, while
prescriptive methodology indicates the most effective means for achieving them. This methodology turns on an 'interpretive' approach (Law,

1974) which involves a process of understanding systems of beliefs from the perspective of the believers. In keeping with a tenet of both the strong programme and lab studies, this approach affirms the empathic possibility that social scientists can both understand the technical content of the sciences they study and communicate intelligently with the producers of that research. To be prescriptive, then, social scientists' (re)constructions must ideally be assessed through a methodology that shows how scientists negotiate and order their intellectual worlds (Mulkay, 1979). To be policy-relevant as well as prescriptive, methodology must illuminate how (social) scientific data (i) are ideologically self-serving and rationalize vested interests, (ii) can perpetuate a conception of science as immune to influences in its environing culture, and (iii) obstruct ethical social action. Armed with such illuminating data, the meta-analyst wields a tool of *ethical* inquiry: the ability to prescribe how data should or should not be used in the process of science policy-making.

To recapitulate: whereas the strong programme makes claims about the negotiation of reality, particularly our conceptions of it, the weak programme emphasizes the actions that people apparently take based on those conceptions. The link between negotiation and practice is the premier conception guiding the weak programme: it is prescriptive and prospective. Therefore, the contexts of negotiation and practice *in situ* become focal points of analysis. No distinctions, however, are made within the programme between internal and external contexts, 'scientific' and 'other' practice. A continuing concern with action embeds the weak programme in a cultural context, science in an institutional context, practice in an organizational and decision-making context. The inherently political character of these contexts impels the issue of 'policy' to the forefront of the meta-analyst's inquiry. Note, too, that although they claim to be self-conscious, proponents of both the strong programme and lab studies deny the role of values within the purview of their investigations. That is, values are considered neither a suitable object of inquiry nor a relevant analytical tool. Instead, they speak of others' 'interests', while maintaining a *value neutrality* — or lack of 'interest' — about the prescriptive content and use of their findings. In short, they subscribe to one of the same epistemological assumptions that they attribute to the category of unreflexive analysts, such as scientometricians.

Because values cannot be purged from reflexive analyses of science, they must be made explicit and applied to the investigation of policy questions. Once social analysts of science are shown to be as self-interested as those whom they study, they will not smugly define as irrelevant the cultural and social values that have normative or ethical implications. It is precisely the role of values that meta-analysts must introduce into their 'interpretive' science studies, and in the process, into science policy.

Meta-analysis and cases of science policy-making

1. Cancer controversies
Although social scientists have had less to say about cancer as a dread disease than biologists, National Cancer Institute directors, and science journalists, a few have examined the social and policy aspects of the US 'war on cancer' (for a review, see Studer and Chubin, 1980). From its inception, the rhetoric of the cancer mission (Chubin and Studer, 1978) engendered questions about ethical decision-making in science, such as disputes among experts regarding the nature of carcinogens and accept-able levels of risk (Gillespie et al., 1979), and the role of the courts in regulating risk (Bazelon, 1979, 1980; Lave and Seskin, 1979; Gori, 1980).

Because social scientists have generally absented themselves from cancer controversies, there has been virtually no meta-analysis of these questions. To remedy this situation, the meta-analyst might ask: what are the transcendent values in the setting of research and funding priorities for cancer? A plethora of evidence suggests that cancer con-troversies are anything but subsiding in the 1980s. The National Cancer Institute (NCI) and the American Cancer Society (ACS) disagree over whether the cancer rate is increasing or decreasing in the US (Smith, 1980). Biometricians and epidemiologists interpret the NCI data differently; the representativeness of surveyed regions is in doubt.

Consider, too, that the Love Canal tragedy illustrates the unenviable task facing the Environmental Protection Agency — to reconcile a fun-damental difference in approach between lawyers and scientists to dread disease. 'The lawyers want quick results that can serve as evidence for law suits; researchers contend that environmental issues as complex as that of Love Canal defy almost any attempts to develop immediately useful data' (Culliton, 1980: 1002). Which views, then, should prevail? How are risk and harm estimated? How much unanimity exists among the experts and in what areas? What, in short, are the sources that feed the controversy?

Still another prospective source of insight into research values is direct observation. For instance, National Institutes of Health (NIH) 'consensus development conferences' bring experts together to debate the meaning of data concerning controversial medical issues so as to provide guidance in the treatment of patients. As reported in *Science* (Marx, 1980), a panel on cervical cancer screening failed to reach consensus. Since it is values — deep-seated, emotionally-held beliefs about the social world and human behaviour — that researchers bring to bear in the interpretation of data, it should be instructive to observe what is claimed, by whom, and to what apparent end at a consensus development conference. This is surely one site where a social scientist can bountifully note what scientists do, say they do, and given archival data, write about doing. Any emerging gulfs between the written and spoken word, offered in different settings to divergent audiences, are measures of values and rhetoric in the reconstruction of intellectual and political history.

Furthermore, if the existence of a technical debate, and not its substance, engenders its further politicization (Nelkin, 1975), the case of cancer controversies suggests that politicization is not intrinsically bad for science. Indeed, analysis of how, why and in what ways politicization occurs may contribute to resolution of the controversies themselves. Such resolution, of course, is anything but straightforward. For whereas scientists see controversy as an ongoing process, the decision-maker must see potential *outcomes*, one of which is closure. The difference between 'controversy' and 'closure' is more than semantic. That democratic societies employ a variety of means for arbitrating disputes and inducing closure says nothing about the morality of such decisions and thus its efficacy for resolving — to the mutual satisfaction of all stakeholders — the controversy. The means, in short, do not justify the ends.

Nevertheless, technical advice may serve as 'a means for defending the legitimacy of policy decisions', the 'willingness of scientists to expose technical uncertainties and to lend their expertise to citizen groups constitutes a formidable political challenge' (Nelkin, 1979: 15). If the exploitation of expertise by the parties to any particular controversy is to be clarified, the methods of the analyst who claims knowledge of that controversy become the clarifying tool. But to be policy-relevant, those methods may unearth the very ambiguities and uncertainties that forestall closure, and indeed, exacerbate the controversy. Such politicization is part of the policy process, and not inherently bad. Politicization may nevertheless *inhibit* closure.

In sum, the interpretations which studies of controversies warrant may complicate the decision-making process. To slow the inexorable movement toward 'procedural' closure, some 'governor' must be applied. Meta-analysis can be this governor; it can aid the policy-maker in recognizing the methodological-ideological underpinnings of the social evidence 'impelling' policy action, or what has been termed the 'unintended consequences of social research' (Studer and Chubin, 1977). Indeed, this is the role prescriptive methodology should play in the study of controversy.

2. Peer review

A second candidate for meta-analysis — peer review — has emerged as a controversy involving two self-interested constituencies — scientists and Congress. Each is attempting to uphold sacrosanct values: science — autonomy, self-governance, and rewards for professional performance; Congress — accountability, egalitarianism, national excellence, and improved quality of life. Can this multitude of often competing values be accommodated by a single peer review system? Mitroff and Chubin (1979), and Roy (1981), among a distinct minority of scientists and science-watchers, think not.

It is in the submission of research proposals for federal funding that peer review becomes particularly odious. For there is a crucial link between scientists' opinions of one another and the situation of competition for scarce resources. Resources afford differential advantages that tend to colour merit, if not obscure it beneath a researcher's reputation. These advantages accumulate; just how they warrant funding decisions and advance careers to the *detriment* of science is unknown. What collusive role do scientists play in sanctioning the priorities and criteria of funding agencies, programmes, and editors? Because social scientists have differed on the propriety of voicing such concerns regarding peer review (Cole et al., 1978; Chubin, 1980), this site is ripe for meta-analysis and reform.

As recently reported in *Science* (Chubin, 1982c), in a suit originally brought against the Department of Health and Human Services, George Kurzon, MD, sought disclosure, under the Freedom of Information Act (FOIA), of 'the names of scientists who have made grant applications to the National Cancer Institute and whose applications have been turned down'. Kurzon took this action contending that the peer review system does not work well where the scientist is unconventional in his or her thinking. The case in point was that of Albert Szent-Gyorgi (see Vogt, 1979). The government argued that the names of scientists denied grants are immune from the provisions of the FOIA. On 21 August 1980, the District Court of Massachusetts upheld the government's position. In support of his appeal, Kurzon solicited an affidavit from Chubin. (For a summary, see Chubin, 1982d, as paraphrased below.)

The chief issues of concern in the Kurzon suit were recently studied by the National Commission on Research (1980), a private non-profit organization founded in 1978 by the American Council on Education, the American Council of Grant Colleges, and the Social Science Research Council.

The Commission's May 1980 report lists among 'the inadequacies of the peer review process which have been cited most often by critics' two of direct relevance to this suit: 'traditionalism and conservatism of peer reviewers and inability or unwillingness to recognize and recommend support for highly innovative, high-risk proposals' (p. 8). 'NIH and NSF acknowledge that there is sometimes a tendency for individual peer reviewers to be too conservative', but nevertheless consider the problem to be 'manageable' (p. 8).

Others both within and outside federal agencies have been more specific and alarming in their criticisms of peer review. For example, the current director of NCI, Dr Vincent T. DeVita, Jun., admitted in a conversation with Daniel S. Greenberg, Washington correspondent of *The New England Journal of Medicine*, that 'the cancer research system is unreceptive to unorthodoxy' (Greenberg, 1980: 1014). Dr DeVita qualifies his admission in several ways, reminding us that 'the peer review system is just people, and people always look a little bit suspiciously at the person who is way out at the edge'.

Another issue of concern raised by the suit is the alleged stigma that scientists who have been denied NCI support would suffer if their names were released as a result of this suit. But it would seem that such stigma, in this time of static or shrinking federal funding for research, has substantially diminished. The damage suffered by a rejected would-be principal investigator is offset by other proposals, often submitted to a variety of agencies, some of which *are* eventually supported. One must risk rejection in the public process of competing for scarce resources, be they journal space for reporting research findings or federal funding that enables those researches to proceed. If a scientist willingly competes in the research arena, he/she accepts the risk of failing as well as succeeding and persevering in the face of hardship and delay. No committed researcher abandons his/her investigations for fear that rejection will bring stigmatization and do

irreparable harm to future investigations. To claim, therefore, that
disclosure of one's attempt to compete for those funds is an invasion
of privacy seems inimical to the public interest — the same public
whose tax dollars would subsidize the researcher's investigation were
his/her proposal funded. Such a one-sided 'disclosure of successes'
policy, as embodied in the FOIA and applied to the competition for
public funding, is (in principle) unjustified.

Chubin's conjectures, however, warrant systematic study. That is
why he agreed to participate in the Kurzon suit and to conduct research
along the lines suggested below if and when the data sought were
released. Only if the experiences of would-be principal investigators
whose proposals have been denied support (or given too low a priority
rating to receive support though approved by an NIH study section)
are reconstructed, can the effects of peer review be measured. Was
the research denied support by NCI pursued? Was non-NIH support
subsequently secured? What was the would-be principal investigator's
funding history prior to the NIH decision? And on the review side,
what did study section members cite as reasons for recommending that
the research not be supported? In short, are innovative approaches seen
as wild speculations lacking any empirical support? Only research utilizing data previously *not* in the public domain could address questions
such as these.

On 22 May 1981, the First Circuit Court of Appeals sustained
Kurzon's appeal, reversing the district court's decision. The names
and addresses of scientists declined in the last two years for NCI funding were recently released. This will allow research on the effects of
peer review — wasteful and facilitative alike. It will also make some
scientists squirm by subjecting one of their private rituals to public
scrutiny. But it is far better, to the meta-analyst, to seek reform of a
system than to disregard or bemoan its existence. Participation in a
legal proceeding makes explicit the kinds of behaviour that scientists
routinely display in their interactions with fellow scientists: promotion
of their interests. The context and stakes may have changed, but the
process is fundamentally the same.

Although Chubin's account may smack of hubris or self-righteous-
ness, it transfers an academic question of scientific norms and practice
to the context of controversy and so-called extra-scientific adjudication
that, as we saw in the case of cancer, is becoming commonplace. These
personal observations, however, are overshadowed by the social and
legal consequences of the Kurzon suit. Such consequences show that the
role of social scientist and citizen are inseparable, that programmatic

calls for 'reflexivity', as in the strong programme, are an invitation to scholarly rumination only, and not a call to critical action in the sense of political reform that Gouldner's (1970, 1976) 'reflexivity' stirs. Meta-analysis, in sum, raises the spectre that ideology can be 'scientific'. Perhaps the fear of relativism originates here. For the weak programme places science on a different footing altogether — a turf stripped of its social trappings — which inhabitants of the strong programme arena, as well as (obviously) the non-relativists in the scientometrics arena, refuse to negotiate. Our cases of science policy-making illuminate the promise of future negotiation which the meta-analyst, as we see it, relishes.

3. Meta-analysis and scientific knowledge

Orthodox historians, philosophers, psychologists, and sociologists of science tend to want science to stand still and remain in good health while they study it. But while they are studying science — usually after idealizing it, in part by purifying it of its social trappings — science is changing. They marvel at its 'success' without considering the contribution of pragmatic criteria, 'tinkering', and trial-and-error technology to the 'success' of 'pure' science. Finally, they act as the apologists and ideologues of science. In their sometimes zealous efforts to capture and frame ideals (of scientific method, of scientific knowledge, of scientific theory), students of science are especially apt to forget that science is subject to all the pathologies and perversions that can transfigure and misdirect social organization and its value-correlates: over-specialization, bureaucratization, ecclesiasticism, authoritarianism, professional closure, excessive competition, elitism, co-optation (especially by military and industrial interests), hierarchism, dogmatism, and so on. Science is peculiarly subject to 'algorithmitis' (a variation on Gresham's law: successful procedural rules drive out understanding, that is, bad science drives out good science), numberitis, and scientism.

The failure to develop a problematic or critical view of science is widespread among sociologists of science. The most curious instance of *this* pathology is the reception Kuhn's (1970) work has received from sociologists. Kuhn's failure to treat the social dimensions of science critically, and as *sociologically* problematic, has gone unnoticed among most sociologists of science. Various aspects of the social organization of science (e.g. intersubjectivity) are taken-for-granted as guarantors of 'good' science. They *should* be treated critically because they are *organized* activities that come in different forms, and are

subject to a variety of transformations. Some of these forms and
transformations may be 'better' for science than others. This realization motivates, in part, the search for an epistemologically relevant
sociology of science. In our terms, this is a search for a political programme. Let us see, then, how lab studies and evolutionary epistemology
are related to each other and to our programme.

Lab studies, following Knorr's summary, suggest that scientific
facts are idiosyncratic hybrids constructed by means of decisions composed of rationalities-and-contingencies in a process carried out in the
slack of a historical contingency-space. 'Local contingency spaces
mapped out by a variety of factors', according to Knorr (1977: 674),
'rule out the one-dimensional rationality which is so readily attributed
to scientists.' Scientists 'tinker'. This idea is compatible with the notion
of natural selection as a tinkering process sketched by Jacob (1977).
The tinkerer principle states that similar problems tackled by different
people in different environments will yield different solutions. But the
limited-number-of-possibilities principle is a warning: there is an extreme where there is one possibility and an extreme where the number
is effectively unlimited — and these extremes are relevant at various
levels of 'abstraction'.

It is also important to note that there are multiple and overlapping
contexts of adaptation and *transformation*. They are not necessarily
co-ordinated or compatible, and their spatial and temporal boundaries
vary. Selection processes in these contexts are competitive. Selection
criteria on the level of everyday life are necessarily more limited and
narrower than criteria on the evolutionary-devolutionary level. Therefore, our choices on the everyday level with respect to selection-and-
retention may be at odds with the choices demanded by the requirements
for adaptive and transformative activities, and for maintaining or raising
the degree of adaptability of transformative potential populations. We
conceive of history as a reservoir of adaptive and transformative strategies in flux which we can survey and draw on in our problem-solving
activities. These strategies are not 'things of the past' but 'things of the
present', not things to respect, but things to scan, play with, succeed
and fail with, discard, reclaim, and transform.

We must always ask about the utility of a strategy or the relevance
of an epistemology or world view: in what sense is it relevant or useful?
In what context, within what spatial and temporal boundaries, for
whom, and with what costs and risks to environments, populations,
and individuals?

Profiling the promise:
the weak programme and the future of meta-analysis

Like all sciences, meta-science must be appraised for its deeds, not just its claims. Such appraisal is premature, but proposing the criteria for *future* evaluations of the weak programme is certainly not. We propose five criteria as particularly applicable to the weak programme, though any programme that promises policy-relevance, if not guidance, and a methodology for delivering on such a promise, could be similarly evaluated. Implicitly, this happens all the time; we prefer to make such evaluation explicit.

Taken together, the five criteria share research sites, problem foci, epistemological assumptions, and prescriptive imperatives with the three research programmes discussed above. Since these programmes are committed to analyses of science and technology, and not meta-analyses of science *policy*, their intents cannot be faulted retroactively. Their prospective uses in the fourth ring, even by those who shrink from the label 'meta-scientist', are welcomed. The weak programme has fluid boundaries, its entrance requirements revolve about what one does and how – not about who one is, where one was trained, or what one claims to be doing.

Our five criteria, then, are:

1. the study of process *and* product;
2. a contextual perspective;
3. an evolutionary epistemology;
4. a future-orientation; and
5. an unremitting criticism, or 'constructive examination', of values in policy making.

The first criterion embraces the decade-old admonition that science, like any other institutionalized activity, should not be studied as a 'black box' (Whitley, 1972). To the meta-analyst this means that what scientists say and do vary with their interests and the listening audience. Furthermore, the gulf between rhetoric and artifact is where the often unseen and untold negotiation unfolds. Meta-analysts must bridge the gulf. For the scientometrician fixes only on what goes into the box – the 'received view' of resources, people, and problems – and what comes out the other end – papers, discoveries, citations, and prizes. Scientometricians celebrate these artifacts and grandly infer the processes they never observed. They feed the scientists' own mythology about rationality and progress. They therefore play into the policy-maker's hands by delivering simplistic, manipulable findings of the 'how much, how often' variety. Reaffirming the excellence of the few in science without specifying the conditions of their handiwork and the science meccas whence they came just perpetuates elitist science policy. Stratification becomes the operating principle of grandeur. A contextual perspective places *scientists-as-workers* into organizations, institutions, and material cultures (Johnston, 1976; Whitley, 1977). Unlike the strong programme, the weak programme does not identify legitimate actors in science, and more generally, in technical controversies on the basis of credentials. The culture helps define (1) who is an interested party, (2) the scope of that interest, (3) the struggle of all parties to demarcate their expertise, and (4) dependence of the parties on other institutions to validate and support their practice. In the contextual perspective, identifying the 'transepistemic' connections (Knorr, 1982) that link scientists to patrons and adversaries alike is the key to understanding why and how negotiations occur. Representing this process — from the lab bench to the court room — to the policy-maker is the onerous task of the meta-inquirer. The sheer multiplicity of actors, views, and interests militates against elegant synopses and quick-fix policy recommendations concerning careers, research programmes, and national funding priorities in R&D (Studer and Chubin, 1980). Infusing scepticism about organizational goals and efficiency, given targeted missions or the search for short-term applications, just compounds the policy-maker's problem.

An evolutionary epistemology underlies the aforementioned focus on practice. From the mundane to the controversial, science — depending on one's historical allegiances — has moved inexorably for some time. While philosophers debate the 'progressive' content of science (e.g. Lakatos and Musgrave, 1970), others argue for the inherently adaptive mechanisms that propel research (for a summary, see Richter, 1972). Whether or not the 'natural selection' — 'survival-of-the-fittest' metaphors have been stretched beyond current biological science licence, the meta-analyst rejoices in the restoration of science to its 'proper' place as a cultural activity. In it, the scientist is again seen as a tinkerer, a creative craftsperson who proceeds not by methodological rigour alone, but by curiosity, luck, serendipity, and yes, a well-endowed chair or long-term research grant. Such a picture of resourceful and timely creativity, however, gives small comfort to the policy-maker who must light a few 'research trails' (Chubin and Connolly, 1982) among many with the benefit of limited allocations. Predicting the pay-off in knowledge, discovery, and invention is a risky business, so risky that it fuels the interminable 'basic-applied' debate (National Science

Foundation, 1980). This merely justifies certain policy decisions and precludes others. In times of fiscal restraint, it jerks policy towards conservatism — greater centralization of resources and support of proven investigators, programmes, and institutions.[5] Evolutionary epistemology reminds us of the politics of life, not just science. Meta-analysis supplies yet another reminder.

A future orientation denotes that the weak programme goes beyond platitudes about 'policy-relevance', and pledges a commitment to interventionist or activist science. Futurists, evaluation researchers, social forecasters, impact assessors, and the like, all anticipate the future (see Rescher, 1981, for a review). Their pronouncements are prescriptive, sometimes doomsdaying, and always provocative. Typically, these prognosticators disdain interrogations of the past through either documents or first-person recollections. They could learn something from the strong programmers about reconstructing the past; the strong programmers could take heed about projecting the future. We do not endorse the methods of the futurist, such as Delphi, scenarios, and mathematical modelling, but we urge those most predisposed to predicting developments in science and technology — the scientometricians — to augment their pedestrian positivism with methods that introduce new variables, data sources, and interpretive possibilities.[6] Methods that allow the 'case study' to be seen as more than a stereotyped exploratory tool (Yin, 1981), and ethics as a vital policy consideration (instead of a nuisance, or at best, an afterthought), need to be recognized as timeless inputs to the policy process. One makes this case, however, with examples in hand, not studies in preparation. The meta-analyst must compile them, digest them, and beseech the policy-maker with them. To influence the future of policy, we must leave the confines of our disciplinary, and even multidisciplinary, moot courts, and walk the corridors of power (Salomon, 1972).

Once in these corridors, the meta-analyst's role is to challenge conventional policy wisdom and jar the policy-maker into perceiving a complex (and if our efforts succeed unexpectedly, a 'multiple') reality. We do that through an unremitting commitment to value-criticism — an examination of our own and others' values and interests. This self-consciousness is an intellectual check on our politics, if you will. It thrusts us into partisan struggles within the culture *as partisans* — with a difference. The difference is our realization that those struggles are value clashes over value-laden problems. In seeking to understand the process by which the clashes came to be, and the values underpinning them, we also seek to influence outcomes. More specifically, we desire resolution with 'due process' — with an airing of viewpoints, of all available information, of all the uncertainty that accompanies the views of the experts, the policy-makers, the interested public, and the social institutions entrusted with mediation and resolution. Scepticism is our chief ally, for claims-making is a political act. Research 'protocols' for dissecting this act (Markle and Petersen, 1981) may assist in our meta-inquiry. But more crucial perhaps is the decision to be on-site, to tackle the messy problem, to function as a meta-scientist (Wartofsky, 1980). To decide this is to become a factor in the problem, not to recoil in horror as an intellectual issue graduates to the status of social problem or public controversy. The decision is a personal and professional one (though the meta-scientist sees no difference). But how does one explain the value of value-critical meta-analysis to one charged with the formulation or implementation of policy? How does one communicate that values are the *policy-maker's* ally — or at worst, an ineluctable (albeit uninvited) companion? How can the meta-analyst challenge the authority of science, which according to Nelkin (1975: 28), 'must give way to a more open understanding of the social, political, and ideological values that have always influenced its own development'? A 'more open understanding' of values prescribes inquiry into what has always been there. By removing the mantle of privilege, the shroud of mystery, that science has enjoyed for decades, the meta-analyst makes explicit to the policy-maker that which both self-interested scientists and commentators on their unique cultures have endeavoured to describe — on *their* own terms. That is, their values have been immune from those who move in other arenas, attached to other programmes that seldom intersect their own. For them, intellectual self-sufficiency within a hallowed social institution safeguards the practice of science unfettered by the politics of the 'rest' of the world. For the meta-analyst, science *is* politics, and the rest of the world, however conceptualized, is programmatically inseparable from research on science and technology. Value-criticism *is* the message and the science policy-maker is presumed to be listening. The future of meta-analysis is staked on this presumption — and the confidence that listening makes a difference.

Epilogue

Conclusions about the weak programme cannot be drawn here. As a mode of inquiry in science studies, meta-analysis is virtually untested.

As a hybrid of three strong research programmes — the strong programme, lab studies, and scientometrics — the weak programme remains
a promise, and we think a promising alternative, for the policy-maker.
By offering three illustrations of the application of meta-analysis to
science and science policy-making, we have suggested that problems of
science and technology dominated by uncertainty and activating
partisan struggles in various sectors of our culture are appropriate
sites for the meta-scientist. By outlining five criteria which derive
from the three strong programmes, yet which can be synthesized
for analytical purposes not initially intended, we have specified our
own expectations for transforming the fourth ring into a fully fledged
arena dedicated to 'post-disciplinary' science studies — for want of
familiar terms, a sociology of knowledge utilization (Weiss and
Bucuvalas, 1981) or a philosophy of policy science.

Despite the outcomes of future appraisals by ourselves and others,
we would assert for now that the post-Mertonian, post-Kuhnian moot-
ing of science studies is an exercise in policy futility. Value-critical
analysis of problems that originate outside a research programme, and
resist definitional or operational control by programme adherents,
forms the research agenda for meta-inquiry.

We conjecture that all 'successful' strategies in human action share
certain characteristics. 'Science' appears to be a symbol for the set of
characteristics shared by 'successful' strategies. We conjecture furthermore that modes of inquiry going by the *usual* labels — science,
witchcraft, mysticism, astrology, etc., or more generally rational,
irrational, etc. — are constituted of *all* the modes of inquiry in varying
proportions. Now if we examine the widely discussed Azande 'poison
oracle' case alongside science as we new post-disciplinarians have
come to view it, we may readily reach the conclusion of Barry Barnes
(1974: 41):

> We possess no rationality criteria which universally constrain the operation
> of human reason, and which also discriminate existing belief systems, or
> their components into rational and irrational groups. Variability in institu-
> tionalized beliefs cannot be explained by a conception of external causes
> producing deviations from rationality. Likewise, the culture of natural science
> cannot be distinctive because of its rationality, in a universal rather than a
> conventional sense.

However, we *can* discriminate (demarcate, perhaps) on the basis of
the scale and scope of past successes. For there is a general strategy
found in all 'successful' belief systems: to the degree that the strategy

is 'successful', to that degree will this general strategy prevail (this is
a first approximation conjecture). This general strategy is distinguished
by its *capacity* for critical, reflexive, meta-inquiry. This distinguishes
the Azande case from *some* cases of what we have indiscriminately
labelled 'science'.

Picture the scene in Wittgenstein's *On Certainty* (1972: 61e); he
and a philosopher are sitting in a garden. In recalling this scene, we
take the liberty of joining Wittgenstein and the philosopher. Now the
philosopher says again and again, 'I know that's a tree', pointing to a
nearby tree. We say again and again, 'I know that's a social construction', pointing to the same tree. A woman arrives and hears all this.
Wittgenstein tells her: 'These fellows aren't insane. We are only doing
philosophy [and sociology].' This garden dialogue is effectively interminable. In order to address the agenda of a relevant epistemology,
we must leave the garden and muck about in a different sort of environment. Outside of the garden, human beings are everywhere. They
implicate themselves in, and thereby realize the causal (and other)
connections between what philosophers distinguish as 'things in the
world' and 'terms that refer'. Humans constantly (and perversely, some
intellectuals believe) interfere with attempts to treat aims such as
'truth' or 'success' without reference to their existence. The recognition
that we cannot eradicate the human and social element in discourse,
inquiry, and knowledge is a prerequisite to advancing any epistemological programme in science studies.

'Epistemology' disguises theological, apologetic, and ideological
quests. Epistemologies shorn of theology and apology can be classified
as critical or conformist ideologies of knowledge and science. A critical
epistemology is not based on the a priori assumption that 'science' is
the paradigmatic mode of inquiry. It is resistant to the idea that the
best way to study science is to use 'scientific methods'. This resistance
is a necessary condition for the *critical* study of science. A conformist
epistemology is based on the notion that science is the paradigmatic
mode of inquiry, and that the best way to study science *is* to use scientific methods. The objective of a conformist epistemology is to nourish
and faithfully reproduce science-as-it-is along with its social trappings.
A critical epistemology creates the possibility for a transformation of
science-as-it-is and its social trappings.

There are some dangers, too, of which we should beware in our
efforts to work out a changed vocabulary. (1) Science is a specific and
delimited epistemic activity; it is one type of inquiry. Anything epistemologically relevant for science will not necessarily transfer to other

modes and will be irrelevant for an *evolutionary* epistemology. (2) While science with its social trappings is *one* type of inquiry, it is not *monolithic*. (3) Since epistemic activities exist within transepistemic fields it is impossible to get an accurate portrait of science by focusing exclusively *on* 'science'.

If we are willing to leave Wittgenstein's garden and construct a critical epistemology, we will have to engage in criticism and renewal with respect to 'facts', technological processes, specific theories, types of theory, and conceptual frameworks (cf. Hooker, 1975). We will have to assess critically the allocation of resources among different arenas of criticism. And we will have to confront currently institutionalized structures of research and criticism. We will be actively engaged in designing and experimenting with social structures; the tinkerer principle will, if adhered to, help to appraise programmes of design, implementation, and expectation in science studies. Any programme, after all, is what it studies, to what end, and for whom. The strength of the weak programme is a consciousness about these very expectations.

Notes

1. The distinction between 'knowledge-production' and 'knowledge-utilization' may be arbitrary, but such specializations are reinforced by journals such as *Knowledge: Creation, Diffusion, Utilization, Research Policy, Policy Sciences*, and *Policy Analysis*, and by recognition of free-floating experts (of mysterious disciplinary origins) as 'policy analysts'.
2. A clear statement of the propensity for 'objective inquiry' and its resultant data — inevitably describable as 'valid', 'reliable' and 'replicable' within narrow confidence limits — can be found in Narin (1979).
3. Recent calls on the editorial page of *Science* for solidarity among *all* sciences, in the face of recent federal budget slashes of support of social science research in the US, is a case in point.
4. An exception proves the rule: the decentralized process adopted by the National Science Foundation to produce a *Five-Year Outlook on Science and Technology* has been unusual. As a congressionally-mandated report, however, its relegation to NSF by then-President Carter and his science advisor Frank Press doomed its potential policy impact. It remains a 'reactive' instead of a

'directive' document. Under the Reagan Office of Science and Technology Policy, that might – for better or worse – change (Chubin and Rossini, 1981).

5. Indeed, two officers of the UK's Social Science Research Council have undertaken a 'study of decisions within research funding organizations, in terms of both setting research priorities and of decisions as between individual applications for funds' (Caswill and Healey, 1981, private communication). In late 1981 these officers visited their US counterpart, NSF, as well as a smattering of academic researchers, on a fact-finding mission. They report (Chubin, private communication) finding few 'facts', but encountered an impenetrable smoke-screen of rhetoric at NSF.

6. With the era of 'evaluation research' upon us, surmounting the stereotypes surrounding qualitative versus quantitative analysis is a necessity. For a healthy start toward methodological ecumenism, see Reichardt and Cook (1979).

References

Barnes, Barry (1974) *Scientific Knowledge and Sociological Theory*, London: Routledge and Kegan Paul.

Barnes, Barry (1977) *Interests and the Growth of Knowledge*, London: Routledge Direct Editions.

Barnes, Barry and Shapin, Steven (eds) (1979) *Natural Order: Historical Studies of Scientific Culture*, London and Beverly Hills: Sage.

Bazelon, David L. (1979) 'Risk and Responsibility', *Science*, 205 (20 July): 277–80.

Bazelon, David L. (1980) 'Science, Technology, and the Court', *Science*, 208 (16 May): 661.

Bloor, David (1976) *Knowledge and Social Imagery*, London: Routledge and Kegan Paul.

Bohm, D. (1976) *Fragmentation and Wholeness*, Jerusalem: VanLeer Jerusalem Foundation.

Bourdieu, P. (1975) 'The Specificity of the Scientific Field and the Social Conditions of the Progress of Reason', *Social Science Information*, 14: 19–47.

Campbell, Donald T. (1974) 'Evolutionary Epistemology', in P. A. Schipp (ed.), *The Philosophy of Karl Popper*, vol. 14–1, LaSalle, Ill.: Open Court.

Campbell, Donald T. (1977) 'Descriptive epistemology: Psychological, Sociological, and Evolutionary', preliminary draft, William James Lectures, Harvard University (Spring).

Campbell, Donald T. (1979) 'A Tribal Model of the Social System Vehicle Carrying Scientific Knowledge', *Knowledge: Creation, Diffusion, Utilization*, 2 (December): 181–201.

Chubin, D. E. (1980) 'Competence is not Enough', *Contemporary Sociology*, 9: 204–7.

Chubin, D. E. (1981a) 'Constructing and Reconstructing Scientific Reality: A Meta-analysis', *International Society for the Sociology of Knowledge Newsletter*, 7 (May): 22–8.

Chubin, D. E. (1981b) 'Values, Controversy, and the Sociology of Science', *Bulletin of Science, Technology, and Society*, 1: 427–36.

Chubin, D. E. (1982a) 'Beyond Invisible Colleges: A Bibliographic Essay', in D. E. Chubin, *Sociology of Sciences: An Annotated Bibliography on Invisible Colleges, 1972–1981*, New York: Garland.

Chubin, D. E. (1982b) 'Collins' Programme and the "Hardest Possible Case"', *Social Studies of Science*, 12: 136–9.

Chubin, D. E. (1982c) 'Reform of Peer Review', *Science*, 215 (15 January): 240.

Chubin, D. E. (1982d) 'Peer Review and the Courts: Notes of a Participant-Scientist', *Bulletin of Science, Technology, and Society*, 2: forthcoming.

Chubin, D. E. and Connolly, T. (1982) 'Research Trails and Science Policies: Local and Extra-Local Negotiation of Scientific Work', pp. 293–311 in N. Elias et al. (eds), *Scientific Establishments and Hierarchies, Sociology of the Sciences Yearbook*, vol. 6, Dordrecht: D. Reidel.

Chubin, D. E. and Rossini, F. A. (eds) (1981) 'Special Issue: The Five-Year Outlook on Science and Technology in the United States', *Technological Forecasting and Social Change*, 20 (September): 97–171.

Chubin, D. E. and Studer, K. E. (1978) 'The Politics of Cancer', *Theory and Society*, 6: 55–74.

Cole, Jonathan R. and Cole, Stephen (1973) *Social Stratification in Science*, Chicago: University of Chicago Press.

Cole, Stephen, Rubin, Leonard, and Cole, Jonathan R. (1978) *Peer Review in the National Science Foundation*, Washington, DC: National Academy of Sciences.

Cole, S., Cole, J. R., and Simon, G. A. (1981) 'Chance and Consensus in Peer Review', *Science*, 214 (14 November): 881–6.

Collins, H. M. (1975) 'The Seven Sexes: A Study in the Sociology of a Phenomenon, or the Replication of Experiments in Physics', *Sociology*, 9: 205–24.

Collins, H. M. (ed.) (1981) 'Knowledge and Controversy: Studies of Modern Natural Science', special issue of *Social Studies of Science*, 11 (February).

Collins, H. M. and Pinch, T. J. (1982) *Frames of Meaning: The Social Construction of Extraordinary Science*, London: Routledge and Kegan Paul.

Cozzens, S. E. (1980) 'Review of Latour and Woolgar's *Laboratory Life*', *4S Newsletter*, 5 (Spring): 19–21.

Culliton, Barbara J. (1980) 'Continuing Confusion over Love Canal', *Science*, 209 (29 August): 1002–3.

Dolby, R. G. A. (1979) 'Reflections on Deviant Science', pp. 9–47 in R. Wallis (ed.), *On the Margins of Science: The Social Construction of Rejected Knowledge*, Staffordshire: University of Keele.

Elkana, Y., Lederberg, J., Merton, R. K., Thackray, A. and Zuckerman, H. (eds) (1977) *Toward a Metric of Science: Essays Occasioned by the Advent of Science Indicators*, New York: Wiley-Interscience.

Feyerabend, P. (1978) *Against Method*, London: Verso.

Gaston, Jerry (1978) *The Reward System in British and American Science*, New York: Wiley.

Gieryn, T. F. (1982) 'Relativist/Constructivist Programmes in the Sociology of Science: Redundance and Retreat', *Social Studies of Science*, 12: 279–97.

Gillespie, Brendan, Eva, Dave, and Johnston, Ron (1979) 'Carcinogenic Risk Assessment in the United States and Great Britain: The Case of Aldrin/ Dieldrin', *Social Studies of Science*, 9 (August): 265–301.

Goodfield, June (1981) *An Imagined World: A Story of Scientific Discovery*, New York: Harper and Row.

Gori, Gio Batta (1980) 'The Regulation of Carcinogenic Hazards', *Science*, 208 (18 April): 256–61.

Gouldner, A. W. (1970) *The Coming Crisis of Western Sociology*, New York: Basic Books.

Gouldner, A. W. (1976) *The Dialectic of Ideology and Technology*, New York: Seabury Press.

Greenberg, D. S. (1980) 'A Conversation with Vincent T. DeVita, Jr., M.D.', *The New England Journal of Medicine*, 303 (23 October): 1014.

Hargens, Lowell (1978) 'Theory and Method in the Sociology of Science', pp. 121–39 in J. Gaston (ed.), *Sociology of Science*, San Francisco: Jossey-Bass.

Hooker, Clifford A. (1975) 'Philosophy and Meta-Philosophy of Science: Empiricism, Popperianism and Realism', *Synthese*, 32: 177–231.

Jacob, F. (1977) 'Evolution and Tinkering', *Science*, 196 (10 June): 1161–6.

Johnston, Ron (1976) 'Contextual Knowledge: A Model for the Overthrow of the Internal/External Dichotomy in Science', *Australian and New Zealand Journal of Sociology*, 12 (October): 193–203.

Knorr-Cetina, Karin D. (1977) 'Producing and Reproducing Knowledge: Descriptive or Constructive?', *Social Science Information*, 16: 669–96.

Knorr-Cetina, Karin D. (1981a) 'The Ethnography of Laboratory Life: Empirical Results and Theoretical Challenges', *International Society for the Sociology of Knowledge Newsletter*, 7 (May): 4–9.

Knorr-Cetina, Karin D. (1981b) *The Manufacture of Knowledge: An Essay on the Constructivist and Contextual Nature of Science*, Oxford: Pergamon.

Knorr-Cetina, Karin D. (1982) 'Scientific Communities or Transepistemic Arenas of Research? A Critique of Quasi-Economic Models of Science', *Social Studies of Science*, 12: 101–30.

Kuhn, Thomas S. (1970) *The Structure of Scientific Revolutions*, revised edition, Chicago: University of Chicago Press.

Lakatos, I. and Musgrave, A. (eds) (1970) *Criticism and the Growth of Knowledge*, Cambridge: Cambridge University Press.

Latour, B. (1980) 'Is it Possible to Reconstruct the Research Process? Sociology of a Brain Peptide', pp. 53–73 in K. D. Knorr et al. (eds), *The Social Process of Scientific Investigation, Sociology of the Sciences Yearbook*, vol. 4, Dordrecht: D. Reidel.

Latour, Bruno and Woolgar, Steve (1979) *Laboratory Life: The Social Construction of Scientific Facts*, London and Beverly Hills: Sage.

Laudan, Larry (1977) *Progress and Its Problems*, Berkeley: University of California Press.

Lave, L. B. and Seskin, E. P. (1979) 'Epidemiology, Causality, and Public Policy',

American Scientist, 67 (March–April): 178–86.

Law, John (1974) 'Theory and Methods in the Sociology of Science', *Social Science Information*, 13: 163–72.

Lindsey, Duncan (1978) *The Scientific Publication System in the Social Sciences*, San Francisco: Jossey-Bass.

MacKenzie, Donald (1978) 'Statistical Theory and Social Interests: A Case Study', *Social Studies of Science*, 8: 35–83.

Markle, Gerald E. and Petersen, James C. (1981) 'Controversies in Science and Technology: A Protocol for Comparative Research', *Science, Technology, and Human Values*, 6 (Spring): 25–32.

Marx, Jean L. (1980) 'Consensus – More or Less – on the Pap Smear', *Science*, 209 (8 August): 672.

Mitroff, I. I. and Chubin, D. E. (1979) 'Peer Review at NSF: A Dialectical Policy Analysis', *Social Studies of Science*, 9 (May): 199–232.

Mulkay, Michael J. (1979) *Science and the Sociology of Knowledge*, London: Allen and Unwin.

Mulkay, Michael J. (1980) 'Sociology of Science in the West', *Sociology*, 28 (Winter): Part One (pp. 1–116), Bibliography (pp. 133–84).

Mullins, Nicholas C. (1973) *Theory and Theory Groups in Contemporary American Sociology*, New York: Harper and Row.

Mullins, N. C., Hargens, L. L., Hecht, P. K., and Kick, E. L. (1977) 'The Group Structure of the Cocitation Clusters: A Comparative Study', *American Sociological Review*, 42 (August): 552–62.

Narin, Francis (1976) *Evaluative Bibliometrics: The Use of Citation Analysis in the Evaluation of Scientific Activity*, New Jersey: Computer Horizons Inc.

Narin, Francis (1979) 'Objectivity versus Relevance in Studies of Scientific Advance', *Scientometrics*, 1 (September): 35–41.

National Commission on Research (1980) *Review Processes: Assessing the Quality of Research Proposals*, Washington, DC (May).

National Science Board (1979) *Science Indicators 1978*, Washington, DC: National Science Foundation.

National Science Foundation (1980) *Categories of Scientific Research*, Washington, DC: NSF 80–28.

Nelkin, Dorothy (1975) 'The Political Impact of Technical Expertise', *Social Studies of Science*, 5 (February): 35–54.

Nelkin, Dorothy (1979) 'Science, Technology, and Political Conflict: Analyzing the Issues', pp. 9–22 in D. Nelkin (ed.), *Controversy: Politics of Technical Decisions*, London and Beverly Hills: Sage.

Pinch, Trevor (1977) 'What Does a Proof Do if it Does not Prove?' pp. 171–215 in E. Mendelsohn et al. (eds), *The Social Production of Scientific Knowledge*, *Sociology of the Sciences Yearbook*, vol. 1, Dordrecht: D. Reidel.

Pinch, Trevor (1980) 'Theoreticians and the Production of Experimental Anomaly: The Case of Solar Neutrinos', pp. 77–106 in K. D. Knorr et al. (eds), *The Social Process of Scientific Investigation*, *Sociology of the Sciences Yearbook*, vol. 4, Dordrecht: D. Reidel.

Radnitzky, G. (1970) *Contemporary Schools of Metascience*, second edition, New York: Humanities Press.

Radnitzky, G. (1974) 'Towards a Systematic Philosophy of Scientific Research', *Philosophy of the Social Sciences*, 4: 369–98.

Reichardt, C. S. and Cook, T. D. (1979) 'Beyond Qualitative versus Quantitative Methods', pp. 7–32 in T. D. Cook and C. S. Reichardt (eds), *Qualitative and Quantitative Methods in Evaluation Research*, London and Beverly Hills: Sage.

Rescher, Nicholas (1981) 'Methodological Issues in Science and Technology Forecasting: Uses and Limitations in Public Policy Deliberations', *Technological Forecasting and Social Change*, 20 (September): 101–12.

Restivo, S. (1981a) 'Notes and Queries on Science, Technology, and Human Values', *Science, Technology and Human Values*, 6 (Winter): 20–4.

Restivo, S. (1981b) 'Commentary: Some Perspectives in Contemporary Sociology of Science', *Science, Technology and Human Values*, 6 (Spring): 22–30.

Richter, Maurice N. (1972) *Science as a Cultural Process*, Cambridge, Mass.: Schenkman.

Roy, Rustrum (1981) 'An Alternative Funding Mechanism', *Science*, 211 (27 March): 1377.

Salomon, J. J. (1972) 'The Mating of Knowledge and Power', *Impact of Science on Society*, 22 (January–June): 123–32.

Smith, R. Jeffrey (1980) 'Government Says Cancer Rate is Increasing', *Science*, 209 (29 August): 998–1002.

Studer, Kenneth E. and Chubin, D. E. (1977) 'Ethics and the Unintended Consequences of Social Research: A Perspective from the Sociology of Science', *Policy Sciences*, 8: 111–124.

Studer, Kenneth E. and Chubin, D. E. (1980) *The Cancer Mission: Social Contexts of Biomedical Research*, London and Beverly Hills: Sage.

Travis, G. D. L. (1980) 'On the Construction of Creativity: The Memory Transfer Phenomenon and the Importance of Being Earnest', pp. 165–93 in K. Knorr et al. (eds), *The Social Process of Scientific Investigation, Sociology of the Sciences Yearbook*, vol. 4. Dordrecht: D. Reidel.

Traweek, Sharon (1981) 'Culture and the Organization of the Particle Physics Communities in Japan and the United States', paper presented at the conference on Communication in Scientific Research, Simon Fraser University (September).

Turner, Stephen P. and Chubin, Daryl E. (1979) 'Chance and Eminence in Science: Ecclesiastes II', *Social Science Information*, 18: 437–49.

Vogt, T. M. (1979) 'Szent-Gyorgyi's Research', *Science*, 203 (30 March): 1293.

Wartofsky, Marx W. (1980) 'The Critique of Impure Reason II: Sin, Science, and Society', *Science, Technology, and Human Values*, No. 33 (Fall): 5–23.

Weiss, Carol H. with Bucuvalas, Michael J. (1981) *Social Science Research and Decision-Making*, New York: Columbia University Press.

Whitley, R. D. (1972) 'Black Boxism and the Sociology of Science: A Discussion of the Major Developments in the Field', pp. 61–92 in P. Halmos (ed.), *The Sociology of Science, The Sociological Review Monograph*, 18 (September).

Whitley, R. D. (1974) 'Cognitive and Social Institutionalization of Scientific Specialties and Research Areas', pp. 69–95 in Richard D. Whitley (ed.), *Social Processes of Scientific Development*. London: Routledge and Kegan Paul.

Whitley, R. D. (1977) 'The Sociology of Scientific Work and the History of Scientific Developments', pp. 21–50 in S. S. Blume (ed.), *Perspectives in the Sociology of Science*. Chichester: Wiley.

Wittgenstein, L. (1972) *On Certainty*, New York: Harper Torchbooks.

Woolgar, S. (1980) 'Discovery: Logic and Sequence in a Scientific Text', in K. Knorr et al. (eds.), *The Social Process of Scientific Investigation, Sociology of the Sciences Yearbook*, vol. 4, Dordrecht: D. Reidel.

Woolgar, S. (1981a) 'Science and Ethnomethodology: A Prefatory Statement', *International Society for the Sociology of Knowledge Newsletter*, 7 (May): 10–15.

Woolgar, S. (1981b) 'Interests and Explanation in the Social Study of Science', *Social Studies of Science*, 11 (August): 365–94.

Yin, Robert (1981) 'The Case Study Crisis: Some Answers', *Administrative Science Quarterly*, 26 (March): 145–52.

Zenzen, M. and Restivo, S. (1982) 'The Mysterious Morphology of Immiscible Liquids: A Study of Scientific Practice', *Social Science Information*, 21: 447–73.

Zuckerman, H. (1970) 'Stratification in American Science', pp. 235–57 in E. O. Laumann (ed.), *Social Stratification: Theory and Research for the 1970s*, Indianapolis: Bobbs-Merrill.

Zuckerman, H. and Miller, R. B. (eds) (1980) 'Science Indicators: Implications for Research and Policy', special issue of *Scientometrics*, 2 (October): 327–448.

4

An Empirical Relativist Programme in the Sociology of Scientific Knowledge

H.M. Collins
University of Bath, UK

Introduction

Setting out a programme of research involves, among other things, setting up rules of practice which define and regulate that programme. However, since rules do not contain the rules for their own application, and since the application of a rule in a new situation does not depend on careful specification but on unexplicated *competence*, to set out a programme is to face the problem of reducing an indefinite number of possible supporting and clarifying comments to a subset of useful guidelines. What this should contain is not obvious at the outset. What is more, the *applicability* of rules, and their precise meaning only becomes clear as a body of practice builds up with their application. With the empirical relativist programme that I am trying to represent we are now in a doubly fortunate position. Firstly, we have a number of case studies which between them have generated the practice of the programme as they have gone along. Secondly, we have a set of alternative practices which differ from this and show us some of the things that are worth spelling out explicitly.

It is the latter felicitous circumstance that has given rise to the appendices of this chapter, and has inspired much of the main part of it too. Five years ago it would not have occurred that the resurgence in the sociology of scientific knowledge would take some of the forms that have emerged recently. It would not therefore have seemed important to present an explicit commentary on many points. Programmes, it appears, are best generated out of practice and example, and best proclaimed and systematized with at least some degree of hindsight.[1]

Pluralism and progress

The growth point of sociology of science during the last ten years has been the sociology of scientific knowledge, and the defining characteristic of this new work has been the 'symmetrical' approach (Bloor, 1976). That is to say, scientific knowledge has been approached in the same way irrespective of its perceived success, truth, progressiveness, rationality and so forth. In the large majority of instances where this attitude has informed actual empirical work, the resulting studies have had, only partly coincidentally, a new character. The studies have been, typically, studies of the development of (relatively) self-contained units of scientific knowledge. Whereas the concerns of the traditional sociology of science encouraged the study of scientific institutions as defined by professional criteria — science as a whole system, the discipline, the individual laboratory or research team — the new focus encourages the study of passages of scientific activity defined by their common cognitive goal — building a laser, detecting gravity waves, detecting J-rays, discovering the nature of a biological mechanism. Even where the studies have described themselves as 'laboratory studies' or 'anthropological studies', many of their most interesting contributions emerge out of research on passages of laboratory work which are defined by a cognitive goal — discovering the structure of a new compound, researching the nature of a food processing operation.

Since science consists in a large part of such cognitively defined knowledge generating passages of activity (linked at a higher level, of course), the new sociology of science has found itself in the fortunate position of being able to generate any number of fairly small, manageable, self-contained studies. The subject has, as it were, a 'granular' structure. This has helped to maintain a vigorous empirical tradition. Also, it has made the subject a testing ground for sociological method and professional practice. It is a microcosm of the good, the bad and the ugly in modern sociology.

Unfortunately, a granular structure can have disadvantages. This chapter appears in a book of 'perspectives'. Encouraged by our 'late-1960s' Kuhnian sophistication, it is all too easy to fall into a relaxed pluralism about differing 'perspectives' when we discover that we disagree. Ironically, pluralism can be afforded only when the questions are big ones — Marxism versus functionalism and so forth — but it has a high cost if every new methodological wrinkle, or minor variation of fieldwork location is described as a fresh start to the subject.[2] Under these circumstances the granules will never add up to anything.

Because of this it seems worthwhile not just to accept a plurality of perspectives but to attempt to try to define some overall goals with reference to which the various different styles of work in the area can be examined. Some recent styles have been characterized by claims to their novelty, originality, immaculate methodology, logical necessity and so forth. A new entrant to the field must feel confused about what is going on, what is basic and what is of more minor significance.

The sociology of scientific knowledge

I see the mainstream concern of the sociology of scientific knowledge as being the *sociology of knowledge* and I see the concentration on science as being a consequence of its suitability as a social laboratory for the exploration of ideas about knowledge in general. It is suitable because it has readily accessible knowledge-producing institutions and because it is the canonical knowledge-producing institution. It is then in a sense the easiest case to study (because it is the most accessible) while, in experimental programme terms, it is the 'hardest case' for study (Collins, 1982a). Within the sociology of *scientific* knowledge thus perceived, the aim of a piece of work will be to contribute to our understanding of the construction of scientific knowledge and, by extension, construction of all knowledge. One part of this overall programme will be to apply our understanding to particular instances of scientific history, while another part will be to show how the history of particular cases supports more general ideas. The whole programme should certainly be able to cope with particular cases, but the understanding of particular cases is certainly not the whole programme.[3]

Living and interpreting social and scientific life

Given this as the mainstream concern of the subject there is no better starting point for characterizing work that has been done with this view in mind than the two central tenets of Bloor's 'Strong Programme':[4]

...[impartiality] with respect to truth and falsity, rationality or irrationality, success or failure. Both sides of these dichotomies...require explanation.

and

...[symmetry] in...style of explanation. The same types of cause...explain, say, true and false beliefs. (Bloor, 1976: 5)

Of course a tenet, like a rule, does not apply itself and experience has shown that different readings are possible even of these apparently straightforward prescriptions. For example, we have argued (Collins and Cox, 1976) that one implication of symmetry is that the natural world must be treated as though it did not affect our perception of it. This reading, it turns out, was not intended by David Bloor. To try to clarify the position, let us bear in mind that the driving force behind the relativist/symmetrical approach is the idea that what counts as the truth can vary from place to place and from time to time.

To get an impression of what can be *done* with this idea, it is useful to see how it was arrived at. The view has various roots in modern sociological thought. These include the later philosophy of Wittgenstein (1953) and its application to anthropology and the social sciences (Winch, 1958; Wilson, 1970) and the phenomenological approach to sociology (e.g. Schutz, 1964, 1967).[5]

These philosophies point out that the meaning of thoughts and of acts is integral with cultural context. For example, to make a 'likeness' of a person in one society is to flatter, whereas in another it is to threaten magically. Of course, in another society, with different conventions of representation, the 'same' set of marks might not even be taken as a likeness.

It is vitally important to note that we are not able to obtain from those with different ways of seeing a description of the way that they manage to see differently. For example, we are not able to explain to someone, who cannot see it, what it is about Figure 1 that enables us to see it as a face. We can be fairly sure that it would not be possible for some peoples — say peoples that were not used to the conventions of black and white two-dimensional representation, or peoples who were hairless, to see it as a face, and we would not be able to explain to them how to see the figure as we do. In seeing the figure as a face, we see it as similar to other faces in ways that we cannot fully articulate. These ways would be referred to as taken-for-granted by phenomenologists, for in the normal way we just live with them without thinking about them. A Wittgensteinian would say that we use rules of seeing

FIGURE 1

Most people take a while to see this as a face. Try and work out what it is that enables you to see it thus at one time when you couldn't see it thus before. Try to explain it to someone who cannot see it.

similarity to see the face, but again we are not able to say what these rules are. It is not just seeing that has these characteristics, but all action. The meaning of all action is given by taken-for-granted rules (see also Knapp, 1981).

This is one way that a thing can appear true at one time or place and false at another; that is, if the taken-for-granted rules of seeing, or measuring or acting in all manner of other ways, were different at the two different times or places. If what was at issue was what was shown in Figure 1, then at one time it might be merely a field of snow covered mountains (which is what the photographer is said to have seen when he photographed it) at another time it might be a face (as it has been for me since about two hours after I first saw it) or at still another time it might be a random black and white pattern. The nicest feature of this example is that we can see how foolish it is to ask which of these it *really is*.

Kuhn's (1962) model of science fits this picture perfectly. The different cultures with their taken-for-granted ways of seeing and acting are different paradigms. A paradigm is coexistent with the rules of seeing and rules of measuring and thinking that give it its physical objects and scientific laws.[6] Different natural objects are precipitated by different paradigms. What may be true in one, may be false in another.

In science as in life the rules that give activity its meaning are not articulated. They are effortlessly followed in a 'natural way'. Indeed, when one follows the rules things come so naturally that one is unaware that anything is being achieved in following them. It will not be obvious that to see some set of marks as an object is any kind of accomplishment. Only when the rules go wrong does it become obvious that everyday life (and, for the scientist, this includes expert scientific life) involves doing anything skilful.[7] Otherwise our giving of meaning to objects — our interpretative practices — are so automatic that we do not notice that any interpretation is involved. We tend to think that what we see must always have been what we see it *as*. That which we bring to the act of seeing is invisible and this gives the meaning of things an 'external' quality. In the sciences the apparent externality of things seen is celebrated and reinforced by the notion that anyone would see the same things if they looked in the same place. If anyone would see the same thing, then its sameness must be a product of *it*, rather than a product of the see-er.[8] When something is thought of like this it is often referred to as a 'datum'. A datum is something that speaks for itself. It doesn't require interpretation to be a datum.[9]

Of course, like everything else data has no meaning outside of an interpretative context. Without this it is just random marks on paper, or whatever. If it is spoken, then it is literally 'noise'. But to notice that data has no meaning outside of its interpretation requires that interpretations normally given in a matter-of-course, taken-for-granted, 'natural' way are suspended. Only then is what is regularly achieved without difficulty or conscious effort seen to be an achievement. In Schutz's terms, what we are then doing is suspending our 'natural attitude' (Schutz, 1964: 104ff.). We need then to suspend our natural attitude to the *natural* world so as to be able to notice the ways that it is constructed and interpreted. We need to suspend that common-sense and philosophical view of science that gives us certainty about scientists dealings with nature. What we need is radical uncertainty about how things about nature are known. This radical uncertainty is relativism. Any alternative view can be crippling to a vigorous exploration of the social construction of the natural world – and indeed to a proper understanding of the role of the natural world in forming our view of it (see Gieryn, 1982; Collins, 1982b, for a more full discussion). Though this point can be argued as an epistemological principle the important thing is to adopt it as a methodological imperative.

Native competence

A radical uncertainty about things is not the same as ignorance. I do not have a radical uncertainty about the meaning of say, equine dressage, I have a profound ignorance of it. To develop radical uncertainty it is first necessary to develop understanding and then suspend that understanding. The sort of understanding necessary is the understanding of the native member – an understanding that makes the meanings, perceptions and acts of the native member follow naturally as a matter of course. It is an understanding of the taken-for-granted rules of the culture under investigation. This is often called 'native competence'. Without native competence the acts or symbols that are part of the native society remain uninterpreted – pieces of behaviour or junk or perhaps marks indistinguishable from noise.

In the sociology of scientific knowledge the researcher will need to develop as far as possible the native competences of the scientific group under study. The greatest possible technical familiarity with the scientific area is called for. But, since a crucial characteristic of taken-for-granted rules is that they cannot be fully explicated, an acquaintance

with the area through the technical literature will not suffice. The
sociologist needs, insofar as it is possible, to acquire the tacit knowledge of native/scientist members. Tacit knowledge is best acquired
through face-to-face contact. Indeed the only method of acquiring
full native competence that we know of is participation in the area
under study.[10]

Participation will *change* the sociologist. The sociologist will become, at least in part, like a native member. The sociologist will thereby
become unlike the readers of the papers in which he or she presents
findings. Herein lies a difficulty, for the material presented in such
papers can only be properly understood by someone with a share in
the native competence of the scientists in question. The *data* are not
meaningful outside of this interpretative context. The data consist of
more than just a set of scientists' utterances; the data include that
which the sociologist *understands*, but cannot explicate, about the
construction of scientific knowledge in the area in question. The sociologist has come to *understand* through participation, but all that the
sociologist can present to readers is a series of utterances.

Not all available utterances could or should be presented. Selective
presentation is a technical necessity, but in addition a certain studied
selectivity is advisable. The rules of selection are those used by, say,
the geologist presenting the meanderings of rivers with a photograph
of the most meandered river he can find, or the high energy physicist
presenting the neatest possible bubble chamber photograph. To confuse
scientists' utterances presented in this way with the whole of the data,
is like confusing photographs with rivers or with subatomic particles.
The observations, skills and knowledge upon which the theories of
river meanders and high energy physics rest is not contained in photographs alone.

Ultimately, the argument for all of these things rests on the cogency
of the theory behind what is claimed and, above all, on independent
replication of the findings.[11] Because of its 'granular structure', the
sociology of scientific knowledge offers unusually good opportunities
for replication (unusually good for sociology that is — see Bell, 1974)
and much has been independently confirmed (Collins, 1981a).

Of course, any sociologist who wants to replicate previous work
must develop the same native competences as the original investigator.
(It will be unusual for the very same passage of scientific activity to be
researched in this degree of detail by any two researchers. But there
is no need for the same area to be looked at in order that confirmatory
findings be generated. Findings ought to be expressed at a level of

generality such that research on similar passages of scientific activity can confirm them — this has been the case with the 'replication studies'.) It is a mistake to think that this need for the replicator to develop special skills makes interpretative sociology inferior or suspect. In this respect it is precisely the same as all the other sciences. To replicate any scientific finding requires the appropriate skills. If the reader of some paper is not to develop those skills and invest the same time and energy into the replicating project as the scientist who first made the claims in question then a certain amount will have to be taken on trust. It is only when we think of a 'datum' in a 'taken-for-granted' way that we are likely to think that it could ever 'speak for itself'.[12]

Having set out this model of interpretative method and its problems we must immediately enter some reservations. The method of full participation can rarely be attained in practice (but see Collins and Pinch, 1982; Fleck, 1935), but a series of depth interviews can be an acceptable substitute (see Collins, 1979, for further discussion). Experience suggests that such a series of interviews, carried through with the object of a more full participation in mind, can serve. In these circumstances the interviewer has contact with the field through the separated experiences of individuals. The interviewer needs to be aware that the prime object of the interview is not to elicit details pertaining to the individual, but to *tap* the body of rules and understandings that comprise the individual as a scientist.[13]

Three types of scientific activity

The Wittgensteinian/phenomenological/Kuhnian model of scientific activity as well as precipitating certain methods also directs our attention when we look at science. There are three sorts of things that scientists do that need to be examined. Scientists work away within their own natural attitude (paradigm) collecting 'data' and producing results in an unproblematic taken-for-granted way. This seems to be exactly what Kuhn meant by 'normal science'. It is certainly well worth studying this activity (my own attempt is to be found in Collins, 1974, and Collins and Harrison, 1975). Another thing that scientists do is to try to overturn the taken-for-granted rules and replace them with a completely new set (see Collins and Pinch, 1982, for an attempt to research this type of activity). The third thing is in between the other two. That is, scientists sometimes produce results that do not fit very well within the paradigm and become involved in controversy as they try to make major changes in what is taken for granted without reforming the whole structure (my own attempts to look at this sort of activity include Collins, 1975 and 1981c).[14] Interestingly, there seems to be nothing in the phenomenological/ Wittgensteinian literature that has to do with *change* in our taken-for-granted ways of seeing. One thing that makes science such an excellent location for making original contributions to the study of knowledge is that it is full of passages of change. The outcome of a change is the construction of new ways of looking at the world — a new piece of knowledge. In science studies there is the opportunity to do empirical work which goes beyond the analyses of the quality and maintenance of everyday life; there is an opportunity to study the modification, destruction and reconstruction of ways of life and their knowledge.

Concerning the study of 'normal science', the difficulty is in suspending the natural attitude. Normal science has such well-established credentials and methods for externalizing its objects that it is hard to make them seem strange and less than certain. It is perhaps no coincidence that one of the first extended field studies of normal science from a sociology of knowledge viewpoint was carried out in an anthropological mood (Latour and Woolgar, 1979). Recently an increasing number of such studies are being carried out. They have the advantage that the single laboratory setting is a reasonable field location for this type of work. (See in this volume Knorr-Cetina, ch. 5, for a summary of some recent studies, and Lynch et al., ch. 8.)

The study of change is rather different. The study of revolutionary change has special problems most of which are to do with locating a suitable fieldwork site (Collins, 1979b; Collins and Pinch, 1982; Krige, 1981). It is easier to examine attempts at large but not revolutionary developments associated with scientific controversy. As before, the ingredients of a study of this sort are technical competence and an ability to suspend the beliefs and ways of seeing that follow as a matter of course from this competence. In the case of a scientific controversy, however, *participants* find that the taken-for-granted rules are thrown into question automatically by the discovery that they no longer produce unproblematic outcomes. Thus, in seeing the world through the scientists' eyes at a time of controversy, one automatically suspends the layman's attitude to science that is so debilitating. (It will be noted that I am equating most scientists' views of the natural world with the layman's view. I think this is true for cases of the development of knowledge in which the scientist is not immediately involved — see Collins, 1981d.)[15] We might say that the scientific controversy operates as an 'autogarfinkel' for scientific knowledge. Controversy is then a very good location for research. Another aspect of scientific change also becomes clear when controversy is examined. Change cannot be understood merely by paying attention to the way that scientists interpret their worlds. A comprehension of the scientists' interpretative competences is a vital part of the enterprise, but whether a change comes about or not is a consequence of more than what happens in any single location, *even though any single location is the seat of all that there is to be known about the general features of scientists' interpretative practices.* Whether a change comes about is a consequence of the way that attempted innovations are treated by the larger scientific community.[16]

In the first place, attempted changes will be examined and argued about by the relatively small set of experts in the specific area of science in question — what I have called the 'core-set' (Collins, 1981d).[17] To begin to understand the process of change, this set of experts and their different laboratories and other institutions must be taken as the minimum unit for investigation. The interaction of these laboratories and experts will determine the outcome of an attempted change and it is this set that gives a new way of seeing its scientific imprimatur. It is this set that confirms, or otherwise, that what is treated as data by one scientist may be treated as data by others. They give it its external quality. (I have previously argued (1982b) that the outcome of the core-set's negotiations over what is acceptable is co-extensive with a well-replicated observation.) The core-set does not work in isolation of course. The ways in which debate is brought to a close is very much a matter of the core-set's relationship to the wider scientific and social environment.[18]

Three stages of research on change in science

Elsewhere (Collins, 1981b) I have outlined what I have called 'stages' in the empirical programme of relativism. The first stage is the empirical documentation of the interpretative flexibility of experimental results. This part of the work has shown what part experimental data play in the practice of science, and what part is played by the touchstones of certainty such as replication. The second stage I have suggested is concerned with the way that the limitless debates made possible by the unlimited interpretative flexibility of data are closed down. The mechanisms of closure have been found to include various rhetorical presentational and institutional devices working within a context of 'plausibility' and other conservative forces (Travis, 1981; Collins, 1981c; Harvey, 1981a; Pickering, 1981). I also look forward to a 'third stage' which will relate the mechanisms of closure to the wider social and political structure.

A very great deal of work has already been done on the relationship of the wider social and political structure to scientific knowledge. A number of studies emerging from Edinburgh and other centres have shown how political interests of one sort or another inform scientists' views about the natural world.[19] Another set of work, not unrelated, is concerned with showing the way that scientific knowledge is used in debates which occur within the public arena concerning pollution and so forth.[20] In looking forward to a third stage I had something slightly different in mind, however. I can probably best explain what this is by giving a sketch of what a third-stage explanation would look like, though *I do not intend that this be taken as anything other than a model.*

Model of a third stage explanation

One complaint offered to me by scientists in the gravitational radiation controversy (Collins, 1975, 1981c) concerned the unfair advantage that one side had in terms of their access to publicity. It was suggested that while scientists on one side had to work with the minimal resources of a university science department, a vocal element on the other side had at their disposal the resources of a large industrial company. Thus the scientists on one side of the controversy were able to make their views widely known by taking advantage of secretarial, printing, and mailing resources, and through the offices of a public relation's department with a press officer, while the other side's counter-arguments were broadcast only in the conference setting and the regular scientific journal. We can easily see that such a one-sided presentation of evidence could well be influential both directly — in affecting opinions of scientists active in the debate — and indirectly — in affecting the opinions of those concerned with funding and so forth but not belonging to the core-set.

If we assume that this feature was a significant factor in the closure of the gravity wave debate in favour of the non-existence of high fluxes of gravity waves (I am *not* able to say how significant it really was) we might then ask how it came about that the representatives of that side of the argument came to have the greater resources. We could ask, for example, if the non-existence of high fluxes of gravity waves was the outcome that was the more likely to be favoured by the industrial sector of American science. We could speculate that the non-existence of gravity waves would preserve the greatest body of current scientific understanding and agreements (Pickering, 1981), whereas if the high flux hypothesis turned out to be correct, the work of the scientific sector of industry would be thrown into chaos on many fronts. What had previously been taken to be adequate understandings of the behaviour of materials, signal processing techniques, thermodynamic noise etc. *could* all have been thrown into doubt. Confidence in the regular ways of doing things at the technological end of science might have been shattered (remember, this is speculation only). In these circumstances it would not be surprising to find the negative view emerging from, and being heavily supported by, currently successful elements of the industrial sector.

This model explanation uses the notion of interests (e.g. Barnes, 1981); it explains why the industrial sector of science should have conservative interests; it shows how these wider conservative interests might lead to a negative evaluation of the existence of high fluxes of gravity waves through the current theoretical network and the maintenance of the maximum number of previous scientific agreements (see Pickering, 1981) and the plausibility structure (Harvey, 1981b) surrounding experimental physics; *and* it shows how the conservative side managed to emerge victorious with the aid of superior rhetorical resources. All the separate elements of this model explanation are currently available in the literature, except that part which shows in detail how the side with what turned out to be the victorious viewpoint *also* had access to the resources for closing the debate in its favour and how it used those resources at the research front. That is the link between the mechanism which constrains debate and the wider sociopolitical structure. This sort of explanation recognizes the features that make for stability in science while also allowing for the possibility of large-scale change so that the conservative outcome does not seem inevitable.

Wider issues

The new sociology of scientific knowledge, as described above, is not a purely abstract subject. It has consequences, though these have been

little developed or explored. Critics have suggested that the consequences are all negative — that the subject is a prescription for anarchy
in science. This is not true. The subject leaves pure science very nearly
as it is; in the main it simply redescribes it. The consequences are
indirect but, nevertheless, of some importance. They arise out of our
growing expertise in *comparing* areas of science, itself a consequence
of what I called the granular structure of the subject, and the way that
objects of study are defined by cognitive boundaries.

Evaluation and funding of science

In the first few paragraphs of this chapter I noted that this attentiveness
to passages of scientific activity, demarcated by reference to cognitive
boundaries rather than institutional or professional boundaries, was a
hallmark of the new sociology of scientific knowledge. It is not difficult
to see why this is. Groups of scientists defined by reference to institutional settings or professional affiliation will be engaged on passages of
work at a variety of stages of development and with varying degrees of
potential. If we fail to notice the cognitive structure of this work — if
we treat it all as cognitively amorphous — we will not notice what
comes to be counted as successful and what does not, and we certainly
will not be able to develop ideas about how these differences come
about. Thus, even if we choose an institutionally defined setting for
our fieldwork location, we will need to pay close attention to the cognitive structure of the work within that institution. Perforce we will need
to compare different types of scientific work and develop the language
and concepts to make this possible. We are going to have to think in terms
such as 'revolutionary science', 'low risk science', 'extraordinary science',
'science done in order to maintain or develop a body of tacit knowledge',
'replication of others' findings' and so forth. This new vocabulary ought
to have some impact on evaluation and funding decisions.

Currently, with only the language of institutionally based sociology of
science to work with, evaluative questions take forms such as 'How many
papers are produced by this or that institution?'; 'What is the cost per
paper emerging from this or that institution?': 'How many pieces of good
quality work have been produced by this or that institution?'. A new
language might make it possible to ask questions to do with, for example,
the balance of different types of cognitive activity within a discipline —
'Is expertise being maintained?'; 'Is work being unnecessarily duplicated?';
'How much money should we make sure we spend on high risk projects

even though 90 percent of it will lead nowhere?' Currently there is no systematic way of talking or thinking about these things.

Science in the public arena

Another area of consequence for the new subject is in those places where science is brought into the public arena. We have already mentioned the interesting work done in looking at science in the setting of such things as debates over pollution. With a few exceptions (e.g. Robbins and Johnston, 1976; Wynne, 1982), the relativist perspective does not seem to have informed this work to a marked extent, at least this has certainly not been made explicit.[21]

Within the relativist programme we accept (stage 1) that the scientific view belonging to both sides of a controversy can be defended indefinitely and that *even in the purest of sciences*, if debate is to end, it must be brought to a close by some means not usually thought of as strictly *scientific* (stage 2). Naturally, the same state of affairs will apply where the science is less 'pure'. There is no need to discover a *bias* in order to establish this point. It is an unavoidable characteristic of all science in which there is commitment to more than one viewpoint. The findings of the relativist programme should have an impact on general attitudes to the role of science in these sorts of debates. Also, the findings help to elucidate the mechanisms used to close down or maintain the scientific side of public controversy.

Actually, the sociology of scientific knowledge has consequences wherever scientific authority is offered to back up arguments in any non-scientific arena. Take, for example, the use of scientific evidence in court rooms — forensic science (see Smith, 1981). Forensic evidence is sometimes challenged and sometimes it is not. We should be looking to see if there are areas of forensic science which are more regularly challenged than others, and we should be asking if unchallenged forensic evidence which is taken to justify a prison sentence would be taken to justify a radical conclusion *within* science. We should be in a position to make comparisons between procedures *within* science and in places where scientific evidence is given in a lay setting (Wynne, 1982).[22]

We are also in a strong position to explore where scientific authority is challenged in support of heterodox views. So long as scientific authority is legitimated by reference to inadequate philosophies of science, it is easy for laymen to challenge that authority. It is easy to show that the practice of science in any particular instance does not accord with the canons of its legitimating philosophies. The fears of those who object to relativism on the grounds of its anarchic consequencies are being realized, not as a result of relativism but as a consequence of an over-long reliance on the very philosophies that are supposed to wall about scientific authority. These walls are turning out to be made of straw. If new walls are to be constructed, they will need to have their foundations laid in scientific practice — in our understanding of the role of the tacit elements of scientific expertise, and the way this expertise, not a philosophical system, can give justification to an opinion about the natural world.

Consequences for science

Lastly, since the findings of the subject should be of consequence wherever comparison between procedures in different sciences is at issue, it is inevitable that the practice of the sciences themselves will not remain completely untouched. This is quite simply because methods in some areas of science are often justified by citing canonical versions of method in other parts of the scientific enterprise. In the social sciences, for example, we have grown accustomed to methodological debates which rest on versions of our relationship with the natural sciences. Irrespective of the position taken in these debates — that the social sciences should aspire to identity with the natural sciences, or that they are fundamentally different — a proper understanding of the methods of the natural sciences must be a precursor to a sensible argument. There is little point in arguing that the social sciences should or should not aim to reproduce the methods of the most successful of the sciences when the version of those methods that is held up as the exemplar is a myth. In this sort of way, the sociology of scientific knowledge must affect the conduct of science even within the walls of the scientific institution itself.[23]

Appendices

APPENDIX 1
Special Relativism

One of the things that sociologists of scientific knowledge are becoming very skilled at is suspending taken-for-granted ways of seeing. As we have learned to suspend more and more, the subject has advanced. Bruno Latour put it this way:

> Soon, however, it was evident that most of the terms employed in order to describe 'internal' factors, were actually amenable to sociological analysis and accounted by concepts so far used to describe 'external' factors. The notion of replication of an experiment was reduced by H. Collins...to the sociology of controversies; the writing of an article was explained by Latour ...and Knorr...in rhetoric or semiotic terms; the notion of 'proof' had been further reduced to social factors by Pinch...and Harvey. Even the small word 'problem' had been made amenable to sociological explanation by Callon.... Indeed, the whole process of fact construction has been shown to be accountable inside a sociological framework. (Latour, 1980: 53)

We might add to Latour's list the opening up to sociological examination of the notion of contradiction, calibration, control group, and statistical analysis. Indeed, one profitable direction for sociological inquiry is to re-explain all the methods of science in sociological terms.

The same abilities can be used to re-examine the basis of our own subject of course. Indeed, it must be obvious that this type of analysis can be applied to any sort of generalizing ability. We can use this fact either to maintain a philosophical awareness of the nature of our own scientific activities and to maintain a methodological sharpness, or we can use it as a rather undiscriminating critical lever. Because of the universal applicability of this type of analysis, it ought to be clear that the mere demonstrability of the socially analyzable nature of any explanatory category should not be allowed to count, by itself, as a criticism of the use of that category. It amounts to no more than being 'more reflexive than thou'. A criticism that can be so easily applied to everything, is not really a criticism of anything. It is, rather a kind of philosophical puzzle – like the problem of induction.[24]

It should also cause little surprise if we lose our balance as researchers if we try to suspend everything at once. It is often taken to be a devastating philosophical criticism of relativist work that if it were true, then there would be no warrant for believing the outcomes of the studies themselves since they would be equally open to re-analysis (see Laudan, 1982; Collins, 1982a). There are many replies to this sort of point but perhaps the most curious thing about it is that it should be applied to sociological work while leaving philosophers untroubled about the reflexive possibilities within their own discipline. After all, if there is a problem of induction, how can a philosopher know that the words he or she writes on the page to explain it will keep their shape and message until tomorrow? An awareness of one's own procedures is a valuable methodological astringent, but when we are doing the sociology of science, as opposed to talking about it, it is as well not to suspend the taken-for-granted rules of the method of sociological research adopted. It is only the natural world which should be held in doubt (special relativism).

Mulkay (1981) has recently developed a criticism of much work in the sociology of science which rests on what appears to be the differential interpretability of different sorts of data.[25] He claims that if conventional work is replaced by 'discourse analysis' — the analysis of scientists' accounts of their work — certain major methodological difficulties will be obviated. He argues that discourse analysis marks an end to 'vassalage' in the sociology of science. In a later paper Mulkay and Gilbert (1982a) write:

> Because one of its central points is that it is impossible to 'tell it like it is in science', discourse analysis will seem like an abrogation of professional responsibility to one who defines the task of the sociologist as doing precisely this. But what *wise* man does not retreat from an analytical impasse or seek an exit from an Analytical Tower of Babel?

It turns out that the phrase 'telling it like it is in science' encompasses all previous work in the sociology of scientific knowledge. The argument is that since scientists regularly produce conflicting versions of scientific reality, sociologists' attempts to provide definitive versions rest on selective reporting, and what amounts to 'defining meaning by fiat'. To solve this problem we must instead analyze the differences in the accounts produced.

This would be a powerful argument if it were the case that Mulkay and Gilbert had somehow discovered a realm of 'pure data' that did not require interpretation — that is, a secret world of non-indexical expressions (Barnes and Law, 1976). Under these circumstances — unique in the body of science (but see note 12) — we would certainly want to go along with them. But, of course, scientists' accounts are no more or less transparent than any other data. To see that an account says that a scientist is prejudiced, or to see that two accounts are in conflict, is an interpretative exercise. To use the data Mulkay and Gilbert must understand enough about science, and about oxidative phosphorylation (their research area) in particular, to know when a piece of discourse is about that subject. They must also understand enough about regular ways of interacting in the English language to recognize taken-for-granted ways of expressing prejudice etc. and they must understand enough about the particular setting of the particular piece of discourse they are analyzing to make sense of it. They need to understand — as we have put it (Collins and Pinch, 1982: 191) — all those things that enable them to distinguish a statement about the prejudiced acts of a scientist engaged in the oxidative phosphorylation controversy from, say 'The Bluebells of Scotland' played on a comb and paper. Merely stepping back one stage in what is to count as data does not avoid the necessity of understanding and interpreting human action.

The interesting thing is the way that some material does not seem to require interpretation so that its meaning appears to be somehow 'external' to us. We can see how this comes about by suspending for a moment our natural attitude to the interview data presented in Mulkay and Gilbert's papers. The first thing we notice is that the papers offer only one interpretation of each quotation – that of Mulkay and Gilbert. Yet this is claimed to be the only available interpretation since selective reporting has been studiously avoided. Of course, selective reporting has been avoided in the sense that only Mulkay and Gilbert's interpretations have ever been collected. It is very easy to show that different interpretations of their interview data are possible. This can be done by extracting isolated quotations and asking people what they are all about.[26] Selective reporting has been obviated in the papers by 'selective observation' and this gives an appearance of inevitability to the interpretations.

Secondly, Mulkay and Gilbert can rely on their interpretations being readily accepted by their readers, because the focus of analysis is such that only very widely distributed interpretative competence is called upon. Because, as they insist, they are not talking about science, but only about such things as how scientists apportion blame, account for their own success, cite philosophers, make jokes and so forth, their work requires a minimum of esoteric abilities to produce *an* interpretation. The preferred interpretation will therefore seem immediately reasonable. This is not to say that the interpretation requires no such abilities – I have already argued that Mulkay and Gilbert's own interpretations of the quotations rest on a certain level of understanding about oxidative phosphorylation and its scientific context – but that the social actions discussed are of the sort that are common property. A reader of one of their papers will then feel immediately at home with the material, and feel that there is little more that needs to be known about science per se in order to have a grasp on the whole situation under discussion. Where the sociologist is attempting to say more about science proper – to 'tell it like it is' in Mulkay and Gilbert's words – he or she needs to develop the esoteric competences of the scientists' subjects as far as possible in order to understand what is going on. As I have argued above, there will be a big gulf between the sociologists' competence in regard to the subject matter under discussion and readers' popular competence. In this respect, sociology of science is like every other discipline.[27]

Of course, none of this is meant to imply that Mulkay and Gilbert's interpretations of their material are defective. To suggest this would be to fall into the 'more-reflexive-than-thou' mode of argument. On the contrary, it is hard to believe that they learned nothing from their extensive fieldwork with scientists and therefore it seems reasonable to yield to their privileged position when it comes to the nuances of the oxidative-phosphorylation debate and to their understanding of the settings and moods of their conversations with scientists. What we have learned is firstly that discourse analysis must stand on its own feet, not on the claimed 'defects' of other programmes. Discourse analysis can no more 'remedy these defects' than any other generalizing activity. Secondly, there is no reason not to use the material and interpretations presented in the discourse analysis papers in comparison with other studies. In the main, oxidative-phosphorylation scientists' conflicting accounts of the experimental work of others seems largely confirmatory of previous reports (e.g. Collins, 1975, 1976, 1981a).

APPENDIX 2
The role of the individual and a response to ethnomethodology

I have already argued that the main task of the interviewer working on the sociology of scientific knowledge is to tap into the everyday life of scientist actors.
Details pertaining to the individual interviewee – personal biography, individual
motive and so forth – play a subservient role to this task (Collins, 1981f). I have
also argued that the minimum unit for the analysis of scientific change is the
core-set. To try to work out how core-sets operate, we must perforce talk to
individuals, but we should read what they say as reflecting processes at the
core-set level – the mechanisms of closure of debate, for example.[28] Even the
individual laboratory can play only a limited role as a fieldwork location in the
study of scientific change. I now want to explain this point further by responding
to a recent interesting paper by Garfinkel, Lynch and Livingston (1981; hereafter
GLL).[29]

GLL discuss the analysis of a section of conversation recorded in tape. The
conversation consists of remarks by scientists who were, at that moment, 'discovering' the first optical pulsar. It seems that the tape recorder was left running
while this momentous event was taking place, and that the scientists in question
– Cocke and Disney – were not too aware that their comments were being
recorded. GLL write:

> On the evening of the discovery of the optical pulsar at Steward Observatory,
> January 16, 1969, by John Cocke, Michael Disney, Don Taylor and Robert
> McCallister, a tape recording in which they reported their series of observations
> was left running and before it ran out recorded the evening's 'conversations'
> from Observation 18 through 23. This unique document, on file at the Center
> for History and Philosophy of Physics at the American Institute of Physics,
> was made available for our examination. (p. 131)

The paper goes on to analyze in a very interesting way the nature of scientists'
work as scientists. At least part of the aim is to answer for science what GLL
call Shils's complaint:

> Shils' complaint to Strodtbeck: In 1954 Fred Strodtbeck was hired by the
> University of Chicago Law School to analyse tape recordings of jury delibera-
> tions obtained from a bugged jury room. Edward Shils was on the committee
> that hired him. When Strodtbeck proposed to a law school faculty to adminis-
> ter Bales Interaction Process Analysis categories, Shils complained: 'By using
> Bales Interaction Process Analysis I'm sure we'll learn what about a jury's
> deliberations makes them a small group. But we want to know what about
> their deliberations makes them a jury.' (p. 122)

Though GLL's ideas are not new to the sociology of scientific knowledge – which
has been influenced from the beginning by Garfinkel's work – their treatment of
the nature of what scientific competence consists in, is one of the best. For
example, a single footnote (26) captures a great deal of what we have spent
several pages trying to explain at the beginning of this paper.

By vulgar competence we understand embodied practices whose efficacy has achieved an ordinariness and 'equipmental transparency' that allows no call for credentials. (p. 140)

We can also use this footnote as a point of departure for our analysis of what this type of work *cannot* achieve.

The term 'competence' is used frequently throughout the paper, and it is important to see how it is used. It is used in the sense of 'native competence' (as I use it in my discussion of Mulkay and Gilbert above) and *not* in the sense of *competently performed experiment* (Collins, 1975). In the latter sense, competence is assigned or denied to experimental performance, often as a consequence of whether experimental results are in accord with or disagree with the ideas of the speaker. In this sense, Cocke and Disney's work would be described as 'competent' by one who believed in pulsars and thought they had discovered a pulsar, and 'incompetent' if it turned out that their experiment had gone wrong in some way.[30] However, in the sense of competent used by GLL, Cocke and Disney's work was competent however it turned out. Thus, the contents of the tape recording *and GLL's analysis of it* − indeed the whole of GLL's paper − would be precisely the same even if what Cocke and Disney had 'discovered' through their evening of shop work was something that was not an optical pulsar. Suppose, for example, that it later turned out that Cocke and Disney had been looking at an artifact − the result of a fault in their oscilloscope − and that this was the scientific consensus. Under these circumstances everything that GLL wrote about Cocke and Disney's work would remain unchanged and would be equally valid! On all the occasions that GLL use the term *competent* of Cocke and Disney's work of that night, it would still be just as applicable!

We can learn from this that GLL's project is one that would apply the same analysis to all qualities of knowledge and is therefore an analysis at too high a level of abstraction to deal with scientific change. There are no activities and exercises of competence etc. in Cocke and Disney's night's work of which one could say 'it was the particular way, or quality with which they applied this ability, or that competence or that ploy that led to their discovery, or led to their discovery being accepted as a discovery'. We can see this because they would have done and said the same things even if they were not making a discovery.

The problem here is in the fieldwork location: if what Cocke and Disney had found turned out to be an artifact, this would happen in the interaction between them and their critics in the more extended scientific debate that followed their night's work. To know what it is about Cocke and Disney's night's work that makes them scientists is a very interesting question. To know what it is that makes them scientists who believe they have made a great discovery is also interesting. But to know what it is about their work that makes them scientists who *are making* a great discovery, one needs to look elsewhere. What it is that made it that they were making a great discovery is to be found outside their night's work.[31]

APPENDIX 3
Reconstructing the paranormal:
a reply by H. M. Collins and T. J. Pinch

The editors have very kindly allowed us two pages in which to respond to chapter 7 below by Mulkay, Potter and Yearley (hereafter MPY) in view of its long criticism of our paper 'The Construction of the Paranormal: Nothing Unscientific is Happening' (1978). We will restrict our comments to what appear to be substantive mistakes, or significant misreading of arguments or intentions.

1. *The notion of 'forum'.* A forum is intended to be a place or location. It includes easily identified locations such as particular journals, and more abstract locations such as the 'idealized experiment'. (This is a similar notion to the 'experimental space'.) It is important that *forums are not identified by reference to the acts which are normally located within them.* Either sort of act may take place within either forum even though this is not usually evident. A main thrust of the paper is to identify occasions when contingent acts are allowed *to be seen* to take place within the constitutive forum and vice-versa. In the paper forums are identified by a common-sense (native-competence) view of science backed up by 'old fashioned philosophic orthodoxy' — e.g. an experiment ought to constitute new knowledge; the constituting of new knowledge should not be coextensive with gossip. The paper is not deeply concerned with demonstrating the general point that contingent acts partly or wholly constitute scientific knowledge. Merton, Barber, Collins and Wynne are cited to support this view which, it is taken, requires little further argument.

MPY are mistaken in thinking that the main thrust of the paper is to argue that contingent acts influence scientific knowledge; they are mistaken in thinking that forums are defined by the type of acts to be found within them. The paper rests on an analysis of the regular style of description, and regular apparent location of acts of different sorts. It is more ambitious than some more recent work insofar as it suggests: (i) certain sorts of descriptions are generally to be found in certain places; (ii) sometimes these general rules break down; (iii) the reasons for breakdown have to do with the nature of the science under discussion; (iv) the maintenance of the normal boundaries and breakdowns of the normal boundaries may have consequences for our beliefs about the natural world.

2. *Bias and the category of 'orthodoxy'.* 'Construction of the Paranormal...' may be a biased paper, but this is not shown by MPY. The term 'orthodox' does not necessarily carry a negative connotation in science (e.g. 'orthodox interpretation of quantum theory'); we ourselves use the term with approval on page 242 when we compare Rhine's work with orthodox psychological experiments. 'Orthodox scientist' is not a term used by parapsychologists to describe other scientists, it is a term used only by ourselves to contrast with work in the paranormal. In the phrase 'old fashioned philosophic orthodoxy', only 'old fashioned' carries a negative connotation.

In other places where we talk about parapsychologists doing good and careful scientific work we are of course referring to current convention in experimental design and we head the section 'using the symbolic and technical hardware of science'. In general, using actors' categories does not necessarily lead to bias unless actors epistemological evaluations are also taken over.

3. *Truth of claims revealed by one or two experiments.* This is not a view restricted to parapsychologists. We took it to be a view belonging to 'old fashioned philosophic orthodoxy'. Also many *critics* have designed ideal experiments with a view to 'settling the matter once and for all'. In accusing us of bias in this regard, Mulkay appears to have overlooked the correct interpretation, to be found in his 1979 book (p. 84).

4. *Categories of parapsychologist and critic embarrassingly overlap.* The categories do overlap, but as we state, this would only cause a problem for *neat quantitative fieldwork* (this phrase is replaced by a rather misleading ellipsis in MPY's quotation). Nearly all generalizing activity encounters overlapping categories. This does not prevent generalization.

5. *Historical controversies are bound to appear to be found in the constitutive forum.* MPY say that we must inevitably place the controversies surrounding Bohm and Barkla in the constitutive forum because they are past controversies. It is suggested that the predominant source of information on past controversies is published information and this will give the appearance that such controversies were predominantly constitutive. However, since we place some past controversies in the contingent forum too, this point seems ill-founded. Our attempt to categorize controversies refers to the major debates. It is, of course, literally inconceivable that a passage of scientific activity could occur without being associated with some contingent acts.

Notes

1. Every rule has its exceptions. It is clear that David Bloor's 1976 'Strong Programme' has had a great deal of influence, most of it good, even though it was set out before much work of a 'symmetrical' sort had been done.

2. A good metaphor is to be found in the joke about the man who was asked how decisions were reached in his household. He replied that he made all the big decisions while his wife made all the small ones. He decided who should be the next President of the United States, what was the best policy for Cuba and Vietnam, and even whether there was life on other planets. She decided which school the children should go to, whether he could change job, and when they would move house!

3. Here I offer a rather more generous definition of what is to count as sociology of knowledge than my friend Steve Shapin. See his otherwise excellent (1982) review article.

4. As I have suggested elsewhere (Collins, 1981e), Bloor's other two tenets serve to confuse rather than add to his programme.

5. I hope to look more closely at the origins of relativistic sociology of science in a review article 'Science as a Social Construct' for *Annual Review of Sociology*, 1983.

6. For a longer analysis of the relationship between Wittgenstein, phenomenology and Kuhn's model, see Collins and Pinch (1982).

7. It is Garfinkel (1967) who invented the technique – often referred to as 'garfinkeling' – where taken-for-granted reality is disturbed deliberately in order to make the rule-following character of day-to-day existence more evident. Figure 1 is another device for revealing the act of seeing as an exercise of skill.

8. Of course, whether everyone would really see the same thing is the topic of the replication studies (e.g. Collins 1981a).

9. Though the deliberate act of assembling data into a certain pattern is often referred to as 'interpreting the data', the latter sort of interpretation is visibly an act of expertise and rather different to the other sort of interpretation. In this sense, data are interpreted in order to turn them into something else; they were already data.

10. For the special difficulties associated with paradigm discontinuity in the scientific arena, see Collins (1979) and Collins and Pinch (1982).

11. Reflexive impulses, it should be noted, are being studiously ignored. Irrespective of the nature of replication – as revealed by studies of science – replicability is what gives a finding its data-like 'external' quality.

12. The conversational analysts make this rather interesting claim with regard to their work. It may well be justified, in which case conversational analysis is a truly unique science. Perhaps the only science in which replication of results would be entirely irrelevant.

13. In practice, I have found that the best way to do this is to make one's technical competence clear by making some perceptive comment requiring a good technical grasp, early in the interview. Once it is possible to begin to talk (something like) 'scientist to scientist' the gauche quality of these unnatural settings soon dissolves. I have found that the 'being instructed' phase of interviews does not last long in fields that I understand reasonably well (cf. Gilbert, 1980; Pinch, 1981).

14. This separation into three parts is a purely analytic exercise. There are overlaps. Normal science may involve more radical elements of change; extraordinary science may turn into revolutionary science, and so forth.

15. A number of sociologists of science (e.g. Latour, Woolgar, Pickering) have argued that I am wrong to think that scientists are less aware of the constructed nature of knowledge even when they are not immediately involved in that construction. This does not accord with my fieldwork experience.

16. This is probably why the phenomenological/interpretative literature does not deal adequately with change.

17. See Frankel (1976) for a discussion of the parallels between those attempting scientific change and revolutionary political groups. Michael Lynch, in casual conversation, suggested that a name should be given to the procedure whereby interviews are conducted at all laboratories involved in a controversy. 'Core-sampling' yielding a 'core-sample' would be nice!

18. In this respect the sort of work described here, when compared to other recent approaches, is indistinguishable from the work of the 'Edinburgh School'. The differences are on small points of methodology and on minor philosophical issues.

19. For a very full review of this sort of work, see Shapin (1982).

20. For discussion of this point, see Chubin (1982), Collins (1982a), Wynne

(1982), Robbins and Johnston (1976), Gillespie, Eva, and Johnston (1979), Nowotny (1977), Mazur (1981), Nelkin (1975, 1978, 1979), Petersen and Markle (1979), and Markle and Petersen (1980).

21. This is not to say that some of it is not informed by an approach that is entirely compatible with relativism (Gieryn (1982) is an example).

22. Collins and Pinch (1979) have begun such an analysis where we explore the way that scientific authority is invested in laymen. Sometimes we found that magicians are invested with scientific authority. Sometimes the media are allowed to make authoritative pronouncements on matters of scientific fact. What is questioned, and who is allowed to question it, seems to depend on the status of the science as much as the status of the contesting parties.

23. I have not attempted a complete review of the relevant literature in this paper. To appreciate the programme it is certainly necessary to read some case studies. The best collection of empirical papers is Collins (1981a). A good review of a large part of the subject may be found in Shapin (1982). Most of the relevant work will also be picked up by following the notes appended to the papers in Collins (1981a). I hope also to review the literature on 'Science as a Social Construct' in a forthcoming volume of *Annual Review of Sociology*. Currently the best available text which brings together a good section of the relevant literature is Mulkay (1979).

24. See the debate between Barry Barnes and Steve Woolgar in *Social Studies of Science*, 11 (3 & 4) (1981), for more material relevant to this point.

25. The other papers presented in this book were not available when I wrote this chapter.

26. I did do this using the first extract from Mulkay and Gilbert's paper 'Accounting for Error' (1982b). Two people produced an interpretation roughly similar to the authors' after some hesitation and difficulty. One produced a rather different interpretation. Limitations of space prevent the reproduction of the tape-recorded dialogue here. It is also salutary to try such an experiment on oneself. Isolate one extract and do not look at it for a period of about a month. Then re-read it out of context. It is quite hard to recapture what it was meant to say in the first place.

27. Take any account of an experiment in the physical sciences as presented in a scientific journal. Unless the reader has the skills, equipment and time to test the claims made in the paper − and this is almost never the case − the results presented have to be taken on trust. Mulkay seems to want to eliminate this feature of science. He thinks that most previous work in the sociology of science depends on trusting scientists' word about what is going on and he calls this vassalage. Actually, it is *sociologists' comprehension* of scientists' worlds that is in question and only they who need to be taken on trust.

28. I think there is even more confusion over the role of single experiments. A great deal of effort has been put into arguing about the 'cause of correct beliefs' (see, e.g. Laudan, 1977). The cause of individual beliefs is not a matter of great concern for the programme. If individuals reached their conclusions about the natural world purely from 'objective observations' or the 'purest reasoning', we would still have to study the way that a consensual conclusion was reached from a set of varied views. (Consensual nearly always means 'large majority' since it is rare for the upholder of heterodox views to relinquish them entirely (see Langmuir, 1953; Collins, 1981d).)

29. I should make it clear that this discussion is only necessary because there is widespread confusion as to the relationship between ethnomethodology and the sociology of knowledge. It is not clear whether ethnomethodology is meant to be a different subject to sociology with different aims or a replacement for sociology with the same or similar potential.

30. In any particular case of controversy, what the victorious side think of as competence in this sense will eventually become everyone's native competence. This is how new knowledge is incorporated into the body of science.

31. Before leaving the brief discussion of GLL it is worth making one more related, though not central, point. This concerns the significance of the tape recording for GLL's work. When GLL refer to the tape as a 'unique document', one's immediate reading — not dispelled in any way by GLL — is that the tape is unique in that it records the moment of a great discovery. That is, it seems to be unique because it records something that was indeed a discovery. But since the tape would have served exactly the same purpose if it had not recorded a discovery, its uniqueness cannot reside in this. Its value for sociological purposes, resides in the fact that it is a recording of a *supposed* discovery.

Furthermore, we need to be very careful about what it is that the tape contains as a representation of the night's work. GLL were not present on the night. The tape is a very fragmentary record. It is short; it contains a record of only one part of one night's work of what was a sequence of nights' work; this sequence itself forms only a small part of the scientific careers of only the scientists involved. We have a record only of some speech and some notes. Even inside narrow aims, as it stands GLL's paper is a very ambitious interpretative exercise. It is rather important not to adopt a fetishistic approach to these scientific fragments. We would not, after all, want to make too much of a tape recording of the word 'Eureka'.

I point this out so that researchers should not be too depressed at the small prospect of finding similar recordings, and should not feel that GLL's access to this particular fragment of record puts them in a uniquely privileged research position. Similar things may be learnt from interactions surrounding any supposed discovery, and it is not impossible to arrange to be present at the time of such events. That Cocke and Disney's work turned out to be scientifically important is entirely beside the point from a sociological viewpoint, though admittedly it will help to attract the attention of scientists to the area. Nevertheless, participant observation of less celebrated passages of scientific activity (of the sort that the GLL group continue to do with great dedication — see also Collins and Pinch, 1982) will give rise to equally useful, and perhaps more complete records of the process of supposed discovery.

References

Barnes, S. B. (1981) 'On the "Hows" and "Whys" of Cultural Change (Response to Woolgar)', *Social Studies of Science*, 11 (4): 481–98.

Barnes, S. B. and Law, John (1976) 'Whatever Should be Done with Indexical Expressions?' *Theory and Society*, 3: 223–37.

Bell, C. (1974) 'Replication and Reality or the Future of Sociology', *Futures* (June): 253–60.

Bloor, David (1976) *Knowledge and Social Imagery*, London: Routledge and Kegan Paul.

Chubin, Daryl E. (1982) 'Collins's Programme and the "Hardest Possible Case"', *Social Studies of Science* 12 (1): 136–9.

Collins, H. M. (1974) 'The TEA Set: Tacit Knowledge and Scientific Networks', *Science Studies*, 4: 165–86.

Collins, H. M. (1975) 'The Seven Sexes: A Study in the Sociology of a Phenomenon, or the Replication of Experiments in Physics', *Sociology*, 9 (2): 205–24.

Collins, H. M. (1976) 'Upon the Replication of Scientific Findings: A Discussion Illuminated by the Experiences of Researchers into Parapsychology', *Proceedings of 4S/ISA Conference*, Cornell University, November 1976.

Collins, H. M. (1979) 'The Investigation of Frames of Meaning in Science: Complementarity and Compromise', *Sociological Review*, 27: 703–18.

Collins, H. M. (ed.) (1981a) 'Knowledge and Controversy: Studies in Modern Natural Science', special issue of *Social Studies of Science*, 11 (1).

Collins, H. M. (1981b) 'Stages in the Empirical Programme of Relativism', *Social Studies of Science*, 11 (1): 3–10.

Collins, H. M. (1981c) 'Son of the Seven Sexes: The Social Destruction of a Physical Phenomenon', *Social Studies of Science*, 11 (1): 33–62.

Collins, H. M. (1981d) 'The Role of the Core-Set in Modern Science: Social Contingency with Methodological Propriety in Science', *History of Science*, 19: 6–19.

Collins, H. M. (1981e) 'What is TRASP?: The Radical Programme as a Methodological Imperative', *Philosophy of the Social Sciences*, 11: 215–24.

Collins, H. M. (1981f) 'Members Talk in Participatory Research', paper prescribed to Conference on Accounts of Action, Surrey University, December 1981.

Collins, H. M. (1982a) 'Special Relativism – The Natural Attitude', *Social Studies of Science*, 12 (1): 136–9.

Collins, H. M. (1982b) 'Knowledge, Norms and Rules in the Sociology of Science', *Social Studies of Science*, 12 (2): 299–309.

Collins, H. M. and Harrison, R. (1975) 'Building a TEA Laser: The Caprices of Communication', *Social Studies of Science*, 5: 441–5.

Collins, H. M. and Cox, G. (1976) 'Recovering Relativity: Did Prophecy Fail?', *Social Studies of Science*, 6: 423–44.

Collins, H. M. and Pinch, T. J. (1978) 'The Construction of the Paranormal: Nothing Unscientific is Happening', pp. 237–70 in R. Wallis (ed.), *On the Margins of Science: The Social Construction of Rejected Knowledge*, Sociological Review Monograph No. 27, University of Keele.

Collins, H. M. and Pinch, T. J. (1982) *Frames of Meaning: The Social Construction of Extraordinary Science*, London: Routledge and Kegan Paul.

Fleck, Ludwik (1979) *Genesis and Development of a Scientific Fact*, Chicago: University of Chicago Press (first published in German in 1935).

Frankel, E. (1976) 'Corpuscular Optics and the Wave Theory of Light: The Science and Politics of a Revolution in Physics', *Social Studies of Science*, 6: 141–84.

Garfinkel, H. (1967) *Studies in Ethnomethodology*, New Jersey: Prentice-Hall.

Garfinkel, H., Lynch, M. and Livingston, E. (1981) 'The Work of a Discovering Science Construed with Materials from the Optically Discovered Pulsar', *Philosophy of the Social Sciences*, 11: 131–58.

Gieryn, Thomas F. (1981) 'Cognitive Authority of Science', paper presented at the 6th Annual Meeting, Society for Social Studies of Science, Atlanta.

Gieryn, Thomas F. (1982) 'Relativist/Constructivist Programmes in the Sociology of Science: Redundance and Retreat', *Social Studies of Science*, 12 (2): 279–97.

Gilbert, G. Nigel (1980) 'Being Interviewed: A Role Analysis', *Social Science Information*, 19 (2): 227–36.

Gillespie, B., Eva, D. and Johnston, R. (1979) 'Carcinogenic Risk Assessment in the United States and Great Britain: The Case of Aldrin/Dieldrin', *Social Studies of Science*, 9: 265–301.

Harvey, Bill (1981a) 'Plausibility and the Evaluation of Knowledge: A Case-Study of Experimental Quantum Mechanics', *Social Studies of Science*, 11 (1): 95–130.

Harvey, Bill (1981b) 'The Interpretation of Quantum Mechanics: A Case-Study in the Sociology of Science', PhD thesis, University of Edinburgh.

Knapp, W. S. (1981) 'On the Validity of Accounts About Everyday Life', *Sociological Review*, 29: 543–62.

Krige, John (1981) *Science, Revolution and Discontinuity*, Hassocks, Sussex: Harvester Press/Humanities Press.

Kuhn, T. S. (1962) *The Structure of Scientific Revolutions*, Chicago: University of Chicago Press.

Langmuir, I. (1953) edited by R. N. Hall, 1968, 'Pathological Science', *General Electric R and D Center Report*, Number 68-C-035, New York.

Latour, Bruno (1980) 'Is it Possible to Reconstruct the Research Process? Sociology of a Brain Peptide', pp. 53–76 in K. D. Knorr, R. Krohn and R. Whitley (eds), *The Social Process of Scientific Investigation, Sociology of the Sciences Yearbook*, vol. 4, Dordrecht: D. Reidel.

Latour, Bruno and Woolgar, Steve (1979) *Laboratory Life: The Social Construction of Scientific Facts*, London and Beverly Hills: Sage.

Laudan, L. (1977) *Progress and Its Problems*, London: Routledge and Kegan Paul.

Laudan, L. (1982) 'A Note on Collins's Blend of Relativism and Empiricism', *Social Studies of Science*, 12 (1): 131–2.

Markle, G. E. and Petersen, J. C. (eds) (1980) *Politics, Science and Cancer: The Laetrile Phenomenon*, Boulder, Colorado: Westview.

Mazur, A. (1981) *Dynamics of Technical Controversy*, Washington: Communications Press.

Mulkay, Michael (1979) *Science and the Sociology of Knowledge*, London: George Allen and Unwin.

Mulkay, Michael (1981) 'Action and Belief or Scientific Discourse? A Possible Way of Ending Intellectual Vassalage in Social Studies of Science', *Philosophy of the Social Sciences*, 11: 163–72.

Mulkay, M. J. and Gilbert, G. Nigel (1982) 'What is the Ultimate Question? Some Remarks in Defence of the Analysis of Scientific Discourse', *Social Studies of Science*, 12 (2): 309–19.

Mulkay, M. J. and Gilbert, G. N. (1982b) 'Accounting for Error', *Sociology*, 16: 165–83.

Nelkin, D. (1975) 'The Political Impact of Technical Expertise', *Social Studies of Science*, 5: 35–54.

Nelkin, D. (1978) 'Threats and Promises: Negotiating the Control of Research', *Daedalus*, 107: 191–209.

Nelkin, D. (ed.) (1979) *Controversy: Politics of Technical Decisions*, London and Beverly Hills: Sage.

Nowotny, H. (1977) 'Scientific Purity and Nuclear Danger: The Case of Risk Assessment', pp. 243–64 in E. Mendelson, P. Weingart and R. Whitley (eds), *The Social Production of Scientific Knowledge*, *Sociology of the Sciences Yearbook*, vol. 1, Dordrecht: D. Reidel.

Petersen, J. C. and Markle, G. E. (1979) 'Politics and Science in the Laetrile Controversy', *Social Studies of Science*, 9: 139–66.

Pickering, Andrew (1981) 'Constraints on Controversy: The Case of the Magnetic Monopole', *Social Studies of Science*, 11 (1): 63–93.

Pinch, T. J. (1981) 'The Sun-Set: The Presentation of Certainty in Scientific Life', *Social Studies of Science*, 11 (1): 131–58.

Robbins, D. and Johnston, R. (1976) 'The Role of Cognitive and Occupational Differentiation in Scientific Controversies', *Social Studies of Science*, 6: 349–68.

Schutz, A. (1962) *The Problem of Social Reality*, *Collected Papers*, vol. I, The Hague: Martinus Nijhoff.

Schutz, A. (1964) *Studies in Social Theory*, *Collected Papers*, vol. II, The Hague, Martinus Nijhoff.

Shapin, S. (1982) 'History of Science and its Sociological Reconstructions', *History of Science*, 20: 157–211.

Smith, Roger (1981) *Trial by Medicine*, Edinburgh: Edinburgh University Press.

Travis, G. D. L. (1981) 'Replicating Replication? Aspects of the Social Construction of Learning in Planarian Worms', *Social Studies of Science*, 11 (1): 11–32.

Wilson, Bryan R. (ed.) (1970) *Rationality*, Oxford: Blackwell.

Winch, P. (1958) *The Idea of a Social Science and its Relation to Philosophy*, London: Routledge and Kegan Paul.

Wittgenstein, L. (1953) *Philosophical Investigations*, Oxford: Blackwell.

Woolgar, S. (1981) 'Critique and Criticism: Two Readings of Ethnomethodology', *Social Studies of Science*, 11 (4): 504–14.

Wynne, B. (1982) *Nuclear Decision – Rationality or Ritual?* London: British Society for the History of Science.

5

The Ethnographic Study of Scientific Work: Towards a Constructivist Interpretation of Science

Karin D. Knorr-Cetina
Wesleyan University, USA

Macro- vs. microsociology of scientific knowledge

The sociology of knowledge has been broadly defined as the study of the social or existential conditioning of thought (Mannheim, 1954). In recent years, the sociology of knowledge has been revived within social studies of science. A number of research programmes focus on what one could loosely describe as the social conditioning of scientific knowledge. What unites the protagonists of these new sociologies of scientific knowledge is a common interest in the technical objects of knowledge produced in science as a target of analysis and explanation. The programmes differ markedly in regard to the analytical perspective brought to bear on scientific knowledge.

One major divide between relevant studies can be linked to the difference between macroscopically-oriented congruence models and microscopically-inclined genetic approaches. The classical approach of the sociology of knowledge is clearly a *congruence approach*: it depends upon the identification of a similarity or an isomorphism between collectively sustained goals (social interests) which the analyst imputes to a social group, and the beliefs promoted by individuals affiliated with this group. As an example, recall Marx's attempt to relate individuals' economic or philosophical ideas to their 'bourgeois' interests (1913). Though not the only macroscopically inclined approach to the sociology of scientific knowledge (see Restivo, 1981, and Chubin and Restivo, this volume) it has recently gained prominence through the contemporary use of an interest model by Barnes and his collaborators in a variety of case studies (Barnes, 1977; Barnes and Shapin, 1979; Barnes, this volume). Furthermore, the analysis aims at objective (class) relationships rather than at subjectively acknowledged social conditions. Since inferences regarding individual cases cannot be unproblematically derived from macroscopic congruency claims, causal or functional imputations remain on a social-structural level. The question not answered by this approach is exactly wherein, at what junctures, and how contextual factors such as social interests enter particular knowledge objects (Mills, 1963: 454ff.). Congruence approaches as described above infer that such influences have taken place from perceived similarities between imputed aspects of the content of knowledge objects. They do not specify the causally connected chain of events out of which an object of knowledge emerges congruent with antecedent social interests or with other social acts. Furthermore, interest models traditionally speak to the question why particular individuals or groups hold particular beliefs, in accordance with the original formulation of the problem of the sociology of knowledge as a problem of the social conditioning of thought (not knowledge). Thus the question why scientist X prefers theory Y is analyzed by reference to the social interests Y^1 for which this scientist stands. Yet individuals may hold beliefs for various reasons quite independently of whether and how these beliefs come to be held to be 'true' (Woolgar, 1981).

Thus even if we learn convincingly why particular individuals or groups believe in a set of propositions, we have not received an answer to the question whether and how these propositions in themselves embody social factors, nor to the question whether and how social factors influence the survival of and acceptance of knowledge claims. In other words, the epistemological question how that which we come to call knowledge is constituted and accepted is not addressed in the above model.[1] To attack this question, we are pressed to examine the genesis and transformation of our objects of knowledge at a level sufficiently close to the actual practices of scientists to be able to differentiate between knowledge-constitutive procedures and rationales. For example, we will have to ask the question whether scientific consensus is formed solely on the basis of evidential considerations. Or else we have to ask whether knowledge-constitutive laboratory selections can be fully accounted for in terms of technical rationales. I believe that these questions require us to adopt a *genetic* and *microlevel* approach to the problem of the social conditioning of scientific knowledge.

Two distinctive, genetic and microscopically oriented approaches relevant to the sociology of scientific knowledge have emerged in recent years.[2] Their foremost difference lies perhaps in the part of scientific practice they have chosen to analyze. The first approach focuses on *scientific controversies* as a strategic anchoring point for the study of consensus formation, that is, of the mechanisms by which knowledge claims come to be accepted as true (see the studies collected in Collins, 1981, and Knorr et al., 1980: 77–193). The second approach has chosen direct observation of the *actual site of scientific work* (frequently the scientific laboratory) in order to examine how objects of knowledge are constituted in science. Both approaches are social in that they consider the objects of knowledge as the outcomes of processes which invariably involve more than one individual, and which normally involve individuals at variance with one another in relevant respects. In contrast to the interest model, they do not seek to establish the potentially social causes of particular scientists' belief-preferences, but rather focus on the processes of interaction between scientists and others within which and through which scientific beliefs take shape. Happily, the distinctive features of the interest model, the study of controversy, and the ethnography of scientific work are complementary rather than contradictory. Thus, knowledge of the (social) interests which may inform participants' theoretical preferences can supplement an inquiry into how knowledge is socially negotiated during controversy, by pointing out why it is likely that particular individuals hold particular beliefs. Conversely, an inquiry into how knowledge objects are construed in scientific work can presumably inform a structural interest explanation as to whether, when and how interest-based theoretical inclinations have entered laboratory selections.

In what follows I will discuss the ethnographic study of knowledge production at the actual site of scientific action as one manifestation of the genetic and microscopic orientation to the sociology of scientific knowledge (for the study of scientific controversy, see Collins as well as Chubin and Restivo, this volume). In particular I will focus on what has come to be called *the programme of constructivism* (Restivo, 1981; Gieryn, 1982). This programme is supported by the results of several laboratory studies — though not all of these studies will necessarily share my pursuit of or characterization of constructivism. I will mainly draw upon the six major studies of which some results are currently available in print or preprint (Knorr-Cetina, 1977, 1979a, b, 1981,

1982a, b; Knorr-Cetina and Knorr, 1982; Latour, 1979, 1980a, b, 1981; Latour and Fabbri, 1977; Latour and Woolgar, 1979; Law and Williams, 1982; Lynch, 1976, 1979, 1982; Garfinkel et al., 1981; McKegney, 1979, 1980, 1982; Williams and Law, 1980; Zenzen and Restivo, 1979, 1982). The reader may also be interested in studies in progress (e.g. Traweek, 1981), or in studies which refer to scientific work, but testify to a non-ethnographic orientation (e.g. Thill, 1972; Goodfield, 1981; Chubin and Connolly, 1982). I will refer to the studies cited in accordance with their geographical origin as the Troy study (TR) for the work of Zenzen and Restivo, the Keele study (KE) for the work of Law and Williams, the Burnaby study (BU) for the work of McKegney, the Irvine (IR) study for the work of Lynch, the La Jolla study (LA) for the work of Latour and Woolgar, and the Berkeley study (BE) for the work of Knorr-Cetina. The scientific fields investigated in these studies are the biochemistry, microbiology and technology of plant proteins (BE), research into the brain's endocrine system (LA), neurotransmittors (IR), mammalian reproductive ecology (BU), cell biology (KE), and the colloid chemistry of immiscible liquids (TR). While the Troy, Burnaby, Keele and Irvine studies involve university research, the La Jolla and Berkeley studies were done at large, publicly financed research institutes.

In the remaining pages, I will take up in turn the following aspects of the constructivist conception of science: first, the artifactual character of the reality within which and upon which scientists operate; second, the selectivity embodied in knowledge production and the 'decision-impregnatedness' of scientific operations; third, the occasioned and contextually contingent character of research selections; fourth, the socially situated character of constructive operations; and fifth, some epistemologically relevant implications of the constructivist programme.

The constructivist interpretation: scientific reality as artifact

Several laboratory studies refer to the *constructive* nature of scientific activities in the sense of a notion introduced in an early publication of the Berkeley study and developed further in the corresponding monograph (BE, 1977: 670; BE, 1981: ch. 1; LA, 1979: 236ff.; IR, 1979: ch. 8). The constructivist interpretation is opposed to the conception of scientific investigation as descriptive, a conception which locates the problem of facticity in the relation between the products of science and an external nature. In contrast, the constructivist interpretation considers the products of science as first and foremost the result of a process of (reflexive) fabrication. Accordingly, the study of scientific knowledge is primarily seen to involve an investigation of how scientific objects are produced in the laboratory rather than a study of how facts are preserved in scientific statements about nature.

To begin our project let us look for a moment at the site of scientific action. In the laboratory scientists operate upon (and within) a highly preconstructed artifactual reality. It is clear that measurement instruments are the products of human effort, as are articles, books, and the graphs and print-outs produced. But the source materials with which scientists work are also preconstructed. Plant and assay rats are specially grown and selectively bred. Most of the substances and chemicals used are purified and are obtained from the industry which serves the science or from other laboratories. The water which runs from a special faucet is sterilized. 'Raw' materials which enter the laboratory are carefully selected and 'prepared' before they are subjected to 'scientific' tests. In short, nowhere in the laboratory do we find the 'nature' or 'reality' which is so crucial to the descriptivist interpretation of inquiry. To the observer from the outside world, the laboratory displays itself as a site of action from which 'nature' is as much as possible excluded rather than included.

The instrumentally achieved character of the experience of modern natural science has led Peirce (1931–35, vol. 5: 457; vol. 7: 340) to suggest that scientific attributes such as the 'hardness' of a diamond are entirely constituted with regard to a system of possible instrumentation, for example by the possibility of another stone being rubbed against the diamond. Protophysics has proposed that major parts of modern physics are better described as technology, that is, as knowledge about how to affect things technically rather than as knowledge which depicts nature (e.g. Janich, 1978: 13ff.). Habermas has referred to the phenomenon in terms of the 'transcendental viewpoint of possible technical control' reflected in modern science (1971: 99). In the scientific laboratory this instrumentality manifests itself not only in the nature of the 'things' upon which scientists operate, but also in the preoccupations of scientific action. Our ordinary contemplation of the moon in a cloudless night differs from the scientist's 'observations' of masses and chemical compositions, of brain impulses and intestine contents, in that instrumentally accomplished observations intercept natural courses of events. The scientist's concern with 'making things work' is a mundane reflection of this ongoing instrumental interception. It is a preoccupation documented in several laboratory studies (e.g. BE, 1977: 670; 1981: 7; IR, 1979: 151, 158ff.).

> The vernacular formulation of 'making it work' suggests a contingency of results upon 'skilled production'. Performing successful research in the context of a complicated array of instrumental and organic contingencies is no easy matter, and even the most skilled technicians relegate a considerable number of their attempts to do experimental and observational work to 'failure'...the work proceeds in circumstances that are seen as, at times, capricious and beyond control, though it is the member's task to construct a rationale for actions in terms of 'effects' contingent upon such actions. Consequently, making it work entails a selection of those 'effects' that can be traced to a 'rational' set of contingencies, and a discarding of 'attempts' that are bound to fall short of such 'effects'. Making it work is thereby a kind of skilled work, but one that is never fully under control. (IR, 1979: 161)

According to the Berkeley study, the concern with making things work (instrumentally) is what we find in the laboratory instead of the quest for truth customarily ascribed to science:

> If there is a principle which seems to govern laboratory action, it is the scientists' concern with making things 'work', which points to a principle of success rather than one of truth. Needless to say, to make things work – to produce 'results' – is not identical with attempting their falsification...[nor does] the scientist's vocabulary of how things work, of why they do or do not work, of steps to take to make them work...reflect some form of naive verificationism, but is in fact a discourse appropriate to the *instrumental manufacture* of knowledge in the *workshop* called a 'lab'. (BE, 1981: 7f.)

The decision-ladenness of constructive operations

We have seen that the products of science can be seen as first and foremost the result of a process of fabrication which manifests itself in the artifactual character of scientific reality and in the instrumental nature of scientific operations. Let us now look more closely at the process of fabrication itself. To consider a product as first and foremost the result of a process of production is to imply that what happens in the process of production is not irrelevant for the products obtained. As the Berkeley study argues, this means that the products of science have to be seen as *highly internally structured* through the process of production, independently of questions of their external structuring through some match or mismatch with 'nature' (BE, 1981: 9ff.).

The decision-impregnated nature of inquiry

How can we conceive of this internal structuring of scientific products? The activities observed in the laboratory not only involve tools and materials which are highly preconstructed, they also involve decisions and selections. The choice of a particular measurement device, a particular formulation of chemical composition, a specific temperature or of the timing of an experiment is a choice among alternative means and courses of action. These selections, in turn, can only be made with respect to other selections: they are based on translations into further selections, the so-called decision criteria. For example, the question which statistical function a scientist chooses to approximate experimental data usually involves a choice between several criteria of statistical fit, as well as choices between criteria such as 'simplicity' (often invoked when a linear function is preferred), 'comparability' (e.g. when the same function is chosen to approximate different data sets), or 'precision' (BE, 1981: 10). Thus scientific products can be seen as internally constructed in terms of several orders or levels of selectivity: they are structured not only with respect to the composite laboratory selections through which they are generated, but also with respect to the translations incorporated within those selections.

Scientific arguments often revolve around such second order selections, as exemplified in the La Jolla study's account of the change of criteria which determined at different points in time, what counted as an 'isolation' of the Thyrotropin Releasing Factor (LA, 1979: 120ff.; see particularly Collins, this volume). To reach a decision, we need a decision criterion or a translation into a second order selection. To challenge a decision, we refer to the possibility of alternative selections.

> Selections can be called into question precisely because they *are* selections; that is, precisely because they involve the possibility of alternative selections. If scientific objects are selectively carved out from reality, they can be deconstructed by challenging the selections they incorporate. If scientific facts are fabricated in the sense that they are derived from decisions, they can be defabricated by imposing alternative decisions. In scientific inquiry, the selectivity of selections incorporated into previous scientific work is itself a *topic* for further scientific investigation. At the same time, the selections of previous work constitute a *resource* which enables scientific inquiry to proceed: they supply the tools, methods, and interpretations upon which a scientist may draw in the process of her own research. (BE, 1981: 12)

The scientific laboratory consists of materializations of earlier scientific selections; this accounts for its artifactual character. 'The mass spectrometer is the reified part of a whole field of physics; it is an actual piece of furniture which incorporates the majority of an earlier body of scientific activity....Every time a statement stabilizes, it is reintroduced into the laboratory (in the guise of a machine, inscription device, skill, routine, prejudice, deduction, programme, and so on)' (LA, 1979: 242f.). It is clear that previous scientific selections thus change the conditions of further decision-making − they set the scene at the site of action. In this sense, scientific products are not only *decision-impregnated*, they are also *decision-impregnating*.

The decision-impregnating character of scientific products

How is it that scientific products become decision-impregnating? According to the La Jolla study, 'facts are constructed through operations designed to effect the dropping of modalities which qualify a given (scientific) statement' (LA, 1979: 237). The La Jolla study lists five types of statements which range from linguistically marked conjectures or speculations (type 1), knowledge claims by one author (type 2) and qualified general assumptions ('Oxytocin is generally assumed to be...,' type 3) to uncontroversial 'facts' still associated with an author (type 4) and unqualified taken-for-granted knowledge (type 5). Laboratory activity is portrayed 'as a constant struggle for the generation and acceptance of particular kinds of statements', namely statements of type 4 which associate an acknowledged fact with the name of the scientist(s) to whom this 'finding' is attributed (LA, 1979: 75ff., 88):

> The problem for participants was to persuade readers of papers (and consti-
> tuent diagrams and figures) that this statement should be accepted as fact.
> To this end rats had been bled and beheaded, frogs had been flayed, chemi-
> cals consumed, time spent, careers had been made or broken, and inscription
> devices had been manufactured and accumulated within the laboratory. This,
> indeed, was the very raison d'etre of the laboratory.

Thus, the constructive operations with which we have associated scientific work can be defined as the sum total of selections designed to transform the subjective into the objective, the unbelievable into the believed, the fabricated into the finding, and the painstakingly constructed into the objective scientific fact. The transformational aspect of the constructivist interpretation does not refer solely to the moulding and shaping of things in the hands of scientific craftsmen (Ravetz,

1971), or to the phenomenon that selectivity itself is transformed in scientific work through the process of 'literary inscription'. The transformations mentioned above imply a *symmetry break* in the sense that the natural becomes dissociated from the social once other selections are effectively ruled out, or once scientists have been persuaded to consider certain propositions as factual descriptions.

Bringing space and time back in: the occasioned character of constructive operations

If the products of scientific work reflexively embody several orders of selectivity, then a major question for us is how the respective selections are accomplished in the laboratory. If laboratory selections emerge from translations into further selections, then laboratory studies confront the question of how the respective translations are made. How do scientists rule out and bring in alternative possibilities, how do they reach and break up closure in ongoing work? If ethnographers of science had hoped to come up with a set of parameters which neatly specify this process they were quickly disappointed. A day in the laboratory will usually suffice to impress upon the observer a sense of the disorder within which scientists operate, and a month in the lab will confirm that most laboratory work is concerned with counteracting and remedying this disorder. As the authors of the Troy study describe their experience: 'Zenzen was surprised that the research was "messy"; Restivo was surprised to find things "messier" than he had anticipated' (TR, 1979: 3).

It is perhaps the single most consistent result of laboratory studies to point to the indeterminacy inherent in scientific operations, and to demonstrate the *locally situated, occasioned* character of laboratory selections. The phenomenon has been noted since the earliest publications of laboratory observations (BE, 1977: 674f.), and confirmed in all ethnographic studies currently available in print. I have mainly used the notions of indexicality, of opportunism and of contingency and idiosyncrasy in this connection (BE, 1979: 356ff.; BE, 1981: ch. 2); the Irvine study refers to circumstances and the indexical properties of laboratory work (IR, 1979: 16ff., 410, ch. 7); the La Jolla study uses the notions of circumstances (LA, 1979: 239), opportunism and idiosyncrasy (LA, 1980); the Troy study focuses on social contingencies (TR, 1979: 19ff.), and the Burnaby study refers to the unique situation and local peculiarities from which hypotheses originate (BU, 1979: 19).

*The situationally contingent, circumstantial or indexical
logic of scientific work*

Laboratory studies demonstrate that scientific products are 'occasioned' by the circumstances of their production. 'Occasioned' here means that the circumstances of production are an integral part of the products which emerge. Thus we are not just referring to contextual factors which 'influence' work which in its core is non-contextual. To quote from the Berkeley study:

> This contextual location reveals that the products of scientific research are fabricated and negotiated by particular agents at a particular time and place; that these products are carried by the particular interests of these agents, and by local rather than universally valid interpretations; and that the scientific actors play on the very limits of the situational location of their action. In short, the contingency and contextuality of scientific action demonstrates that the products of science are hybrids which bear the mark of the very indexical logic which characterizes their production.... (BE, 1981: 58)

The occasioned character of scientific work first manifests itself in the role played by *that which visibly stands around* at the research site, that is by facilities and measurement devices, materials which are in stock, journals and books in situ in the library, or specialized laboratories with specially trained technicians. It quickly touches upon less material objects such as the kind of routine analyses offered by service laboratories, office and laboratory hour regulations, or things for which one can get money easily within the organization. Circumstances of this sort are simple but consequential in that they reappear in the instrument chosen for a particular measurement, in the kind of analysis made, in a chemical ingredient selected, or in a problem formulation.

Test animals and other source materials equally are a constant cause of occasioned selections. For example, rats which are about to be 'sacrificed under nembutal anesthesia by intracardial perfusion' (to cite an excerpt from the field notes of the Irvine study), tend to squirm, squeak, kick, try to bite, and wriggle free. Thus they tend to cause troubles which require unmethodical remedies. For five rats, the Irvine study lists

> troubles in the animal's attempt to escape (Rat #1), failure of the animal to easily 'go under' the anesthetic (Rats #2, 3), 'toughness' of heart tissue to puncturing in the procedure (Rat #3), a leak sprung in fluid's course through the vascular system (Rat #5). The troubles pointed to the circumstantial character of each animal in its operative situation – to the troubles

inherent in the animal's frantic attempt to avoid compliance, to the arrangements of equipment and their possibilities for falling apart. (IR, 1979: 424)

Variability caused by raw materials is a dreaded source of nuisance for the scientists. As the head of a laboratory put it: 'The big variability is getting the raw material. We have never been able to get the same raw material again...it's the same in microbiology. You have to scratch yourself in the same place every time you play, and everything has to be the same, or else the accounts are meaningless' (BE, 1981: 68f.). The Troy study provides a comprehensive list of variable circumstances which affected the nature and the direction of the laboratory work observed (TR, 1979: 11).

The indexicality and the occasioned oscillation of rules and decision criteria

Let us now turn to a somewhat less tangible aspect of indexical construction: to local interpretations and the variation of rules and decision criteria. Decision criteria are often considered to be universal principles which circumscribe a variety of concrete selections. The criteria of 'simplicity', 'feasibility' and 'costs' provide frequently cited examples of such general principles. Yet seemingly universal decision criteria have variable indexical meanings, and they appear in concrete laboratory constructions in their indexical form. To be sure, the instruments needed in an experiment, the energy consumption, labour intensity or duration of a process, even the health hazards involved can all be translated into financial expenses and called 'costs'. Yet the product bears the mark of *concrete* selections such as the choice of a toxic versus non-toxic chemical, or of a laser-beam operated microscope (through which particle structure can be explored) versus a 'normal' electron microscope (which renders pictures of the particle surface). It is the concrete selection in which 'that which stands around' reappears, and it is the concrete translation in which time- and space-bound circumstances of broader relevance (such as the year-to-year policy of the Food and Drug Administration) come to bear. General criteria are post hoc and ex ante schematizations of higher order selections which become meaningful and consequential only in their indexical form, as circumstantially occasioned selections.

Criteria oscillations in scientific inquiry can be tied to this indexicality. In its record of the creation of a few hundred analogs of somatostatin out of 2.6×10^{22} possible analogs, the La Jolla study describes a series of occasioned shifts in selection criteria which decided from one analog to the next which modification to try. For example:

> modification 167 combines two different modifications invented earlier. One of the rules is to delete one after another each amino acid and see what happens. One of the other programmes is to replace the levorotatory form that exists in nature, with a dextrorotary form. From these two rules, however, you cannot *deduce* modification 167 because it cannot be obtained through systematic screening except by manufacturing thousands of analogs. The modification 167 is not a chance encounter though...JR makes up a small rule: 'combine successful modification'; and then follows another explicit constraint: 'go to the analogs that are most helpful for diabetes — and so justify our one million dollar grant'. So, they devise des-Asn^5 D-Trp^3 that is...immediately patented by the lawyers of the non-profit institute in which JR works. (LA, 1980: 61).

What determines the final string of analogs created is not one consistently applied criterion, but problem translations which are made up 'in going along', and which manifest themselves in the above shifts between 'rules'. Glaring inconsistencies often result from such situated choices. In the following example the whole point of a long-term research effort is subverted by such choices.

> The entire thrust of (research on single cell proteins) is the notion that protein suitable for human consumption can be isolated from the cells of certain highly abundant microorganisms. Unfortunately, the necessary disruption of the cell wall can only be accomplished by a homogenisation method using liquid CO_2 as a coolant, a method which costs about $10,000 per 1,000 grams of microbial protein. Moreover, the resulting protein is chemically modified in order to become more suitable for human consumption. And before this process of modification can proceed, the protein is dissolved by means of potentially toxic organic compounds. Thus, the picture we get from these long term research efforts is that of a 'cheap' protein which is tremendously expensive to produce, and which is made 'suitable for human consumption' by the use of toxic substances. (BE, 1981: 77)

Needless to say, scientists adjust their research goals to suit the selections made, and they adjust their selections to suit new circumstances created by their research. If selections are seen as time- and space-bound indexical selections, such shifts and oscillations will not be surprising. If the logic of research is an opportunistic logic, consistency according to formal criteria cannot be endemic to constructive operations. This is of course not to say that we cannot find any consistent selections or selection criteria in the process. But this consistency appears to be primarily linked to self-referential efforts at *consistency-making* and cannot be simply presupposed.

The socially situated character of constructive operations

To call the logic of inquiry opportunistic is to point to the occasioned character of selections and to the scientists' self-referential definitions of an 'occasion'. Differently speaking, we could say that selections arise out of 'occasions' which are accomplished as 'occasions'. These accomplishments, however, are not in principle individual achievements. The unit of action relevant here is a social unit, composed of (at least) two participants. Moreover, the respective interactions transcend the laboratory site, and appear to be situated in a field of social relations. I will first turn to the interactively accomplished character of constructive operations.

The interactively accomplished character of scientific work

All laboratory studies of which substantial results are available demonstrate the interactive basis of scientific work, whether they address the phenomenon explicitly or not. For example, the Troy study wants 'to convey...the way in which *communication* and contingencies continuously influence the course of scientific research'. It adds more specifically: 'the research adapted itself to...constraints by making use of contingencies; and the way they are made use of is partly a function of communication about them' (TR, 1979: 24f.).

The La Jolla study holds that scientists' activities are directed not towards 'reality' but towards operations on statements, which means towards an agonistic field of social conflict constituted by other scientists and their statements. The practical reasoning of scientists in the laboratory is particularly apt to illustrate the interactive basis of scientific work. In the following example, two scientists negotiate what they choose to accept as negative evidence for a psychobehavioural effect (LA, 1979: 156):

> Wilson: Anyway, the question for this paper is what I said in one of the versions that there was *no evidence* that there was any psychobehavioural effect of these peptides injected I.V...Can we write that down?
> Flower: That's a *practical* question...what do *we accept* as a negative answer?
> (Flower mentioned a paper which reported the use of an 'enormous

amount' of peptides with a positive result.)
Wilson: That *much?*
Flower: Yes, so it depends on the peptides...but it is very important to do...
Wilson: I will give you the peptides, yet we have to do it...but I'd like to
read the paper...
Flower: You know it's the one where...
Wilson: Oh, I have it, OK.
Flower: The threshold is one ug...OK, if we want to inject 100 rats (we need
at least a few micrograms)...it's a practical issue.

For Flower the 'practical' question is what quantity of peptides
Wilson is willing to provide. As the La Jolla study argues, the discussion
'entails a complex negotiation about what constitutes a legitimate
quantity of peptides'. The Irvine study devotes an extended chapter to
the presentation and analysis of transcribed conversations among scientists, which demonstrate in minute detail the subtle shifts through
which agreement is socially accomplished in the laboratory. In the
following extract, the issue is what one 'sees' (IR, 1979: 322):

V: How de yew know they're microglia?
H: Uh: :h
V: I: *mean*
V: (hh) UH YEH KNOW THE'S A BIG QUESTION OF
H: (   )
V: whut i:s microglia, whut is'n microglia an' where does microglia come
from en-
H: (ahts;s ats *fuckin* doesn' make any difference t'me noe)
V: O:h its a big doh- big d(hh)d question an-
( ): hah hah hah hah hah
H: I don't worry bou-
yeh know *thet* s:s (   )
ah yeh know yew c'n use whatever *wo:rd* yew wonna use=
V: =uh:h
H: say uh Del Rio Hortega (pos'tve cells) fer all I care, *right?*
H: Y'see these liddle things (   )
H: Del Rio Hortega positive cells

The irrelevance of specialist communities

Laboratory studies display scientific products as emerging from a form
of *discursive interaction* (BE, 1981: 28f.) directed at and sustained
by the arguments of other scientists. Naturally, the group of relevant others includes many not present in the laboratory itself. The
situational contingencies observed in the laboratory are traversed and

sustained by relationships which constantly transcend the site of action. The scientists' constructive operations are socially accomplished not only in the sense in which they involve in situ face-to-face interaction, but also in the sense that they involve participants' referring to — and calling upon — 'ex situ' relations.

It is probably no exaggeration to say that the notion which has been most frequently associated with the ex situ social organization of science is that of the *scientific community*. Scientific communities are mostly circumscribed by a specialty area and seen as small social systems with inherent boundaries and internal mechanisms of integration. Since the earliest sociological studies of science, these mechanisms have been characterized in terms of economic analogies. Starting from an emphasis on the role of (imperfect) competition (e.g. Merton, 1968) we have moved to precapitalist models of the scientific community in which scientific achievements are exchanged for a variety of rewards (e.g. Hagstrom, 1965), and finally to a capitalist market economy of science originally proposed by Bourdieu (1975). Here the scientific field is the locus of a competitive struggle for the monopoly of scientific credit acquired through the imposition of technical definitions and legitimate representations of scientific objects. The market model has been modified and refined by the La Jolla study, which sees scientists as seekers and investors of credibility. Credibility accrues from credible information, that is, from statements of type 4 or 5 (see above p. 122). It can in turn be converted to money, positions, recognitions, etc., and through these resources into more information, in a cycle in which scientists are not interested in truth, nor their subject matter, nor in recognition per se (Latour, 1979: 49ff.). What is of interest is the acceleration and expansion of the reproductive cycle which produces new and credible information, that is, statements for which the cost of raising objections is as high as possible. 'Reproduction for the sake of reproduction is the mark of pure, scientific capitalism' (LA, 1979: 194f., 207, 213):

> It becomes clear that sociological elements such as status, rank, award, past accreditation, and social situation are merely resources utilized in the struggle for credible information and increased credibility. It is at best misleading to argue that scientists are engaged, on the one hand, in the rational production of hard science and, on the other, in political calculation of assets and investments. On the contrary, they are strategists, choosing the most opportune moment, engaging in potentially fruitful collaborations, evaluating and grasping opportunities, and rushing to credited information.... Their political ability is invested in the heart of doing science. The better politicians and strategists they are, the better the science they produce.

Studies of scientific work which have not adopted the quasi-economic model of specialty fields have either not addressed the issue (IR, 1979), or taken a critical stance (BE, 1981: ch. 4). The Troy study outlines the contours of a 'hierarchical complex model' of the scientists' involvement in different groups held together by the degree and kind of communication entertained — a model most relevant to intraorganizational exchanges (TR, 1979: 23). The Keele study has employed the credibility model to account for the scientists' self-interested activities (KE, 1980). In addition, it has introduced the notion of 'networking' to refer to the tacit structuring activities through which agents establish interrelationships between people, things, and facts in a way potentially transcending scientific fields.

The critique of the capitalist market model of specialty fields can quickly be sketched. First, the notion of action implied by this model is dangerously near to that of classical economic theory, where homo economicus is a conscious maximizer of profits. He or she is either assumed to have an insatiable appetite for property, or is thought to accumulate for the sake of accumulation. In the first case, the behaviour is linked to an implicit assumption about human nature; in the second, it derives from market requirements which result from well-known historical developments. More sophisticated versions of economic man tend toward the latter interpretation, and substitute the idea of 'satisficing' under conditions of limited information for that of rational optimization: actors make do with the first satisfactory solution they come across (March and Simon, 1958).

However, the model remains individualistic and voluntaristic. It ignores the fact that decision outcomes are socially accomplished in context rather than individually calculated, as illustrated in micro-social research (Knorr-Cetina and Cicourel, 1981: 7–47). Moreover, it ignores the fact that outcomes are often not *consciously* calculated, or even intended by any one of the parties involved. To be sure, some economic models of science have tried to avoid these problems by defining their descriptions and imputations as social-structural, and by disclaiming any interest in individual behaviour. Yet to describe a system in intentional terms, such as in terms of interests, accumulation, competition and investment, requires that we assume corresponding individual behaviour, or specify some mechanism to explain system outcomes as not provoked by matching individual actions. Short of such a mechanism, intentionally descriptive system models of economic *behaviour* promote unintelligible reifications.

A second point of criticism is that the capitalist market analogy when applied to science leads to a host of difficulties. The advantage of an analogy is that it brings to bear upon a little-known phenomenon information about a better-known phenomenon which in some sense can be seen as similar to the former. Yet the mechanisms transferred from one phenomenon to the next have to remain internally consistent, or else the transfer amounts to not much more than a substitution of terms (such as 'symbolic capital' for 'recognition'). In Marx's economic theory, the notion of capital is linked to the idea of an accumulation of surplus value, which in turn is inherently connected to the notions of exploitation, class structure, and alienation. To make sense of this structure in a scientific specialty, we would somehow have to distinguish scientists-capitalists from scientists-workers by defining a level of symbolic capital or credibility above which scientists count as capitalists and below which they do not. However, such a procedure would be arbitrary. Part of the difficulty is the notion of symbolic capital itself. Such capital, particularly if it is understood in terms of credibility or operationalized in terms of publications and professional status, is a common, though graded, characteristic of everyone to whom the notion scientist commonly applies. Another and more important part of the difficulty is the restricted reference of the market model, which continues to promote an *internalistic* view of science.

This internalism 'is no longer due to the once dominant distinction between the social and the cognitive side of science, but to a continuing limitation of the perspective to the scientists themselves' (BE, 1981: 134). Scientific communities have turned into markets, and normative and functional integration has been replaced by a competitive struggle. Scientists have become capitalists, but they are still treated as though they were isolated in a self-contained, independent system of their own. Since we cannot define class differences in this system in any justifiable way, we end up with communities of petty capitalists who sustain themselves by somehow exploiting (or not exploiting?) each other. In economic theory, the existence of such community capitalism would certainly be a curiosity, in particular because those who provide the actual resources into which symbolic capital must be converted before it can be renewed are conspicuously absent from the picture.

Finally, it appears that as in previous economic models, this internalism goes together with a (presumably unintended) functionalism. The capitalist market model implies that there is an unequivocal connection between the reproduction of credible information and access to positions, careers, research money, citations and recognition. Yet the assumption that a career in science is made by accumulating scientific 'achievements' and by converting the credit associated with these achievements into resources and positions leads us back directly to Kingsley Davis's famous theory of social stratification according to which those who achieve best earn the better positions in society. While such a system might indeed be called functional, decades of sociological research have shown that it does not exist. The Keele study has seen some of the difficulty:

> Calculations about credibility rarely take place uninfluenced by noncredibility issues. This is, of course, a way of saying that science is constitutively social in a manner even broader than that suggested by the credibility model. To view science as the disinterested search for credibility is, in its own way, as misleading as to view it as the disinterested search for truth. (KE, 1980: 313)

The transepistemic connection of research

Basing his argument on a study of communication patterns in a number of research laboratories, Whitley has recently proposed that such relatively broad organizational units as specialist communities are largely irrelevant and often unknown to the scientists who work in these laboratories (1978: 427), and Edge has called the 'correct definition of a specialty' a meaningless concept to be replaced by a *radically participant-centred* perspective on scientific collectivities (1979: 124).

What, then, do scientists' ex situ involvements as displayed in the laboratory suggest in regard to the social organization of science? The scientists' practical reasoning routinely refers not only to specialty colleagues and other scientists, but also to grant agencies, administrators, industry representatives, publishers, and the management of the institute at which they work. It is clear that the agents invoked do not form a professional membership group. Moreover, scientists, even specialty colleagues, may confront each other in their everyday exchanges in 'non-scientific' roles in which they administer money or decide on professional careers. Similarly, a government official or sales' agent may negotiate with the scientific specialist the methods to be used in a research project, or the proper interpretations of a measurement result.

In short, laboratory reasoning and the involvements in which scientists perceive themselves to be entangled refer us to symbolic relationships which are *transepistemic* (BE, 1982a), that is, to relationships which in principle go beyond the boundaries of a scientific community. These symbolic relations are not primarily determined by characteristics held in common by its members as in the case of a logical class. The social integration which emerges from this picture is based not upon what is shared, but upon what is *transmitted* between agents. Accordingly, relationships between agents are often construed as 'resource'-relationships, in which agents are interested in what is transmitted because they can convert it into something else. For example, results in the literature are taken over in order to be converted into new products of the scientist making the transfer, and they will, in the process, undergo transformations and reconstructions.

The crucial question is, of course, in what sense the observed transepistemic connections of scientists are relevant to the process of inquiry. My answer is that these relationships emerge as the locus in which the decision criteria corresponding to laboratory selections — not necessarily the decisions themselves — are defined and negotiated. Take the case of a grant proposal. It has long been noted that research problems may be an 'external' input to science, for example an input defined by the research priorities a funding agency determines. Yet the funding agency usually does much more than simply promote certain goals. The proposals I looked at go through many fine-grained stages of problem translation and elaboration. It is exactly through these elaborations that scientists and financing agencies negotiate what the problem is and how it is to be translated into research selections.

Some epistemologically relevant implications of constructivism

My claim that transepistemic relationships are the locus in which the decision translations corresponding to laboratory selections are defined and negotiated does not imply that laboratory selections can be *read off* from scientists' contextual involvements. For one thing, the interests and commitments negotiated in these interactions do not unequivocally determine decision translations in the laboratory. Research problems defined in grant proposals become redefined during laboratory investigations, and agreements regarding research choices change in response to the circumstances, the opportunities and the troubles encountered from occasion to occasion. Second, the interests and commitments underlying transepistemic interactions often remain implicit, and at times may be deliberately left unclear. Scientists themselves 'figure', 'think', and 'imagine' what other participants 'have in mind' in regard to their work. But clearly they often do not know precisely what kind of result would meet with interest and satisfaction. Third, it is clear that the preferences emerging from transepistemic involvements depend themselves on the variable circumstances of these interactions. In short, scientists' ex situ involvements are simply marked by the same indexical, occasioned and socially accomplished logic which appears to characterize laboratory action.

I take this phenomenon to be a characteristic feature of social practice in general, and I want to point out some of its epistemologically relevant implications. If the conditions at the research site and the circumstances of scientists' interactions constitute variable occasions out of which laboratory selections arise, then we cannot predict the outcome of these occasions from knowledge of single components of these circumstances. If the respective occasions are marked by a social (interactional) dynamic of its own, then we cannot predict the outcome of the situation from knowing the actors who engage in the negotiation. Thus we are confronted with the somewhat annoying picture of an indeterminacy inherent in social action. The indexicality and the idiosyncrasies of scientific work jeopardize the hope of the philosopher of science to find once and for all the set of criteria which rule scientific selections. The situational contingency and the social dynamic of scientific action resist the attempt of the sociologist to specify once and for all the (social and cognitive, internal and external) factors which determine scientific action.

Strictly speaking, at least two sources of unpredictability can be differentiated. First, social action appears to be *underdetermined* by antecedent constraints (such as goals, rules, or 'structural' conditions). I take this to imply that antecedent constraints become practically meaningful only when interpreted in context, and hence their specific enactment (including their neglect, perversion, or substitution) changes with time- and space-bound conditions. Second, in a given situation social action may be *overdetermined* in that different, interpreted constraints (such as personal goals and technical preferences) exist and are at variance with one another, in which case the outcome of the situation seems to depend on the (unpredictable) dynamics of the clash. Both features account for the negotiated aspects of social life, though conflict is endemic only to the latter condition. Both features describe the essential indeterminancy of social practice in the sense that practice can no longer be conceived as the mere execution of a predetermined order of things, but rather this order is itself a function of local closure reached in practical action.

Perhaps surprisingly, observers of scientific work have seen this indeterminacy in a positive light. They have maintained that the contingencies observed are 'constitutive of the research' (TR, 1979: 24), or that they must be considered the very principle of scientific change (BE, 1981: 11ff.). They have analyzed scientific writing as a material operation of creating order out of noise produced in scientific work (LA, 1979: 245) and have pointed to recent developments in thermodynamics (Prigogyne) and systems theory (von Foerster) to support these observations (LA, 1979: 244ff.; BE, 1981: 10ff.). These developments demonstrate the creation of 'order out of disorder', or more precisely, of information out of noise and of organization out of chance events.

The most useful analogy here is perhaps that of the evolution of the universe, or more restrictively, that of biological evolution. Macro- and microevolution can be seen to originate from self-organizing processes which crucially involve chance mechanisms, an idea with which we are familiar in terms of the biological mechanisms of muta- tion and selection. Put extremely, theories of evolution demonstrate the possibility of conceiving of creation and the progressive develop- ment of things out of nothing, and invoke chance as the most effective mechanism in the process. It is the thrust of the constructivist concep- tion to conceive of scientific reality as progressively emerging out of indeterminancy and (self-referential) constructive operations, without assuming it to match any pre-existing order of the real (BE, 1977: 673; 1981: 4, 18ff.; LA, 1979: 244ff., 250).

If we take the metaphor of the *manufacture* of knowledge seriously, science emerges from the constructivist interpretation as a 'way of world-making' (Goodman, 1978). A factory is a production facility, and not an establishment designed to mimic nature. Nor would it seem that a process of fabrication is best described by a model which one-sidedly conceives of science as problem-solving (Laudan, 1977). The problem-solving model suggests that science is a successful tool for adequately coping with the world, even though we may not want to think of it as correctly representing the world. The vision behind this model is that of a decreasing stock of problems constituted by what we do not yet know about how to handle the world-out-there. The vision behind the constructivist programme as I conceive of it is that of a potentially increasing stock of problems created by science in the process of secreting an unending stream of entities and relations that make up 'the world'. The 'unknown world' as an intentional object of science is itself a function of a constantly changing scientific practice, of what at every moment of scientific work emerges as the known world. But this known world is a cultural object, a world identified and embodied in our language and our practices.

Thus, accepted theories must indeed be considered more than just useful instruments for facilitating measurements and observations, in the sense that they identify for us in our language and practices (and what more could there be?) what 'the world' really is and what it consists of. Yet this 'world' is itself the outcome of a process of inquiry which is construed generatively and ontologically, rather than descriptively and epistemologically. More concretely, inquiry is 'about' ever new procedures in terms of which 'something' can be practically reliably encountered and recognized as an object which displays identifiable characteristics, and which can thereby become incorporated in and constitutive of our future world.

To conclude, the interpretation of science I have advanced entails neither a subjectivist position (see the respective accusations of Bazerman, 1980, and Cozzens, 1980, against the La Jolla study) nor a relativist position in the common (say Mannheim's, 1954) sense of the word. It requires the working out of an *empirical, constructivist epistemology* which conceives of the order generated by science as a (material) process of embodiment and incorporation of objects in our language and practices. Needless to say, the effort to develop such an interpretation of science has only just begun. Quite obviously, I think that the programme will profit from (but need not be bounded by) the microscopic investigation of scientific practice.

Notes

I am grateful to Daryl Chubin, Michael Mulkay and Sal Restivo (who coined the notion 'transepistemic') for helpful comments on an earlier draft of this chapter.

1. This is not to say that references to social or cognitive interests could not be used, say, to explain epistemologically relevant events such as the closure of a controversy. And indeed, Pickering's account of the success of the charm model over the colour model in a recent controversy in quantum physics provides us

with an example of exactly this use of an interest explanation (1980). As I see it, the distinctive difference between Pickering's account and the traditional interest approach lies in the fact that Pickering addresses himself to the question of what causes a consensus formation, and not to the epistemologically irrelevant question of what causes individuals' belief preferences.

2. I am aware of at least two other research programmes which can be characterized by methodological microscopism: one is the ethnomethodological approach to science studies (see Lynch, 1979; Garfinkel et al., 1981; Woolgar, 1980; and Lynch et al. as well as Woolgar, this volume). The other is the emerging discourse analysis of scientific talk and writing as proposed by Mulkay and Gilbert (see Gilbert and Mulkay, 1980; the formulation of the constitutive assumptions of this perspective by Mulkay and Gilbert, 1982, and the works quoted in Mulkay, Potter and Yearley, this volume). While other analysts, and particularly students of laboratory practice, also analyze scientific discourse (Latour and Fabbri, 1977; Latour and Woolgar, 1979; Lynch, 1979; Knorr-Cetina and Knorr, 1982; Knorr-Cetina, 1981: ch. 5; Woolgar, 1980), Mulkay et al. adopt a distinctive methodological and epistemological perspective which appears uninterested in questions of the sociology of knowledge as posed above. The same holds for ethnomethodological analyses of science. I should also like to mention that microsociological studies of science have not developed in isolation. In many respects, Fleck's only lately rediscovered study of the genesis and development of a scientific fact constitutes a forerunner of recent microsociological investigations into the hard sciences (Fleck, 1979; first published in 1935). Furthermore, the 'cognitive' sociology of science which emerged in the wake of the reception of Kuhn has argued the necessity to include the 'cognitive' side of science in sociological investigations since the early 1970s (see e.g. Nowotny, 1973; Weingart, 1976; Edge and Mulkay, 1976). Finally, some of the results of ethnographic studies of science are sustained by work in history and philosophy of science which ranges from Duhem to Kuhn (see the Introduction to this volume) — though most ethnographic studies to date have the character of grounded sociological theory and description and do not link themselves directly to the above work.

References

Barnes, B. (1977) *Interests and the Growth of Knowledge*, London: Routledge & Kegan Paul.

Barnes, B. and Shapin S. (eds) (1979) *Natural Order*, London and Beverly Hills: Sage.

Bazerman, C. (1980) 'Bruno Latour's and Steve Woolgar's *Laboratory Life*, Book Review', *4S Newsletter*, 5 (2): 14–19.

Bourdieu, P. (1975) 'The Specificity of the Scientific Field and the Social

Conditions of the Progress of Reason', *Social Science Information*, 14 (6): 19–47.

Chubin, D. and Connolly, T. (1982) 'Research Trails and Science Policies: Local and Extra-Local Negotiation of Scientific Work', pp. 293-311 in N. Elias, H. Martins and R. Whitley (eds), *Scientific Establishments and Hierarchies, Sociology of the Sciences Yearbook*, vol. 6, Boston/Dordrecht: D. Reidel.

Collins, H. (ed.) (1981) 'Knowledge and Controversy: Studies in Modern Natural Science', special issue of *Social Studies of Science*, 11 (1).

Cozzens, S. (1980) 'Bruno Latour's and Steve Woolgar's *Laboratory Life*, Book Review', *4S Newsletter*, 5 (2): 19–21.

Edge, D. (1979) 'Quantitative Measures of Communication in Science: A Critical Review', *History of Science*, 17: 102–34.

Edge, D. and Mulkay, M. (1976) *Astronomy Transformed*, New York: Wiley.

Fleck, L. (1979) *Genesis and Development of a Scientific Fact*, Chicago: University of Chicago Press (first published in German, 1935).

Garfinkel, H., Lynch, M. and Livingston, E. (1981) 'The Work of a Discovering Science Construed with Materials from the Optically Discovered Pulsar', *Philosophy of the Social Sciences*, 11: 131–58.

Gieryn, T. (1982) 'Relativist/Constructivist Programmes in the Sociology of Science: Redundance and Retreat,' *Social Studies of Science*, 12 (2): 279–97.

Gilbert, G. N. and Mulkay, M. (1980) 'Contexts of Scientific Discourse: Social Accounting in Experimental Papers', pp. 269–94 in K. Knorr, R. Krohn and R. Whitley, *The Social Process of Scientific Investigation, Sociology of the Sciences Yearbook*, vol. 4, Boston/Dordrecht: D. Reidel.

Goodfield, N. (1981) *An Imagined World*, New York: Harper & Row.

Goodman, N. (1978) *Ways of World-Making*, Indianapolis: Hackett Publishing Company.

Habermas, J. (1971) *Knowledge and Human Interests*, Boston: Beacon Press.

Hagstrom, W. O. (1965) *The Scientific Community*, New York: Basic Books.

Janich, P. (1978) 'Physics – Natural Science or Technology?', pp. 3–27 in W. Krohn, E. Layton and P. Weingart (eds), *The Dynamics of Science and Technology, Sociology of the Sciences Yearbook*, vol. 2, Boston/Dordrecht: D. Reidel.

Knorr, K. D. (BE, 1977) 'Producing and Reproducing Knowledge: Descriptive or Constructive? Toward a Model of Research Production', *Social Science Information*, 16: 669–96.

Knorr, K. D. (BE, 1979a) 'Tinkering Toward Success; Prelude to a Theory of Scientific Practice', *Theory and Society*, 8: 347–76.

Knorr, K. D. (BE, 1979b) 'Contextuality and Indexicality of Organizational Action: Toward a Transorganizational Theory of Organizations', *Social Science Information*, 18: 79–101.

Knorr-Cetina, K. D. (BE, 1981) *The Manufacture of Knowledge: An Essay on the Constructivist and Contextual Nature of Science*, Oxford: Pergamon Press.

Knorr-Cetina, K. D. (BE, 1982a) 'Scientific Communities or Transepistemic Arenas of Research? A Critique of Quasi-Economic Models of Science', *Social Studies of Science*, 12 (1): 101–30.

Knorr-Cetina, K. D. (BE, 1982b) 'The Constructivist Programme in Sociology of Science: Retreats or Advances?,' *Social Studies of Science*, 12 (2): 320–4.

Knorr-Cetina, K. D. and Cicourel, A. (eds) (1981) *Advances in Social Theory and Methodology: Toward an Integration of Micro- and Macro-sociologies*, London: Routledge & Kegan Paul.

Knorr-Cetina, K. D. and Knorr, D. W. (1982) 'The Scientist as a Literary Reasoner, or the Transformation of Laboratory Research', in J. O'Neill (ed.), *Science Texts* (forthcoming).

Knorr, K., Krohn, R. and Whitley, R. (eds) (1980) *The Social Process of Scientific Investigation, Sociology of the Sciences Yearbook*, vol. 4, Boston/Dordrecht: D. Reidel.

Latour, B. (1979) 'Le dernier des capitalistes sauvages. Interview d'un biochemiste', Paris: Conservatoire des Arts et Métiers (unpublished manuscript).

Latour, B. (LA, 1980a) 'Is it Possible to Reconstruct the Research Process? Sociology of a Brain Peptide', pp. 53–76 in K. Knorr, R. Krohn and R. Whitley (eds), *The Social Process of Scientific Investigation, Sociology of the Sciences Yearbook*, vol. 4, Boston/Dordrecht: D. Reidel.

Latour, B. (LA, 1980b) 'The Three Little Dinosaurs or a Sociologist's Nightmare', *Fundamenta Scientiae*, 1: 79–85.

Latour, B. (LA, 1981) 'Who is Agnostic or What Could it Mean to Study Science?', in H. Kucklick and R. Jones (eds), *Knowledge and Society*, vol. III, Greenwich, CO: JAI Press.

Latour, B. and Fabbri, P. (LA, 1977) 'Pouvoir et Devoir dans un article des sciences exactes', *Actes de la Recherche en Sciences Sociales*, 13: 81–95.

Latour, B. and Woolgar, S. (LA, 1979) *Laboratory Life. The Social Construction of Scientific Facts*, London and Beverly Hills: Sage.

Laudan, L. (1977) *Progress and Its Problems*, Berkeley: University of California Press.

Law, J. and Williams, R. (KE, 1982) 'Putting Facts Together: A Study of Scientific Persuasion', *Social Studies of Science*, 12 (4): 535–58.

Lynch, M. (IR, 1976) 'Art and Artifact in Microscopy', Irvine, Calif.: University of California (unpublished manuscript).

Lynch, M. (IR, 1979) 'Art and Artifact in Laboratory Science: A Study of Shop Work and Shop Talk in a Research Laboratory', PhD dissertation, Irvine, Calif.: University of California, and London: Routledge & Kegan Paul (1982).

Lynch, M. (IR, 1982) 'Technical Work and Critical Inquiry: Investigations in a Scientific Laboratory', *Social Studies of Science*, 12 (4): 499–534.

McKegney, D. (BU, 1979) 'The Research Process in Animal Ecology', paper presented at the conference on The Social Process of Scientific Investigation, Montreal: McGill University, October.

McKegney, D. (BU, 1980) 'Inquiry into Inquiry: The Case of Wildlife Biology', paper presented at the conference on Science and Technology Studies – Toronto 80, Toronto: University of Toronto, October.

McKegney, D. (BU, 1982) 'Inquiry into Inquiry. Local Action and Public Discourse in Wildlife Ecology', PhD dissertation, Burnaby: Simon Frazer University.

Mannheim, K. (1954) *Ideology and Utopia: An Introduction to the Sociology of Knowledge*, New York: Harcourt, Brace, Jovanovich.

March, J. and Simon, H. (1958) *Organizations*, New York: Wiley.

Marx, K. (1913) *A Contribution to the Critique of Political Economy*, Chicago: Kerr (first published 1859).

Merton, R. K. (1968) 'The Matthew Effect in Science', *Science*, 159 (3810): 56–63.

Mills, C. W. (1963) *Power, Politics and People*, I. L. Horowitz (ed.), New York: Ballantine Books.

Mulkay, M. and Gilbert, G. N. (1982) 'What is the Ultimate Question? Some Remarks in Defence of the Analysis of Scientific Discourse', *Social Studies of Science*, 12 (2): 309–19.

Nowotny, H. (1973) 'On the Feasibility of a Cognitive Approach to the Study of Science', *Zeitschrift für Soziologie*, 2 (3): 282–96.

Peirce, C. (1931–35) *Collected Papers*, C. Hartshorne and P. Weiss (eds), Cambridge, Mass.: Harvard University Press.

Pickering, A. (1980) 'The Role of Interests in High Energy Physics: The Choice between Charm and Colour', in K. Knorr, R. Krohn and R. Whitley (eds), *The Social Process of Scientific Investigation, Sociology of the Sciences Yearbook*, vol. 4, Boston/Dordrecht: D. Reidel.

Ravetz, J. R. (1971) *Scientific Knowledge and its Social Problems*, Oxford: Clarendon Press.

Restivo, S. (1981) 'Some Perspectives in Contemporary Sociology of Science', *Science, Technology and Human Values*, 35: 22–30.

Thill, G. (1972) *La Fête Scientifique*, Paris: Institute Catholique de Paris.

Traweek, S. (1981) 'Culture and the Organization of the Particle Physics Communities in Japan and the United States', paper presented at the conference on Communication in Scientific Research, Burnaby: Simon Fraser University, September.

Weingart, P. (1976) *Wissensproduktion und Soziale Struktur*, Frankfurt: Suhrkamp.

Whitley, R. (1978) 'Types of Science, Organizational Strategies and Patterns of Work in Research Laboratories in Different Scientific Fields', *Social Science Information*, 17: 427–47.

Williams, R. and Law, J. (KE, 1980) 'Beyond the Bounds of Credibility', *Fundamenta Scientiae*, 1: 295–315.

Woolgar, S. (1980) 'Discovery: Logic and Sequence in a Scientific Text', pp. 239–68 in K. Knorr, R. Krohn and R. Whitley (eds), *The Social Process of Scientific Investigation, Sociology of the Sciences Yearbook*, vol. 4, Boston/Dordrecht: D. Reidel.

Woolgar, S. (1981) 'Interests and Explanation in the Social Study of Science', *Social Studies of Science*, 11 (3): 365–98.

Zenzen, M. and Restivo, S. (TR, 1979) 'The Mysterious Morphology of Immiscible Liquids: The Discovery and Pursuit of an Anomaly in Colloid Chemistry', paper presented at the conference on The Social Process of Scientific Investigation, Montreal: McGill University, October.

Zenzen, M. and Restivo, S. (TR, 1982) 'The Mysterious Morphology of Immiscible Liquids: A Study of Scientific Practice', *Social Science Information*, 21 (3): 447–73.

6

Give Me a Laboratory and I will Raise the World

Bruno Latour
École des Mines, Paris

Now that field studies of laboratory practices are starting to pour in, we are beginning to have a better picture of what scientists do inside the walls of these strange places called 'laboratories' (Knorr-Cetina, this volume). But a new problem has emerged. If we are not able to follow up our participant-observation studies far enough to take in questions outside the laboratory, we are at great risk of falling back into the so-called 'internalist' vision of science. From the very beginnings of these microstudies, this criticism was levelled at us by scholars preoccupied by larger problems such as science policy, history of science, or more broadly, what is known as Science, Technology and Society (STS). For such topics, laboratory studies seemed utterly irrelevant. At the time, our critics were largely wrong because we first of all had to penetrate these black boxes, and to get firsthand observations of the daily activity of scientists. This was the foremost priority. The result, to summarize it in one sentence, was that nothing extraordinary and nothing 'scientific' was happening inside the sacred walls of these temples (Knorr, 1981). After a few years of studies, however, our critics would be right in raising again the naïve but nagging question: if nothing scientific is happening in laboratories, why are there laboratories to begin with and

Author's note: Many arguments developed here are commentaries on ideas discussed with my colleague Michel Callon. I wish to thank Mark Smith for his assistance in preparing the manuscript.

why, strangely enough, is the society surrounding them paying for these places where nothing special is produced?

The question appears innocent enough, but is actually a rather tricky one because there is a division of labour between scholars studying organizations, institutions, public policy on the one hand, and people studying micronegotiations inside scientific disciplines on the other. It is truly difficult to see common elements between the analysis of the laetrile controversy (Nelkin, 1979) and the semiotic study of a single scientific text (Bastide, 1981); between the study of indicators for following the growth of R&D and the history of the gravitational wave detector (Collins, 1975); or between the Windscale Inquiry and the deciphering of the mutterings of a few scientists during a chat at a bench (Lynch, 1982); it is so hard to grasp common features among these interests, that people tend to think that there are indeed 'macroscopic' problems, and that the two sets of issues ought to be treated differently, with different methods, by different breeds of scholars. This belief in a *real* difference of scale between macro- and micro-objects in society is common among sociologists (Knorr and Cicourel, 1981), but is especially strong in sociology of science. Many analysts of STS are proud of not entering at all into the content of science and into the microlevel of scientific negotiations, while, at the other end of the spectrum, some analysts claim that they are interested only in controversies between scientists (Collins, 1982), or even claim that there is no society at all or at least no macrosociety about which something serious could be uttered (Woolgar, 1981). The funny thing about this misunderstanding is that it reproduces on slightly different grounds the age-old polemic between 'internalist' and 'externalist' in the study of science and technology. While the debates of earlier times opposed 'social influences' to 'purely internal development' in accounting for the movement of scientific disciplines, people are now opposing 'public policy', 'large-scale economic push and pull' to 'micronegotiations', 'opportunism' and 'laboratory folklore'. The terms have changed, the belief in the 'scientificity' of science has disappeared, but the same respect for the boundaries of scientific activity is manifested by both schools of thought.

The time has now come for the analysts of scientists at work to deal with the naïve but fair criticism put to them by scholars interested in 'macro' issues. But there is of course no way that we can easily conciliate such profoundly different perspectives and methods. In particular, it is impossible for observers used to laboratory studies to leave this firm ground where so much has been achieved and simply dive into 'macro' problems, computing gross national product percentages, citations and rewards and so on. If we do deal with these questions it will be on our own terms.

In this chapter, I would like to propose a simple line of enquiry: that is, to stick with the methodology developed during laboratory field studies, focusing it not on the laboratory itself but on the construction of the laboratory and its position in the societal milieu (Callon, 1982). Indeed, I hope to convince the reader that the very difference between the 'inside' and the 'outside', and the difference of scale between 'micro' and 'macro' levels, is precisely what laboratories are built to destabilize or undo. So much so, that without keeping back the discoveries we made while studying laboratory practices we can reassess the so-called 'macro' problems much more clearly than before and even throw some light on the very construction of macroactors themselves. I simply beg the readers to put aside for a time their belief in any *real* difference between micro- and macroactors at least for the reading of this paper (Callon and Latour, 1981).

I. 'Give me a place to stand and I will move the earth'

To illustrate my argument I will extract an example from a recent study done in the history of science (Latour, 1981a). We are in the year 1881, the French semi-popular and scientific press is full of articles about the work being done in a certain laboratory, that of Monsieur Pasteur at the École Normale Supérieure. Day after day, week after week, journalists, fellow scientists, physicians and hygienists focus their attention on what is happening to a few colonies of microbes in different mediums, under the microscope, inside inoculated animals, in the hands of a few scientists. The mere existence of this enormous interest shows the irrelevance of too sharp a distinction between the 'inside' and the 'outside' of Pasteur's lab. What is relevant is the short circuit established between many groups usually uninterested by what happens inside laboratory walls, and laboratories usually isolated and insulated from such attention and passion. Somehow, something is happening in these dishes that seems directly essential to the projects of these many groups expressing their concern in the journals.

This interest of outsiders for lab experiments is not a given: it is the result of Pasteur's work in enrolling and enlisting them. This is worth emphasizing since there is a quarrel among sociologists of science about the possibility of imputing interests to people. Some, especially the

Edinburgh school, claim that we can impute interests to social groups
given a general idea of what the groups are, what society is made of,
and even what the nature of man is like. But others (Woolgar, 1981)
deny the possibility of such imputation on the grounds that we do not
have any independant way of knowing what the groups are, what
society is after and what the nature of man is like. This dispute, like
most, misses the fundamental point. Of course there is no way of
knowing which are the groups, what they want and what man is,
but this does not stop anyone from convincing others of what their
interests are and what they ought to want and to be. He who is able to
translate others' interests into his own language carries the day. It is
especially important *not* to rely on any science of society or science of
man to impute interests because as I will show, sciences are one of the
most convincing tools to persuade others of who they are and what
they should want. A sociology of science is crippled from the start if
it believes in the results of one science, namely sociology, to explain
the others. But it is still possible to follow how sciences are used to
transform society and redefine what it is made of and what are its aims.
So it is useless to look for the profit that people can reap from being
interested in Pasteur's laboratory. Their interests are a consequence and
not a cause of Pasteur's efforts to translate what they want or what he
makes them want. They have no a priori reason to be interested at all,
but Pasteur has found them more than one reason.

1. Move one: capturing others' interests

How has Pasteur succeeded in capturing the interests of other indif-
ferent groups? By the same method he has always used (Geison, 1974;
Salomon-Bayet, 1982). He transfers himself and his laboratory into the
mist of a world untouched by laboratory science. Beer, wine, vinegar,
diseases of silk worms, antisepsy and later asepsy, had already been
treated through these moves. Once more he does the same with a new
problem: anthrax. The anthrax disease was said to be terrible for
French cattle. This 'terrible' character was 'proven' by statistics to
officials, veterinarians and farmers and their concerns were voiced by
the many agricultural societies of the time. This disease was studied by
statisticians and veterinarians, but laboratory practice had no bearing
on it before Pasteur, Koch and their disciples. At the time, diseases
were local events that were to be studied with all possible attention by
taking into account all the possible variables — the soil, the winds, the

weather, the farming system, and even the individual fields, animals and farmers. Veterinary doctors knew these idiosyncrasies, but it was a careful, variable, prudent and uncertain knowledge. The disease was unpredictable, and recurred according to no clear pattern, reinforcing the idea that local idiosyncrasies had to be taken into account. This multifactorial approach made everyone extremely suspicious of any attempt to cut through all these idiosyncrasies and to link one disease with any single cause, such as a micro-organism. Diseases like anthrax, with all their variations, were typically what was thought not to be related to laboratory science. A lab in Paris and a farm in Beauce have nothing in common. They are mutually uninteresting.

But interests, like everything else, can be constructed. Using the work of many predecessors who had already started to link laboratories and anthrax disease, Pasteur goes one step further and works in a makeshift laboratory right on the farm site. No two places could be more foreign to one another than a dirty, smelling, noisy, disorganized nineteenth-century animal farm and the obsessively clean Pasteurian laboratory. In the first, big animals are parasited in seemingly random fashion by invisible diseases; in the second, micro-organisms are made visible to the observer's eye. One is made to grow big animals, the other to grow small animals. Pasteur (the 'shepherd' in French) is often seen in the enthusiasm of the moment as the inventor of a new animal husbandry and a new agriculture, but at the time these two forms of livestock have little relation to one another. Once out in the field, however, Pasteur and his assistants learn from the field conditions and the veterinarians and start creating these relations. They are interested in pinpointing all the variations in the onset and timing of the outbreaks of anthrax and in seeing how far these could fit with their one living cause, the anthrax bacillus. They learn from the field, translating each item of veterinary science into their own terms so that working on their terms is also working on the field. For instance, the spore of the bacillus (shown by Koch) is the translation through which dormant fields can suddenly become infectious even after many years. The 'spore phase' is the laboratory translation of the 'infected field' in the farmer's language. The Pasteurians start by learning this language and giving one of their own names for each of the relevant elements of the farmer's life. They are interested in the field but still useless and uninteresting for the farmers and their various spokesmen.

2. Move two: moving the leverage point
   from a weak to a strong position

At this point Pasteur, having situated his laboratory on the farm, is
going to transfer it back to his main workplace at the École Normale
Supérieure, taking with him one element of the field, the cultivated
bacillus. He is the master of one technique of farming that no farmer
knows, microbe farming. This is enough to do what no farmer could
ever have done: grow the bacillus in isolation and in such a large quantity that, although invisible, it becomes visible. Here again we have,
because of laboratory practice, a variation of scale: outside, in the 'real'
world, inside the bodies, anthrax bacilli are mixed with millions of
other organisms with which they are in a constant state of competition.
This makes them doubly invisible. However, in Pasteur's laboratory
something happens to the anthrax bacillus that never happened before
(I insist on these two points: something happens *to the bacillus* that
never happened before). Thanks to Pasteur's methods of culture it is
freed from all competitors and so grows exponentially, but, by growing
so much, ends up, thanks to Koch's later method, in such large colonies
that a clear-cut pattern is made visible to the watchful eye of the
scientist. The latter's skills are not miraculous. To achieve such a result
you only need to extract one micro-organism and to find a suitable
milieu. Thanks to these skills, the asymmetry in the scale of several
phenomena is modified: a micro-organism can kill vastly larger cattle,
one small laboratory can learn more about pure anthrax cultures than
anyone before; the invisible micro-organism is made visible; the until
now uninteresting scientist in his lab can talk with more authority
about the anthrax bacillus than veterinarians ever have before.

The translation that allows Pasteur to transfer the anthrax disease to
his laboratory in Paris is not a literal, word-for-word translation. He
takes only one element with him, the micro-organism, and not the
whole farm, the smell, the cows, the willows along the pond or the
farmer's pretty daughter. With the microbe, however, he also draws
along with him the now interested agricultural societies. Why? Because
having designated the micro-organism as the living and pertinent cause,
he can now reformulate farmers' interests in a new way: if you wish to
solve *your* anthrax problem you have to pass through *my* laboratory
first. Like all translations there is a real displacement through the
various *versions*. To go straight at anthrax, you should make a detour
through Pasteur's lab. The anthrax disease *is* now at the École Normale
Supérieure.

But this version of the translation is still a weak one. In Pasteur's lab, there is a microbe, but anthrax infection is too disorderly a thing to be explained with a single cause only. So the outside interests could as well say that the laboratory has no real bearing on the spread of anthrax disease, and that it is just plain arrogance for a scientist to claim that he holds the key to a real disease 'out there'. But Pasteur is able to make a more faithful translation than that. Inside the walls of his laboratory, he can indeed inoculate animals he has chosen with pure, much-diluted culture of anthrax. This time, the outbreak of an epizootic is mimicked on a smaller scale entirely dominated by the charting and recording devices of the Pasteurians. The few points deemed essential are imitated and reformulated so as to be scaled down. The animals die of the microbes, and only of that, and epizootics are started at will. It can now be said that Pasteur has inside his laboratory, on a smaller scale, the 'anthrax disease'. The big difference is that 'outside' it is hard to study because the micro-organism is invisible and strikes in the dark, hidden among many other elements, while 'inside' the lab clear figures can be drawn about a cause that is there for all to see, due to the translation. The change of scale makes possible a reversal of the actors' strengths; 'outside' animals, farmers and veterinarians were *weaker* than the invisible anthrax bacillus; inside Pasteur's lab, man becomes stronger than the bacillus, and as a corollary, the scientist in his lab gets the edge over the local, devoted, experienced veterinarian. The translation has become more credible and now reads: 'If you wish to solve your anthrax problem, come to my laboratory, because that's where the forces are reversed. If you don't (veterinarians or farmers) you will be eliminated.'

But even at this point, the strength is so disproportionate between Pasteur's single lab and the multiplicity, complexity and economic size of the anthrax outbreaks, that no translation could last long enough to keep the aggregation of interest from falling apart. People readily give their attention to someone who claims that he has the solution to their problems but are quick to take it back. Especially puzzling for all practitioners and farmers, is the *variation* of the disease. Sometimes it kills, sometimes not, sometimes it is strong, sometimes weak. No contagionist theory can account for this variety. So Pasteur's work, although interesting, could soon become a curiosity or more precisely, a laboratory curiosity. It would not be the first time that scientists attract attention, only to have nothing come out of it in the end. Microstudies remain 'micro', the interests captured for a time soon go to other translations from groups that succeed in enrolling them.

This was especially true of medicine which at the time was tired of continuous fashions and fads (Leonard, 1977).

But here Pasteur does something on chicken cholera and on anthrax bacillus inside his laboratory that definitively modifies the hierarchy between veterinary science and microbiology. Once a great many microbes are cultivated in pure forms in laboratories and submitted to numerous trials to make them accelerate their growth or die, a new practical know-how is developed. In a few years, experimenters acquire skills in manipulating sets of materials that never existed before. This is new but not miraculous. Training microbes and domesticating them is a craft like printing, electronics, blue-ribbon cooking or video art. Once these skills have accumulated inside laboratories, many cross-overs occur that had no reason to occur anywhere else before. This is not because of any new cognitive attitude, or because suddenly people become conscious of micro-organisms they were unaware of before. It is simply that they are manipulating new objects and so acquiring new skills in a new idiosyncratic setting (Knorr, 1981).

The chance encounter that made possible the first attenuated culture of chicken cholera is well-known (Geison, 1974), but chance favours only well-prepared laboratories. Living causes of man-made diseases undergo so many various trials that it is not that surprising if some of these trials leave some microbes alive but weak. This modification would have been invisible if the laboratory had not tried to imitate the salient features of epizootics by inoculating many animals. The invisible modification of the invisible microbes is then made visible; chickens previously inoculated with the modified strain don't get cholera but they resist inoculation of intact microbes. Submitting cultures of chicken cholera to oxygen is enough to make them less virulent when they are inoculated into the animals. What is made visible through the lab statistics is the chain of weakened microbes, then strengthened microbes and eventually, strengthened animals. The result is that laboratories are now able to imitate the *variation of virulence*.

It is important to understand that Pasteur now does more and more things inside his laboratory which are deemed relevant by more and more groups to their own interests. Cultivating the microbes was a curiosity; reproducing epizootics in labs was interesting; but varying at will the virulence of the microbes is fascinating. Even if they believed in contagion, no one could with this one cause explain the randomness of the effects. But Pasteur is not only the man who has proved the relation of one microbe/one disease, he is also the one who has proved that the infectiousness of microbes could vary under conditions that could be controlled, one of them being, for instance, a first encounter of the body with a weakened form of the disease. This variation in the laboratory is what makes the translation hard for others to dispute: the variation was the most puzzling element that previously justified the scepticism towards laboratory science, and made necessary a clear differentiation between an outside and inside, between a practical level and a theoretical level. But it is precisely this variation that Pasteur can imitate most easily. He can attenuate a microbe; he can, by passing it through different species of animals, on the contrary, exalt its strength; he can oppose one weak form to a strong one, or even one microbial species to another. To sum up, he can do inside his laboratory what everyone tries to do outside but, where everyone fails because the scale is too large, Pasteur succeeds because he works on a small scale. Hygienists who comprise the largest relevant social movement of that time are especially fascinated by this imitated variation. They deal with whole cities and countries, trying to pinpoint why winds, soil, climates, diets, crowding, or different degrees of wealth accelerate or stop the evolution of epidemics. They all see — they are all led to see — in the Pasteurian microcosmos what they are vainly trying to do at the macroscopic level. The translation is now the following: 'If you wish to understand epizootics and soon thereafter epidemics, you have one place to go, Pasteur's laboratory, and one science to learn that will soon replace yours: microbiology.'

As the reader is aware, I am multiplying the words 'inside' and 'outside', 'micro' and 'macro', 'small scale' and 'large scale', so as to make clear the destabilizing role of the laboratory. It is through laboratory practices that the complex relations between microbes and cattle, the farmers and their cattle, the veterinarians and the farmers, the veterinarians and the biological sciences, are going to be transformed. Large interest groups consider that a set of lab studies talk to them, help them and concern them. The broad concerns of French hygiene and veterinary sciences will be settled, they all say, inside Pasteur's laboratory. This is the dramatic short circuit I started with: everyone is interested in lab experiments which a few years before had not the slightest relation to their fields. This attraction and capture were made by a double movement of Pasteur's laboratory to the field and then from the field to the laboratory where a fresh source of know-how has been gained by manipulating a new material: pure cultures of microbes.

3. Move three: moving the world with the lever

But even at this stage, what was in the laboratory could have stayed there. The macrocosmos is linked to the microcosmos of the laboratory, but a laboratory is never bigger than its walls and 'Pasteur' is still only one man with a few collaborators. No matter how great the interests of many social groups for what is being done in one laboratory, there is nothing to stop interests from fading and dispersing if nothing more than laboratory studies happens. If Pasteur stays too long inside his laboratory and, for instance, shifts his research programme using the anthrax microbe to learn things in biochemistry, like his disciple Duclaux, people could say: 'Well after all, it was just an interesting curiosity!' It is only by hindsight that we say that in this year 1881, Pasteur invented the first artificial vaccination. By doing so we forget that to do so it was necessary to move still further, this time from the laboratory to the field, from the microscale to the macroscale. As for all translations it is possible and necessary to distort the meanings but not to betray them entirely. Groups that accepted to pass through Pasteur's hands in order to solve their problems, nevertheless only go through him to their own ends. They cannot stop in his laboratory.

Pasteur, from the start of his career, was an expert at fostering interest groups and persuading their members that their interests were inseparable from his own. He usually achieved this fusion of interests (Callon, 1981) through the common use of some laboratory practices. With anthrax he does just that but on a more grandiose scale, since he is now attracting the attention of groups that are the mouthpiece of larger social movements (veterinary science, hygiene, soon medicine), and about issues that are the order of the day. As soon as he has performed vaccinations in his laboratory he organizes a field trial on a larger scale.

This field experiment was organized under the auspices of the agricultural societies. Their attention had been captured by Pasteur's former moves, but the translation ('solve your problems through Pasteur's lab') implied that *their* problems could be solved and not only Pasteur's. So the translation is also understood in part as a contract, the counterpart of which is now expected from Pasteur. 'We are ready to displace all our interests through your methods and practices so that we can use them to reach our own goals.' This new translation (or displacement) is as hard to negotiate as the first one. Pasteur has vaccine for anthrax in his laboratory at Paris. But how can laboratory practice be extended? In spite of all the niceties written by epistemologists on that point, the answer is simple: only by extending the laboratory itself. Pasteur cannot just hand out a few flasks of vaccine to farmers and say: 'OK, it works in my lab, get by with that.' If he were to do that, it would *not* work. The vaccination can work only on the condition that the farm chosen in the village of Pouilly le Fort for the field trial be in some crucial respects transformed according to the prescriptions of Pasteur's laboratory. A hard negotiation ensues between Pasteurians and agricultural interests on the conditions of the experiment. How many inoculations? Who will be the umpire? And so on. This negotiation is symmetrical to the initial one when Pasteur came to the farm site, trying to extract the few pertinent elements of the disease that he could imitate inside his laboratory. Here, the problem is to find a compromise that extends Pasteur's laboratory far enough — so that the vaccination can be repeated and work — but which is still acceptable to the farming representatives so that it is seen as an extension of lab science outside. If the extension is overreached, the vaccination will fail and Pasteur will be thrown back inside his laboratory by the disappointed farmers. If the extension is too modest, the same thing will happen: Pasteur will be considered to be a lab scientist uninteresting for others' outside use.

The Pouilly le Fort field trial is the most famous of all the dramatic proofs that Pasteur staged in his long career. The major mass media of the time were assembled on three successive occasions to watch the unfolding of what was seen as Pasteur's prediction. 'Staging' is the right word because, in practice, it is the public showing of what has been rehearsed many times before in his laboratory. It is strictly speaking a repetition, but this time in front of an assembled public which has previously invested so much interest and is now expecting its rewards. Even the best performer has stage fright, even if everything has been well rehearsed. Indeed this is what happened (Geison, 1974). But for the media it was not seen as a performance, it was seen as a prophecy. The reason behind this belief shows us exactly why the distinction between inside and outside of the laboratory is so misleading. If you isolate Pasteur's laboratory from the Pouilly le Fort farm, so that one is the inside and the other is the outside world, then of course there is a miracle for all to see. In his lab Pasteur says, 'all vaccinated animals will be alive by the end of May; all the untreated animals will have died by the end of May; and outside the lab the animals die or survive'. Miracle. Prophecy, as good as that of Apollo. But if you watch carefully the prior displacement of the laboratory to capture farmers' interest, then to learn from veterinary sciences, then to transform the farm back into the guise of a laboratory, it is still interesting, extraordinarily clever and ingenious, but it is *not* a miracle. I will show later that most of the mystified versions of scientific activity come from overlooking such displacements of laboratories.

But there is still one step to make so that we reach our point of departure: the anthrax outbreaks and their impact on French agriculture. Remember that I said it was a 'terrible' disease. While saying this I heard my ethnomethodologist friends jumping on their chairs and screaming that no analyst should say that 'a disease is terrible' or that 'French agriculture' exists, but rather that these are social constructions. Indeed they are. Watch now how the Pasteur group is going to use these constructions to their advantage and to France's. Pouilly le Fort was a staged experiment to convince the investors — in confidence and later in money — that the translation made by Pasteur was a fair contract. 'If you want to solve your anthrax problem go through my microbiology.' But after Pouilly le Fort, everyone is convinced that the translation is now: 'If you want to save your animals from anthrax, order a vaccine flask from Pasteur's laboratory, École Normale Supérieure, rue d'Ulm, Paris.' In other words, on the condition that you respect a limited set of laboratory practices — disinfection, cleanliness, conservation, inoculation gesture, timing and recording — you can extend to every French farm a laboratory product made at Pasteur's lab. What was at first a capture of interest by a lab scientist is now extending through a network much like a commercial circuit — not quite since Pasteur sends his doses free of charge — that spreads laboratory products all over France.

But is 'all over France' a social construction? Yes indeed; it is a construction made by statistics-gathering institutions. Statistics is a major science in the nineteenth century, and is what 'Pasteur', now the label for a larger crowd of Pasteurians, is going to use to watch the spread of the vaccine, and to bring to the still uncertain public a fresh and more grandiosely staged proof of the efficacy of the vaccine. Throughout France as it is geographically marked out by its centralized bureaucracy, one can register on beautifully done maps and diagrams the decrease of anthrax wherever the vaccine is distributed. Like an experiment in the Pasteur lab, statisticians inside the office of the agricultural institutions are able to read on the charts the decreasing slopes that mean, so they say, the decrease of anthrax. In a few years, the transfer of the vaccine produced in Pasteur's lab to all farms was recorded in the statistics as the cause of the decline of anthrax. Without these statistical institutions it would of course have been utterly impossible to say whether the vaccine was of any use, as it would have been utterly impossible to detect the existence of the disease to begin with.

We have now reached the point we started from. French society, in some of its important aspects, has been transformed through the displacements of a few laboratories.

II. Topology of laboratory positioning

I have chosen one example but many could be found in Pasteur's career and I am confident that every reader has many more of these in mind. The reason why we do not acknowledge these many examples is to be found in the way we treat science. We use a model of analysis that respects the very boundary between micro- and macroscale, between inside and outside, that sciences are designed to not respect. We all see laboratories but we ignore their construction, much like the Victorians who watched kids crawling all over the place, but repressed the vision of sex as the *cause* of this proliferation. We are all prudish in matters of science, social scientists included. Before drawing some general conclusions about laboratories in the third part, let me propose a few concepts that would make us become less prudish and would help to liberate all the information that we cannot help having.

1. Dissolution of the inside/outside dichotomy

Even in the brief outline given above, the example I have chosen is enough to show that, at worst, the categories of inside and outside are totally shaken up and fragmented by lab positioning. But what word can be used that could help us to describe what happened, including this reversion leading to the breaking down of inside/outside dichotomies? I have used several times the words 'translation' or 'transfer', 'displacement' or 'metaphor', words that all say the same thing in Latin, Greek or English (Serres, 1974; Callon, 1975). One thing is sure throughout the story told above: every actor you can think of has been to some extent *displaced* (Armatte, 1981). Pasteur's lab is now in the middle of agricultural interests with which it had no relation before; in the farms an element coming from Paris, vaccine flasks, has been added; veterinary doctors have modified their status by promoting 'Pasteur's' science and the vaccine flasks: they now possess one more weapon in their black bags; and sheep and cows are now freed from a terrible death: they can give more milk and more wool to the farmer and be slaughtered with greater profit. In McNeil's terms (McNeil, 1976), the displacement of microparasites allows the macroparasites – here the farmers – to grow fatter by feeding off healthier cattle. By the same token all the macroparasitic chain of tax collectors, veterinarians, administrators and landlords prosper by feeding off the richer farmers (Serres, 1980). One last element is pushed out – the anthrax bacillus. Wherever the veterinarian comes the small parasite has to go. In this succession of displacements, no one can say *where the laboratory is* and *where the society is*. Indeed the question 'where?' is an irrelevant one when you deal with *displacements* from a lab in Paris to some farms then back to Paris, drawing along with it the microbes and the farmers' interests; then to Pouilly le Fort where an extended repetition is staged, then to the whole agricultural system through statistics and bureaucracy. But it is clear that the situation of the farms after the moves is not the same as before. Through the leverage point of the lab, which is a moment in a dynamic process, the farm system has been displaced. It now includes a routine annual gesture, part of which used to be a laboratory practice and still is a lab product. Everyone has changed, including the 'whole society', to use common terms. This is why I used in the title a parody of Archimedes's famous motto: 'give me a laboratory and I'll move the earth'. This metaphor of the lever to move something else is much more in keeping with observation than any dichotomy between a science and a society. In other words, it is the same set of forces that drives people inside Pasteurian labs to strengthen microbiology and outside to stage the Pouilly le Fort experiment or to modify French agriculture. What we will have to understand later is why in this *moment* the laboratory gains strength to modify the state of affairs of all the other actors.

Another reason why the inside/outside notion is irrelevant, is that in this example the laboratory positions itself precisely so as to reproduce inside its walls an event that seems to be happening only outside – the first move – and then to extend outside to all farms what seems to be happening only inside laboratories. As in some topological theorem, the inside and the outside world can reverse into one another very easily. Naturally, the three relations outside, inside, outside again, are in no way identical. Only a few elements of the macroscopic epizootics are captured in the lab, only controlled epizootics on experimental animals are done in the lab, only specific inoculation gestures and vaccine inoculant are extracted out of the lab to be spread to farms. That this metaphorical drift, which is made of a succession of displacements and changes of scale (see below p.164), is the source of all innovations is well known (Black, 1961). For our purpose here, it is enough to say that each translation from one position to the next is seen by the captured actors to be a faithful translation and not a betrayal, a deformation or something absurd. For instance, the disease in a Petri dish, no matter how far away from the farm situation, is seen as a faithful translation, indeed *the* interpretation of anthrax disease. The same thing is true when hygienists see as equivalent the trials microbes undergo in Pasteur's lab, and the variations of epidemics that masses of people undergo in a large city like Paris. It is useless trying to decide if these two settings are really equivalent – they are not since Paris is not a Petri dish – but they are deemed equivalent by those who insist that if Pasteur solves his microscale problems the secondary macroscale problem will be solved. The negotiation on the equivalence of non-equivalent situations is always what characterizes the spread of a science, and what explains, most of the time, why there are so many laboratories involved every time a difficult negotiation has to be settled.

For the vaccine to be effective, it has to spread outside in the 'real world out there', as people say. This is what best shows the absurdity of the dichotomy between inside/outside and the usefulness of micro-studies of science in understanding macroissues. Most of the difficulties associated with science and technology come from the idea that there is a time when innovations are in laboratories, and another time when they are tried out in a new set of conditions which invalidate or verify the efficacy of these innovations. This is the 'adequatio rei et intellectus' that fascinates epistemologists so much. As this example shows, the reality of it is more mundane and less mystical.

First, the vaccine works at Pouilly le Fort and then in other places only if in all these places the same laboratory conditions are extended there beforehand. Scientific facts are like trains, they do not work off their rails. You can extend the rails and connect them but you cannot drive a locomotive through a field. The best proof of this is that every time the method of extension of the anthrax vaccine was modified, the vaccine did *not* work and Pasteur got bogged down in bitter controversy, for instance with the Italians (Geison, 1974). His answer was always to check and see if everything was done according to the prescriptions of his lab. That the same thing can be repeated does not strike me as miraculous, but it does seem to be for all the people who imagine that facts get out of laboratories without the extension of lab practices.

But there is a second reason why the laboratories have no outside. The very existence of the anthrax disease in the first place, and the very efficacy of the vaccine at the end of the story, are not 'outside' facts given for all to see. They are, in both cases, the result of the prior existence of statistical institutions having built an instrument (statistics in this case), having extended their network through the whole French administration so as to gather data, and having convinced all the officials that there was a 'disease', a 'terrible' one, and that there was a 'vaccine', an 'efficient' one. Most of the time when we talk about the outside world *we are simply taking for granted the prior extension of a former science* built on the same principle as the one we are studying. This is why lab studies in the end hold the key to the understanding of macro-problems, as I will show at the end of this chapter.

2. *Playing havoc with differences of scale*

But if the inside/outside dichotomy does not hold true, what are we going to say about differences of scale which, the reader should be reminded, are at the origin of many discussions in sociology of science, since it is because of this belief in differences of scale that microstudies are accused of missing some essential points? In the example I sketched out above, we are never confronted with a social context on one hand and a science, laboratory, or individual scientist on the other. We do *not* have a context influencing, or not influencing, a laboratory immune from social forces. This view, which is the dominant view among most sociologists, is exactly what is untenable. Of course, many good scholars like Geison could show why the fact that Pasteur is a Catholic, a conservative, a chemist, a Bonapartist, etc., do count (Farley and Geison, 1979). But this sort of analysis, no matter how careful and interesting, would entirely miss the main point: *in his very scientific work, in the depth of his laboratory, Pasteur actively modifies the society of his time and he does so directly* − not indirectly − *by displacing some of its most important actors.*

Here again Pasteur is a paradigmatic example. As a politician he failed so completely that he was unable to get more than a few votes the few times he tried to get elected senator. But he has along with Carnot, and the Republic itself, the greatest number of streets bearing his name in all French villages and towns. This is also a nice symbol of the studies about Pasteur. If you look for examples of his 'politicking' politics, you will of course find them but they are poor, disappointing, and never in keeping with the importance of his scientific work. The poverty of your findings will make readers say that 'there is something else in Pasteur, in his scientific achievements, that escapes all social or

political explanation'. People who would utter this cliché would indeed
be right. A poor critical explanation always protects science. This is
why the more radical scientists write against science, the more science
is mystified and protected.

To study Pasteur as a man acting on society, it is not necessary to
search for political drives, for some short-term monetary or symbolic
profits or for long-term chauvinistic motives. It is no use looking for
unconscious ideologies or devious drives (drives which, by some mystery, are clear only to the analyst's eyes). It is no use muckraking. You
just have to look at what he does in his laboratory as a scientist. To
summarize a long study in a nutshell (Latour, 1981a), Pasteur adds to
all the forces that composed French society at the time a new force for
which he is the only credible spokesman – the microbe. You cannot
build economic relations without this 'tertium quid' since the microbe,
if unknown, can bitter your beer, spoil your wine, make the mother of
your vinegar sterile, bring back cholera with your goods, or kill your
factotum sent to India. You cannot build a hygienist social movement
without it, since no matter what you do for the poor masses crowded in
shanty towns, they will still die if you do not control this invisible
agent. You cannot establish even innocent relations between a mother
and her son, or a lover and his mistress, and overlook the agent that
makes the baby die of diptheria and has the client sent to the mad
house because of syphilis. You do not need to muckrake or look for
distorted ideologies to realize that a group of people, equipped with a
laboratory – the only place where the invisible agent is made visible –
will easily be situated everywhere in all these relations, wherever the
microbe can be seen to intervene. If you reveal microbes as essential
actors in all social relations, then you need to make room for them,
and for the people who show them and can eliminate them. Indeed
the more you want to get rid of the microbes, the more room you
should grant Pasteurians. This is not .false consciousness, this is not
looking for biased world views, this is just what the Pasteurians *did* and
the way they were *seen* by all the other actors of the time.

*The congenital weakness of the sociology of science is its propensity
to look for obvious stated political motives and interests in one of the
only places, the laboratories, where sources of fresh politics as yet un-
recognized as such are emerging.* If by politics you mean elections and
law, then Pasteur, as I have said, was not driven by political interests,
except in a few marginal aspects of his science. Thus his science is
protected from enquiry and the myth of the autonomy of science is
saved. If by politics you mean to be the spokesman of the forces you

mould society with and of which you are the only credible and legitimate authority, then Pasteur is a fully political man. Indeed, he endows himself with one of the most striking fresh sources of power ever. Who can imagine being the representative of a crowd of invisible, dangerous forces able to strike anywhere and to make a shambles of the present state of society, forces of which he is by definition the only credible interpreter and which only he can control? Everywhere Pasteurian laboratories were established as the only agency able to kill the dangerous actors that were until then perverting efforts to make beer, vinegar, to perform surgery, to give birth, to milk a cow, to keep a regiment healthy and so on. It would be a weak conception of sociology if the reader were only to say that microbiology 'has an influence' or 'is influenced by the nineteenth-century social context'. *Microbiology laboratories are one of the few places where the very composition of the social context has been metamorphosed.* It is not a small endeavour to transform society so as to include microbes and microbe-watchers in its very fabric. If the reader is not convinced, then he can compare the sudden moves made at the same time by socialist politicians, talking on behalf of another crowd of new, dangerous, undisciplined and disturbing forces for whom room should be made in society: the labouring masses. The two powers are comparable in this essential feature: they are fresh sources of power for modifying society and cannot be explained by the state of the society at the time. Although the two powers were mixed together at the time (Rozenkranz, 1972), it is clear that in political terms the influence of Pasteurian laboratories reached further, deeper, and more irreversibly since they could intervene in the daily details of life — spitting, boiling milk, washing hands — and at the macroscale — rebuilding sewage systems, colonizing countries, rebuilding hospitals — without ever being clearly seen as a stated political power.

This transformation of what is the very composition of society can in no way be defined through distinctions of scales and of levels. Neither the historian nor the sociologist can distinguish the macrolevel of French society and the microlevel of the microbiology laboratory, since the latter is helping to redefine and displace the former. The laboratory positioning, as I insisted on earlier, was in no way inevitable. Pasteur could have failed to link his work on microbes to his many clients' interests. Had he failed, then I agree that the distinction of levels would hold true: there would indeed be French agricultural, medical, social, political interests on the one hand, and the insulated laboratory of a disinterested scientist at the École Normale Supérieure on the other. Claude Bernard had such a laboratory. But this was in no way Pasteur's strategy, and still less that of the larger Institut Pasteur, which was always situated in such a way that all the interested commercial, colonial, and medical interests had to pass through their laboratories to borrow the technics, the gestures, the products, the diagnostic kits that were necessary to further their own desires. Laboratories were set up everywhere: on the front line during the first world war in the trenches they largely made possible; before the colonists arrived in the tropics, allowing the very survival of the white colonists and their soldiers; in the surgery ward that was transformed from a teaching amphitheatre into a laboratory (Salomon-Bayet, 1982); in the plants of the food industries in many public health services; inside the small offices of general practitioners; in the midst of farms, and so on. Give us laboratories and we will make possible the Great War without infection, we will open tropical countries to colonization, we will make France's army healthy, we will increase the number and strength of her inhabitants, we will create new industries. Even blind and deaf analysts will see these claims as 'social' activity, but on condition that laboratories are considered places where society and politics are renewed and transformed.

III. How the weakest becomes the strongest

What I have said about the example treated in Part I now leads us to the more general problem of laboratory practice and of the relevance of microstudies for understanding the 'large-scale' problems raised by the field known as Science, Technology and Society (STS). If I were to summarize the argument presented in Part II I could say that a sociology of science hamstrings itself from the start: if, that is, it takes for granted the difference of levels or of scale between the 'social context' on the one hand and the laboratory or the 'scientific level' on the other; and if it fails to study *the very content* of what is being done inside the laboratories. I claim that, on the contrary, laboratories are among the few places where the differences of scale are made irrelevant and where the very content of the trials made within the walls of the laboratory can alter the composition of society. The methodological consequence of this argument is, of course, that we were right in starting with on-the-spot laboratory studies and looking for a sociology of the *contents* of science (Latour and Woolgar, 1979). It is not only the key to a sociological understanding of science that is to be found in lab studies, it is also, I believe, the key to a sociological understanding of society itself, since it is in laboratories that most new sources of power are generated. Sociology of science cannot always be borrowing from sociology or social history the categories and concepts to reconstruct the 'social context' inside which science should be understood. On the contrary, it is time for sociology of science to show sociologists and social historians how societies are displaced and reformed with and through the very contents of science. But to do so, sociologists of scientific practice should avoid being shy and sticking only to the level of the laboratory (for this level does not exist) and being proud of diving inside laboratory walls, because laboratories are the places where the inside/outside relations are reversed. In other words, since laboratory practices lead us constantly inside/outside and upside/down, we should be faithful to our field and follow our objects throughout all their transformations. This is simply good methodology. But to do so without getting dizzy, we should understand in more detail the strange topology that laboratory practices present.

The most difficult problem for understanding this positioning of laboratory practice is to define precisely why it is that in the laboratory and only there new sources of strength are generated. Using the metaphor of the lever, why is a laboratory a solid lever and not a soft straw? In asking this question we are back to the problem of understanding what has been achieved through microstudies of science. Many answers were given by epistemologists before lab studies started pouring in. It was said that scientists had special methods, special minds, or in more culturalist forms of racism, some kind of special culture. It was always in something 'special', usually of a cognitive quality, that this source of strength was explained. Of course, the moment sociologists walked into laboratories and started checking all these theories about the strength of science, they just disappeared. Nothing special, nothing extraordinary, in fact nothing of any cognitive quality was occurring there. Epistemologists had chosen the wrong objects, they looked for mental aptitudes and ignored the material local setting, that is, laboratories. The same thing happened with most of the so-called Mertonian sociology. No special sociological relations could explain anything about the strength of science. The 'norms' faded away like the 'invisible college' and the 'precapitalist recognition of debt', and went into the limbo where 'falsification', and the 'angels' sexes' are put for a well-deserved eternal rest. The first sociologists made the same mistake as the epistemologists. They looked for something special everywhere except in the most obvious and striking place: the settings. Even scientists themselves are more aware of what makes them special than many analysts. Pasteur, for instance, a better sociologist and epistemologist than most, wrote a kind of treatise on sociology of science simply pointing to the laboratory as the cause of the strength gained by scientist over society (Pasteur, 1871).

Laboratory studies have been successful, but so far only in the negative sense of dissipating previous beliefs surrounding science. Nothing special is happening in the cognitive and in the social aspect of laboratory practice. Knorr-Cetina has reviewed this (this volume, ch. 5) and there is nothing much else to add, nothing except that we now have to explain what happens in laboratories that makes them such an irreplaceable source of political strength, strength which is *not* explained by any cognitive or social peculiarities.

In earlier work (Latour and Fabbri, 1977; Latour and Woolgar, 1979), I have indicated a line of enquiry to answer this most tricky of all questions. This approach can be summed up by the sentence: *look at the inscription devices*. No matter if people talk about quasars, gross national products, statistics on anthrax epizootic microbes, DNA or subparticle physics; the only way they can talk and not be undermined by counter-arguments as plausible as their own statements is if, and only if, they can make the things they say they are talking about easily readable. No matter the size, cost, length, and width of the instruments they build, the final end product of all these inscription devices is always a written trace that makes the perceptive judgment of the others *simpler*. The race for the invention of these inscription devices and for the simplification of the inscriptions provided leads either to simple forms (dots, bands, peaks and spots) or, even better, to another written text directly readable on the surface of the inscription. The result of this exclusive interest in inscriptions is a text that limits the number of counter-arguments by displaying, for each difficult displacement, one of these simplified inscriptions (diagrams, tables, pictures). The purpose of the construction of this double text that includes arguments and inscriptions is to alter the modalities a reader could add to the statements. Moving a modality from 'it is probable that A is B', to 'X has shown that A is B', is enough to obtain a scientific 'fact' (Latour and Woolgar, 1979: ch. 2).

This kind of enquiry had the immense advantage of revealing special features of the laboratory — obsession for inscription devices and writing specific types of texts — which left the rest of the setting completely ordinary. To take up Feyerabend's saying: 'in the laboratory anything goes, except the inscription devices and the papers'.

Scientific fact is the product of average, ordinary people and settings, linked to one another by no special norms or communication forms, but who work with inscription devices. This argument which at first appeared reductionist and too simple has since received much more support and is now well established. Semiotics (Bastide, 1981) has demonstrated how far one can go in the content of science by looking at this matter of the text itself, but it is from cognitive anthropology, cognitive psychology, and history of science that stronger support is now coming. The technology of inscribing (writing, schooling, printing, recording procedures) is seen by more and more analysts as the main cause of what was attributed in earlier times to 'cognitive' or 'vague cultural' phenomena. The books of Jack Goody (1977), and above all of Elizabeth Eisenstein (1979), show well the extraordinary fecundity of looking at this material level that had escaped the attention of epistemologists, historians, sociologists and anthropologists alike because inscription technology seemed to them to be too obvious and too 'light'. This mysterious thinking process that seemed to float like an inaccessible ghost over social studies of science at last has flesh and bones and can be thoroughly examined. The mistake before was to oppose heavy matter (or 'large-scale' infrastructures like in the first 'materialist' studies of science) to spiritual, cognitive or thinking processes instead of focusing on the most ubiquitous and lightest of all materials: the written one (Havelock, 1981; Dagognet, 1973).

But if we accept this approach, are we not back again to the micro-level and far from the macroconcerns of all the other analysts in STS, preoccupied by serious things like disarmament, technology transfer, sociology of innovation or history of science? Looking at the inscriptions is interesting one could say, but it leaves us with a long way to go to explain how the strength is gained in laboratories to transform or displace societies. This is precisely why the first laboratory study I made was weak; it was weak for a simple methodological reason. I focused on one laboratory, taking for granted its existence as a unit and its relevance to the outside. So I had no occasion to watch the most puzzling procedure of all, how a set of inscription procedures are made to be relevant to issues which at first sight seem utterly foreign and much too grandiose, complicated or disorderly ever to end up on the top of a desk in a few easily read diagrams and charts discussed quietly by a few white-coated PhDs. The last point of this chapter will be to formulate, thanks to Pasteur's strategy, the simple answer to this puzzle, so simple indeed that it had escaped my attention.

The answer is visible if we bring together the three threads of my argument: the dissolution of the inside/outside boundary; the inversion of scales and levels; and finally the process of inscription. These three themes point to the same problem: how a few people gain strength and go inside some places to modify other places and the life of the multitudes. Pasteur, for instance, and his few collaborators cannot tackle the anthrax problem by moving all over France and gathering an intimate knowledge of all the farms, farmers, animals and local idiosyncrasies. The only place where they are able and good workers is in their laboratory. Outside they are worse at farming than the farmers and worse at veterinary medicine than the veterinarians. But they are expert inside their own walls at setting up trials and instruments so that the invisible actors — which they call microbes — show their moves and development in pictures so clear that even a child would see them. The invisible becomes visible and the 'thing' becomes a written trace they can read at will as if it were a text. This expertise, in their case, is already obtained by a complete modification of the scale. As has been previously explained, the microbe is invisible as long as it is not cultivated in isolation from its other competitors. As soon as it grows uninhibited on an aptly chosen medium, it grows exponentially and makes itself large enough to be counted as small dots on the Petri dish. I don't know what a microbe is, but counting dots with clear-cut edges on a white surface is simple. The problem now is to link this expertise to the health field. I showed the solution earlier by these three-pronged movements that displace the laboratory. The consequence is clear. By these moves an epizootic occurs inside the laboratory walls that is deemed relevant to the macroproblems outside. Again the scale of the problem is reversed, but this time it's the 'macro' that is made small enough to be dominated by the Pasteurians. Before this displacement and inversion that allowed Pasteurians to hook an expertise in setting up inscription devices onto the health field, no one had ever been able to master the course of an epidemic. This 'mastery' means that each event — the inoculation, the outbreak of an epidemic, the vaccination, the counting of the dead and of the living, the timing, the places — becomes entirely readable by a few men who could agree among themselves because of the simplicity of each perceptive judgment they were able to make about simple diagrams and curves.

The strength gained in the laboratory is not mysterious. A few people much weaker than epidemics can become stronger if they change the scale of the two actors — making the microbes big, and the epizootic small — and others dominate the events through the inscription devices that make each of the steps readable. The change of scale entails an acceleration in the number of inscriptions you can get. Obtaining data on anthrax epidemics on the scale of France was a slow, painstaking, and uncertain process. But in a year Pasteur could multiply anthrax outbreaks. No wonder that he became stronger than veterinarians. For every statistic they had, he could mobilize ten of them. Before Pasteur, their statements could be interrupted by any number of other statements just as plausible as theirs. But when Pasteur comes out of his lab with this many figures who is able to mount a serious attack against him? Pasteur has gained strength simply by modifying the scale. So, in discussions about anthrax, Pasteur has two sources of strength: the epizootic and the microbes. His opponents and predecessors had to work 'outside' on a 'large scale', constantly stabbed in the back haphazardly by the invisible agent that made their statistics look random. But Pasteur, by building his laboratory and inserting it in the farms as we have seen, dominates the microbe — that he made bigger — and the epizootic — that he made smaller — and multiplies the experiments at small cost *without leaving his laboratory*. This concentration of forces makes him so much stronger than his competitors that they cannot even think of a counter-argument except in the few cases where, like Koch, they are equipped as well as he is.

To understand the reason why people pay so much for laboratories which are actually ordinary places, one just has to consider these places as nice technological devices to invert the hierarchy of forces. Thanks to a chain of displacements — both of the laboratory and of the objects — the scale of what people want to talk about is modified so as to reach this best of all possible scales: the inscription on a flat surface written in simple forms and letters. Then everything they have to talk about is not only visible, but also readable, and can be easily pointed at by a few people who by doing this dominate. This is as simple and as sufficient as Archimedes's point about moving the earth and making the weakest the strongest. It is simple indeed because making simple moves is what this device is about. 'Accumulated knowledge' people say with admiration, but this acceleration is made possible by a change of scale, which in turn makes possible the multiplication of trials and errors. Certainty does not increase in a laboratory because people in it are more honest, more rigorous, or more 'falsificationist'. It is simply that they can make as many mistakes as they wish or simply more mistakes than the others 'outside' who cannot master the changes of scale. Each mistake is in turn archived, saved, recorded, and made easily readable again, whatever the specific field or topic may be. If a great many trials are recorded and it is possible to make a sum of their inscriptions, that sum will always be more certain if it decreases the possibility of a competitor raising a statement as plausible as the one you are defending. That is enough. When you sum up a series of mistakes, you are stronger than anyone who has been allowed fewer mistakes than you.

This vision of the laboratory as a technological device to gain strength by multiplying mistakes, is made obvious if one looks at the difference between a politician and a scientist. They are typically contrasted on cognitive or social grounds. The first is said to be greedy, full of self-interest, short-sighted, fuzzy, always ready to compromise, and shaky. The second is said to be disinterested, far-sighted, honest, or at least rigorous, to talk clearly and exactly and to look for certainty. These many differences are all artificial projections of one, simple, material thing. The politician has no laboratory and the scientist has one. So the politician works on a full scale, with only one shot at a time, and is constantly in the limelight. He gets by, and wins or loses 'out there'. The scientist works on scale models, multiplying the mistakes inside his laboratory, hidden from public scrutiny. He can try as many times as he wishes, and comes out only when he has made all the mistakes that have helped him gain 'certainty'. No wonder that one does not 'know' and the other 'knows'. The difference, however, is not in 'knowledge'. If you could by chance reverse the positions, the same greedy, short-sighted politician, once in a laboratory, is going to churn out exact scientific facts, and the honest, disinterested, rigorous, scientist put at the helm of a political structure that is full scale and with no mistakes allowed will become fuzzy, uncertain and weak like everyone else. The specificity of science is not to be found in cognitive, social or psychological qualities, but in the special construction of laboratories in a manner which reverses the scale of phenomena so as to make things readable, and then accelerates the frequency of trials, allowing many mistakes to be made and registered.

That the laboratory setting is the cause of the strength gained by scientists is made still clearer when people want to establish elsewhere conclusions as certain as those reached in the laboratory. As I have shown above, it can be said that there is no outside to laboratories. The best thing one can do is to extend to other places the 'hierarchy of forces' that was once favourable inside the first laboratory. I showed this for anthrax but it is a general case. The mystification of science comes most often from the idea that scientists are able to make 'predictions'. They work in their labs and, sure enough, something happens outside that verifies these predictions. The problem is that no one has ever been able to verify these predictions without extending first the conditions of verification that existed in the laboratory. The vaccine extends on the condition that farms are transformed into an annex of Pasteur's lab and that the very statistical system that made anthrax visible in the first place is used to verify if the vaccine had any effect. We can watch the extension of laboratory conditions, and the repetition of the final trial that was favourable, but we cannot watch predictions of scientists extending themselves beyond laboratory walls (Latour and Woolgar, 1979: ch. 4).

If this seems counter-intuitive to the reader, a little reasoning will convince him that every counter-example he can think of in fact conforms to the position stated here. No one has ever seen a laboratory fact move outside unless the lab is first brought to bear on an 'outside' situation and that situation is transformed so that it fits laboratory prescriptions. Every counter-example is a belief that such a thing is possible. But a belief is not a proof. If the proof is given then the two conditions I stated will always be verified. My confidence in this answer is not based on presumption but on a simple scientific belief, shared by all my fellow scientists, that magic is impossible and that action at a distance is always a misrepresentation. Scientists' predictions or previsions are always post-dictions or repetitions. The confirmation of this obvious phenomenon is shown in scientific controversies when scientists are forced to leave the solid ground of their laboratories. The moment they really get 'outside' they know nothing, they bluff, they fail, they get by, they lose all possibility to say anything that is not immediately counter-attacked by swarms of equally plausible statements.

The only way for a scientist to retain the strength gained inside his laboratory by the process I have described is not to go outside where he would lose it at once. It is again very simple. The solution is in *never going out*. Does that mean that they are stuck in the few places where they work? No. It means that they will do everything they can to extend to every setting some of the conditions that make possible the reproduction of favourable laboratory practices. Since scientific facts are made inside laboratories, in order to make them circulate you need to build costly networks inside which they can maintain their fragile efficacy. *If this means transforming society into a vast laboratory, then do it.* The spread of Pasteurian laboratories to all the places that a few decades before had nothing to do with science is good example of this network building. But a look at systems of Standard Weights and Measures, called 'métrologie' in French, is still more convincing. Most of the work done in a laboratory would stay there for ever if the principal physical constants could not be made constant everywhere else. Time, weight, length, wavelength, etc., are extended to ever more localities and in ever greater degrees of precision. Then and only then, laboratory experiments can be brought to bear on problems occurring in factories, the tool industry, economics or hospitals. But if you just try in a thought experiment to extend the simplest law of physics 'outside', without first having extended and controlled all the main constants, you just could not verify it, just as it would have been impossible to know the existence of anthrax and to see the efficacy of the vaccine without the health statistics. This transformation of the whole of society according to laboratory experiments is ignored by sociologists of science.

There is no outside of science but there are long, narrow networks that make possible the circulation of scientific facts. Naturally the reason for this ignorance is easy to understand. People think that the universality of science is a given, because they forget to take into account the size of the 'métrologie'. Ignoring this transformation that makes all displacements possible is like studying an engine without the railway or the freeway networks. The analogy is a good one since the seemingly simple work of maintaining the physical constants constant in a modern society is evaluated to be three times more than the effort of all the science and technology themselves (Hunter, 1980). The cost of making society conform to the inside of laboratories so that the latter's activity can be made relevant to the society is constantly forgotten, because people do not want to see that universality is a social construction as well (Latour, 1981b).

Once all these displacements and transformations are taken into account, the distinction between the macrosocial level and the level of laboratory science appears fuzzy or even non-existent. Indeed, laboratories are built to destroy this distinction. Once it is dissolved, a few people can inside their insulated walls work on things that can change the daily life of the multitudes. No matter if they are economists, physicists, geographers, epidemiologists, accountants, microbiologists, they make all the other objects on such a scale — maps, economic models, figures, tables, diagrams — that they can gain strength, reach incontrovertible conclusions, and then extend on a larger scale the conclusions that seem favourable to them. *It is* a political process. *It is not* a political process. It is since they gain a source of power. It is not since it is a source of fresh power that escapes the routine and easy definition of a stated political power. 'Give me a laboratory and I will move society', I said, parodying Archimedes. We now know why a laboratory is such a good lever. But if I now parody Clausewitz's motto, we will have a more complete picture: 'science is politics pursued by other means'. It is not politics since a power is always blocked by another counter-power. What counts in laboratory sciences are the other means, the fresh, unpredictable sources of displacements that are all the more powerful because they are ambiguous and unpredictable. Pasteur, representing the microbes and displacing everyone else, is making politics, but by other, unpredictable means that force everyone else out, including the traditional political forces. We can now understand why it was and is so important to stick to laboratory microstudies. In our modern societies most of the really fresh power comes from sciences – no matter which – and not from the classical political process. By staking all social explanations of science and technology on the classical view of politics and economics – profit, stated power, predictable evils or goods – analysts of science who claim to study the macrolevels fail to understand precisely what is strong in science and technology. In speaking of scientists who make politics by other means, their boring and repetitive critique is always that they 'just make politics', period. Their explanation falls short. The shortness of it is in the period – they stop where they should start. Why though are the means different? To study these other means, one must get inside the contents of the sciences, and inside the laboratories where the future reservoirs of political power are in the making. The challenge of laboratories to sociologists is the same as the challenge of laboratories to society. They can displace society and recompose it by the very content of what is done inside them, which seemed at first irrelevant or too technical. The careful scrutiny of laboratory scientists cannot be ignored and no one can jump from this 'level' to the macropolitical level since the latter gets all its really efficient sources of power from these very laboratories that have just been deemed uninteresting or too technical to be analyzed.

But we can also understand why students of laboratory practices should not be shy and accept a vision of their own method that would limit them to the laboratory, whereas the laboratory is just a moment in a series of displacements that makes a complete shambles out of the inside/outside and the macro/micro dichotomies. No matter how divided they are on sociology of science, the macroanalysts and the microanalysts share one prejudice: *that science stops or begins at the laboratory walls.* The laboratory is a much trickier object than that, it is a much more efficient transformer of forces than that. That is why by remaining faithful to his method, the microanalyst will end up tackling macroissues as well, exactly like the scientist doing lab experiments on microbes who ends up modifying many details of the whole of French society. Indeed, I think an argument could be made to show that the existence of the macrolevel itself, the famous 'social context', is a consequence of the development of many scientific disciplines (Callon and Latour, 1981). It is already clear to me that this is the only way that sociology of science can be rebuilt in keeping with the constraints now set by laboratory studies. I also think that it is one of the few ways that sociology of science can teach something to sociology instead of borrowing from it categories and social structures that the simplest laboratory is destroying and recomposing. It would be high time, since the laboratory is more innovative in politics and in sociology than most sociologists (including many sociologists of science). We are only just starting to take up the challenge that laboratory practices present for the study of society.

References

Armatte, Michel (1981) *Ca marche, les traductions de l'homme au travail, Mémoire de DEA*, Paris: CNAM-STS.

Bastide, Françoise (1981) 'Le Foie Lavé, analyse sémiotique d'un texte scientifique', *Le Bulletin*, 2: 35–82.

Black, Max (1961) *Models and Metaphors*, Ithaca, NY: Cornell University Press.

Callon, Michel (1975) 'Les Opérations de Traductions', in P. Roqueplo (ed.), *Incidence des Rapports Sociaux sur le Développement Scientifique*, Paris: CNRS.

Callon, Michel (1981) 'Struggles and Negotiations to Define What is Problematic and What is Not: The Sociologic Translation', in K. Knorr, R. Krohn and R. Whitley (eds), *The Social Process of Scientific Investigation, Sociology of the Sciences Yearbook*, vol. 4, Dordrecht: D. Reidel.

Callon, Michel (1982) 'La Mort d'un Laboratoire Saisi par l'Aventure Technologique' (in preparation).

Callon, Michel and Latour, Bruno (1981) 'Unscrewing the Big Leviathan, or How do Actors Macrostructure Reality?', in K. D. Knorr-Cetina and A. Cicourel (eds), *Advances in Social Theory and Methodology Toward an Integration of Micro- and Macro-Sociologies*, London: Routledge and Kegan Paul.

Collins, H. M. (1975) 'The Seven Sexes: A Study in the Sociology of a Phenomenon or the Replication of Experiments in Physics', *Sociology*, 9 (2): 205–24.

Collins, H. M. (1982) 'Stages in the Empirical Programme of Relativism', *Social Studies of Science*, 11 (1): 3–10.

Dagognet, François (1973) *Ecriture et Iconographie*, Paris: Vrin.

Eisenstein, Elizabeth (1979) *The Printing Press as an Agent of Change*, Cambridge: Cambridge University Press.

Farley, John and Geison, Gerald (1974) 'Science, Politics and Spontaneous Generation in 19th Century France: The Pasteur-Pouchet Debate', *Bulletin of the History of Medicine*, 48 (2): 161–98.

Geison, Gerald (1974) 'Pasteur', in G. Gillispie (ed.), *Dictionary of Scientific Biography*, New York: Scribners.

Goody, Jack (1977) *The Domestication of the Savage Mind*, Cambridge: Cambridge University Press.

Havelock, Eric A. (1981) *Aux Origines de la Civilisation Ecrite en Occident*, Paris: Maspéro.

Hunter, J. S. (1980) 'The National System of Scientific Measurement', *Science*, 210: 869–75.

Knorr-Cetina, K. D. (1981) *The Manufacture of Knowledge: An Essay on the Constructivist and Contextual Nature of Science*, Oxford: Pergamon Press.

Knorr-Cetina, K. D. and Cicourel, A. (eds) (1981) *Advances in Social Theory: Toward an Integration of Micro- and Macro-Sociologies*, London: Routledge and Kegan Paul.

Latour, Bruno (1981a) 'Qu'est-ce qu'être Pastorien?' (in preparation).

Latour, Bruno (1981b) *Irréductions: Tractatus Scientifico-Politicus*, Paris: Chezloteur.

Latour, Bruno and Fabbri, Paolo (1977) 'Pouvoir et Devoir dans un Article de Sciences Exactes', *Actes de la Recherche*, 13: 82–95.

Latour, Bruno and Woolgar, Steve (1979) *Laboratory Life: The Social Construction of Scientific Facts*, London and Beverly Hills: Sage.

Leonard, Jacques (1977) *La Vie Quotidienne des Médecins de L'Ouest au 19° Siècle*, Paris: Hachette.

Lynch, Michael (1982) *Art and Artefact in Laboratory Science: A Study of Shop Work and Shop Talk in a Research Laboratory*, London: Routledge and Kegan Paul.

McNeil, John, (1976) *Plagues and People*, New York: Doubleday.

Nelkin, Dorothy (ed.) (1979) *Controversy, Politics of Technical Decisions*, London and Beverly Hills: Sage.

Pasteur, Louis (1871) *Quelques Réflexions sur la Science en France*, Paris.

Rosenkranz, Barbara (1972) *Public Health in the State of Massachusetts 1842–1936, Changing Views*, Harvard: Harvard University Press.

Salomon-Bayet, Claire (1982) 'La Pasteurisation de la Médecine Française' (in preparation).

Serres, Michel (1974) *Hermès III, La Traduction*, Paris: Editions de Minuit.

Serres, Michel (1980) *Le Parasite*, Paris: Grasset.

Woolgar, Steve (1981) 'Interests and Explanation in the Social Study of Science', *Social Studies of Science*, 11 (3): 365–94.

7

Why an Analysis of Scientific Discourse is Needed

Michael Mulkay
Jonathan Potter
University of York, UK
Steven Yearley
St Hugh's College, Oxford

Analysis of scientists' discourse did not begin until the second half of the 1970s and only in the last year or so has this body of analysis begun to grow at all rapidly. Nevertheless, there are now several published papers in which the characteristics and possible advantages of this form of analysis are discussed in general terms (Woolgar, 1979, 1980; Mulkay, 1981; Mulkay and Gilbert, 1982b). What is absent from the literature so far is a careful examination of how previous approaches to the sociology of science have used scientists' discourse as the basis for their own conclusions and a clear demonstration of their failure to explore how scientists employ such discourse as an interpretative resource.

In this chapter we will fill this gap in the literature. We will proceed by taking two studies in which radically different methodologies and epistemological positions are adopted and by showing that neither study copes adequately with scientists' discourse. On the assumption that these studies occupy opposite ends of a methodological continuum and an epistemological continuum in the sociology of science, it is reasonable to conclude that approaches nearer the centre of these continua probably suffer from similar defects. In other words, we will use these studies to argue that virtually the whole of the sociology of science, insofar as it is empirically based, is undermined by basic methodological faults associated with its failure to consider the nature of scientific discourse. In the last section of the paper, we will outline and briefly exemplify an alternative form of analysis, that is, discourse analysis, which can be seen as responding to these methodological problems.

Quantitative analysis of scientific progress

We will begin with a paper by White, Sullivan and Barboni (henceforth WSB): 'The Interdependence of Theory and Experiment in Revolutionary Science: The Case of Parity Violation' (1979). WSB combine in their paper two influential themes in the sociological analysis of scientific knowledge: namely, a quantitative approach and the sociological investigation of philosophical schemes. We will use this study to illustrate certain general problems associated with each of these elements.

WSB use citation analysis to examine the changing relationship between theory and experiment in a specialty of particle physics called 'weak interactions'. Their analysis is 'guided' by Lakatos' philosophical schema for characterizing scientific progress and they focus on the idea that progress can be defined as the theoretical anticipation of experimental results: 'Therefore, according to Lakatos, in progressive research programmes... [t]heory will anticipate experiment, and experiment will be directed by theory' (p. 304). WSB maintain that weak interactions has undergone a scientifically progressive phase following the 'discovery' that one of its previous basic assumptions — the conservation of parity — was untenable. They suggest that the 'V-A theory', which in due course provided a general solution to the anomaly of parity nonconservation, is a remarkably successful theory. The point of their analysis is to show how the interdependence between theory and experiment changed after the 'discovery of parity nonconservation' and at the same time to compare Lakatos' speculations about progressive science with an actual instance. The assumption that weak interactions is progressive is thus essential to the logic of their paper; it is this assumption which allows them to judge the adequacy of Lakatos' analysis by examining its ability to cope with the case of weak interactions.

WSB proceed by categorizing articles and citations in the field of weak interactions between 1950 and 1972 according to whether they were experimental, theoretical or phenomenological. Their citation data are presented in the form of graphs which show the deviation of each year's citations from the frequencies which would be expected if citation were random. WSB suggest that by examining the changes in citations across categories it is possible to measure the dependence of each category upon the others, and thus, the dependence of each kind of scientific activity upon the other two kinds of activity. By plotting these citation ratios over time, WSB attempt to identify the changing patterns of interdependence between theory and experiment and thereby to furnish a dynamic measure of Lakatos' concept of scientific progress.

WSB find that it is only for one short period, immediately after the publication of the theory which led to the abandonment of parity conservation, that their data are consistent with Lakatos' scheme. During this period there was a large increase in the citation of theoretical articles by experimental articles. WSB interpret this to mean that theory was anticipating experiment; as it should in a Lakatosian progressive research programme. However, soon after this, experimentalists seem to have become less concerned with theory, or as WSB put it:

> these data suggest that the number of 'instances verifying excess [empirical] content' were decreasing in frequency. Thus, if we take a very strong position on the relevance of these data, and if we take Lakatos seriously, we must conclude that weak interactions subsequent to 1959 was experiencing a period of 'declining progress'. (p. 323)

WSB describe the specialty of weak interactions as being revolutionary and progressive. Yet according to their operational measures of Lakatos' criteria, progress declined after 1959. As a result of this apparent inconsistency between their results and Lakatos' interpretation of scientific development, WSB suggest that their findings, in conjunction with other recent work, weaken our confidence in the adequacy of the Lakatosian scheme. They point to a parallel between weak interactions and radio astronomy. For the latter discipline also experienced an undeniably progressive period of growth in which 'experiment almost always led theory' (p. 322). Thus neither of these two fields seems to conform to Lakatos' model of progressive science. One response, they accept, could be to retain Lakatos' conception of progress and to classify radio astronomy and weak interactions as non-progressive 'by definition'. But this, they suggest, 'hardly seems sensible', because it would go against participants' strong conviction that these fields are in fact progressive (p. 322). It appears to them, therefore, in view of the accumulating empirical evidence, that Lakatos' model of progressive science is in need of revision.

In their concluding remarks, WSB seem to distinguish between the correctness and the usefulness of Lakatos' speculations. Lakatos may not be right and more appropriate empirical classifications will have to be devised, but his schema did provide a helpful point of departure. WSB emphasize the contribution made by Lakatos' writings in stimulating them to create useful ways of measuring the relationship between important kinds of social action in science. They maintain that these measures have led, independently of Lakatos' philosophical speculations, to a much richer understanding of the dynamics of intellectual change in this specialty (p. 324).

Philosophical concepts, quantitative measures and participants' discourse

Let us now examine in more detail how WSB apply Lakatos' philosophical categories to their specialty. WSB treat this exercise as if it were quite straightforward; various terms in Lakatos' philosophy are taken to refer to certain observable features of weak interactions. Crucial to their argument is the claim that the conservation of parity is part of the 'hard core' − in Lakatos' sense − of weak interactions. For they claim that the overthrow of parity conservation led to the formation of the 'first truly "progressive" research programme in weak interactions' (p. 318). Yet WSB relegate the justification of this claim to a footnote, where they state that there is 'much evidence' that parity conservation was part of the hard core. As an example of such evidence, they quote three lines from a speech given at a Nobel Prize ceremony, in which a participant refers to an assumption about the symmetry of elementary particle reactions which was held 'almost tacitly'.

Lakatos himself writes only in very general terms about the hard core being made up of essential or fundamental assumptions. It is not clear, therefore, what either WSB or Lakatos mean by 'fundamental', although there is nothing to suggest that Lakatos simply means 'tacitly held'. Moreover, WSB's procedure of referring to one brief phrase in a Nobel speech in order to identify a fundamental component of the hard core seems strikingly asociological. We cannot take a Nobel presentation speech as a colourless factual record of the development of weak interactions. It is surely the case that such speeches are designed for the occasion, in such a way that the nature of the 'achievement' being celebrated is fully recognized. Thus it is equally possible to treat the passage quoted by WSB as an example of scientists reconstructing events in a way which makes their award of the prize appear to be entirely appropriate and natural (Mulkay, 1974; Halliday, 1978; Woolgar, 1980). Despite their claim to be checking Lakatos' ideas by means of rigorous quantitative methods, WSB's identification of the hard core in the text of their own paper depends on a highly selective and rather simplistic use of a participants' account of the 'central assumptions of the field'. This leads us on to a more basic question about the equivalence of participants' and analysts' categories, namely: in what sense is weak interactions a research programme or a series of research programmes? Lakatos' seemingly commonplace terminology makes it tempting to equate a research programme with the social units recognized by participants. However, the Lakatosian concept has an explicit philosophical meaning, part of which suggests, for instance, that it refers to a series of theories, each adding clauses to the last (1970: 118). WSB do not acknowledge this in their paper and they do not check whether the entity 'weak interactions', as defined by participants, corresponds systematically with the Lakatosian concept of 'research programme'.

WSB avoid facing this problem of conceptual correspondence directly by simply reinterpreting Lakatos' concepts in participants' terms. Thus, the research programme under investigation is treated as identical to the specialty of weak interactions; the hard core is treated as equivalent to the assumptions of parity conservation/nonconservation; theory and experiment are defined in terms of participants' distinctions between theorists, experimentalists and phenomenologists; and so on. Throughout their text, WSB move frequently and unreflexively between analysts' and participants' categories, usually treating the two kinds of concept as equivalent, whilst consistently adopting participant's terminology, definitions and interpretations as their own.

WSB not only give participants' categorizations precedence by allowing them to subsume Lakatos' philosophical concepts, but they also prefer what they take to be participants' interpretative claims to those of Lakatos wherever there appears to be a discrepancy. This can be seen most clearly in WSB's decision to accept the 'accumulated wisdom' (p. 323) of participants as providing the most convincing index of scientific progress. WSB appear to work on the assumption that if enough participants seem to say the same thing, then the analyst can take their statements as providing sociologically adequate descriptions. If enough scientists say that a field is progressive, then it offends common sense to maintain that it could be otherwise. The point which we want to emphasize is that central parts of WSB's analysis consist of restatements of what they take to be the general view of the field as expressed by participants.

There are several problems with this use of scientists' accounts. First of all, the analysts tend to ignore the diversity of these accounts. Did the participants all say exactly the same thing on all occasions about, for example, the progressive character of the field/programme? If not, how have the analysts obtained their simple summary of participants' views? We cannot answer these questions for weak interactions, but the variability of participants' characterizations of radio astronomy, and their lack of uniformity or of clear consistency, are well documented (Edge and Mulkay, 1976).

This leads us to a second problem, that of temporal reference. To which precise period does the 'accumulated wisdom' of participants refer? WSB find that weak interactions was strongly progressive in the Lakatosian sense only during the period 1957–9 and they conclude that in Lakatosian terms 'weak interactions subsequent to 1959 was experiencing a period of "declining progress" ' (p. 323). This, they suggest, seems inconsistent with participants' characterization of the field as 'progressive'. But WSB offer no careful examination of members' accounts in order to show that these accounts are clearly incompatible with the results of their citation analysis. It may well be that, although participants refer loosely to 'the progressiveness of weak interactions', they would be quite willing to accept that the field was more progressive in the late 1950s than at any other time.

Thirdly there is the question of what participants mean when they refer to 'progress' or when they use some equivalent term. Thus a participant might say: 'Radio astronomy was certainly progressive during its first two and a half decades in the sense that new kinds of data and new realms of study were being rapidly identified. But no major advances in scientific *understanding* occurred then. Thus *real* progress, which of course depended on these earlier observations, occurred only after the mid-1960s when the task of theoretical interpretation began in earnest.' In this hypothetical, but plausible, statement the notion of progress is used in a subtle way to encompass the whole development of the field, yet at the same time to allow for different degrees, phases and facets of progress. By varying the meaning of the term 'progress', the speaker can claim both that radio astronomy has undergone one continuous progressive sequence and that it has been progressive only since the mid-1960s.

These, and many other easily conceived and easily documented, accounts are quite possible. The same kind of possibilities presumably apply equally in the case of weak interactions. Thus participants' interpretative accounts cannot be used in the simple manner exemplified in, but by no means restricted to, WSB's study. The potential diversity of participants' accounts, their lack of temporal precision and the variable meaning of central terms make WSB's procedure, namely, that of using an undocumented summary version of participants' supposed views about progress as their main analytical reference point, fundamentally inadequate.

So far we have seen that WSB either rely on selective examples of participants' actual accounts or summary versions of participants' supposed accounts as they try to conceptualize such basic Lakatosian notions as 'hard core', 'research programme' and 'progress'. A similar failure to deal carefully enough with participants' interpretative work is evident in their quantitative methods. Once again, the way in which they deal with members' accounts undermines their analysis.

WSB do not propose that quantitative methods should replace qualitative methods, but they do see them as providing a 'check' on claims derived from qualitative evidence as well as a 'finely calibrated' assessment of research areas (p. 305). Their study, they claim, contains quantitative findings that prove to be particularly revealing (p. 306). Central to their method is a threefold classification of articles on weak interactions based upon participants' own categories. It is easy to allocate articles to these categories, they suggest, because it is 'well known' that elementary particle physics papers are 'quite easily distinguishable' (p. 306) into those which concern general theory, phenomenology and experiment. WSB appear to mean by this that there seems to be considerable agreement among participants about the usefulness of such a classification of articles. Because they are presupposed in the interpretation of citation data, it is crucial for WSB's paper that these categories are valid and reliable. More specifically, each category of papers is taken as representing a discrete class of social action and the citations between categories of papers are taken to represent interdependence between these classes of action. Thus WSB's measurements of the interdependence of 'theory' and 'experiment' ultimately depend on how they allocated papers to these three categories.

WSB place research papers in the three categories ostensibly by reading the formal text of each paper and by inferring from that text what kind of scientific action was involved in generating the text. Thus a 'basic experimental paper' is one which 'is not explicitly related by its authors to any guiding theoretical work' (p. 307). A 'theory-testing experimental paper' can be recognized when authors include a statement like the following: 'These theoretical considerations have stimulated us to undertake a search for long-lived neutral particles' (p. 307). Phenomenological papers are said to involve ideally 'an interface between theory and experiment' (p. 307). They are treated as a distinct class of theoretical papers whose authors are concerned with 'building mathematical models of fairly narrow categories of empirical data generated by experimentalists' (p. 307). The authors of 'general theoretical papers', in contrast, are dealing with 'the very nature of weak interaction, not with any particular set of particle decays' (p. 308). Finally, there is a 'third generic type of theory article' which WSB call 'applications of general theory'. This type of paper occurs when theorists 'wish to show how some general theory may be applied to particular cases' (p. 308). Such papers are likely to include a statement like: 'A study was made to determine if it is possible to verify the X theory.'

One immediate problem with this procedure is that it appears to take the formal text of the published paper as a reliable guide to the actions involved in producing it and to other actions on which it reports. Yet there is clear evidence that researchers can describe a given set of experiments in quite different terms, depending on the context. For instance, an experiment can be described in the published paper as a new method for measuring the known value of a well-established phenomenon, whilst being described in an interview as a moderately convincing test of a controversial theory (Gilbert, 1976; Gilbert and Mulkay, 1980). We suggest, therefore, that there is no way in which WSB can infer the nature of participants' actions from the formal text alone.

Secondly, the scope of WSB's categories seems extremely vague. This is hardly surprising, given that they are taken over from the everyday discourse of participants. But while such loose terminology may be perfectly adequate for the ordinary interpretative tasks facing participants, it furnishes an insecure basis for WSB's attempt at rigorous quantitative measurement of social action. For instance, it is not easy to see any clear distinction between 'theory-testing experimental' papers, 'applications of general theory' or 'phenomenology' papers dealing with the interface between theory and experiment. It is not even required that the authors of 'experimental' papers publish their own original data. For WSB count as experimental papers those where *experimental* particle physicists have obtained raw data elsewhere and have analyzed it (p. 306).

It is possible that WSB's actual procedure here was to classify articles in terms of an unacknowledged classification of their authors into experimentalists, theorists and phenomenologists. This procedure would mean that experimental papers would be papers published by experimentalists, whether or not the data are their own and whether or not they analyze the data. Theory papers would be papers 'written by theorists' (p. 308), whether or not the theory is applied to particular cases, and so on. Insofar as this description of their method is correct, WSB's identification of 'theoretical action' and 'experimental action' comes to depend on participants' unexplicated uses of the terms 'theorist' and 'experimentalist'.

If, on the other hand, this suggestion is incorrect, then WSB seem to be relying primarily on the versions of action which participants produce in highly conventionalized form for the specific context of formal publication. Either way, WSB's analysis is dependent on assumptions about participants' discourse which have not been examined by the analysts and which consequently influence their analysis and conclusions in unspecifiable ways.

Similar problems beset their citation analysis. They assume that citations can be used as an indicator of 'dependence', or as they put it 'an indicator of the degree to which general theory, phenomenology, and experiment were formally dependent on each other' (p. 306). In a footnote, WSB state that 'formally' here means 'in the published literature' (p. 325). They have, therefore, moved from the Lakatosian conception of dependence of theory on experiment to the much more restricted notion of 'dependence in the published literature'. This (unexplicated) translation allows them to maintain that they are measuring, *solely* by counts of citation, Lakatos' complex analytical terms dealing with scientists' actions and beliefs; for example, theory is treated as dependent on experiment if theoretical articles cite experimental articles. Yet they give no coherent rationale for this. The equation of 'dependence' and 'citation' is established entirely by means of analysts' fiat. That this type of move is commonly made by other citation analysts does not justify it, particularly as in other cases citation data are taken to be a direct indicator of scientists' recognition or even of the quality of cited work (Mulkay, 1981). Each of these variables is quite different and yet no argument is offered as to why citations should measure one rather than another in any given analysis. These analysts simply take over participants' conventionalized versions of cognitive interdependence, which have been produced for the specific context of the formal literature, define them arbitrarily as equivalent to a Lakatosian concept, and treat the ensuing numbers as analytically unproblematic.

Even within WSB's paper there are indications that the notion of dependence is not exhausted by citation counts alone. Referring to a period when cross-citation between 'experimental' and 'theoretical' articles was low, they say that they are:

> not suggesting that general theorists were unaware of experimental data, or that they did not try to influence the conduct of experiments during this period. We suggest only that their current research was not immediately dependent on current experimental results. (p. 322)

This passage makes it clear that WSB are quite aware that there may be connections between 'theory' and 'experiment', that is, between the actions of 'theorists' and 'experimentalists', which are not revealed in their citation counts. This does not, however, lead them to search for more adequate indicators of 'dependence'. Nor does it lead them to state their findings in more modest form. Thus the figure which summarizes their findings on weak interactions is entitled 'The Inter-relationship of General Theory, Phenomenology and Experiment etc.', rather than 'Participants' Versions of Interdependence, as expressed through their Citations to Various Categories of Published Papers' (Gilbert, 1977).

When we look at the manner in which WSB actually use their quantitative data, we find that they do not use it as a check on their qualitative material. Instead, their interpretation of quantitative data is based upon a qualitative assessment of the field; which in turn seems to derive in a largely unspecified manner from participants' accounts (Woolgar, 1976). WSB introduce their quantitative data in the context of a brief intellectual history of weak interactions. If quantitative data were being used to check qualitative material we would expect that, in the case of disagreement, the qualitative analysis would be reworked. Yet, this is not the case.

A good example occurs in the discussion of V-A theory. V-A theory is crucial to WSB's analysis, because they present it as the turning-point in the development of weak interactions. They suggest that the quantitative data support their qualitative estimate that this theory led weak interactions to be thoroughly progressive; that it was 'an intellectual tour de force which *anticipated* experimental results for several years' (p. 318). Their quantitative data consist of ratios which measure the rates of citation between the three kinds of research papers and which are taken to represent interdependence between the corresponding kinds of social action. WSB use a ratio of 1.0 to represent random citation. Less than 1.0 means that one category is citing another less often than would occur if citation were random. More than 1.0 means that a category is being cited more frequently than in a random pattern. The graphs go from 0.0 to 3.0, but the great majority of (non-self referring) data points are in the range of 0.0 to 1.0.

The V-A theory was published in 1957 and is described by WSB as 'extraordinary in the degree to which it seems to meet or exceed all criteria by which theories are generally evaluated' (p. 318). It is surprising to find, however, that WSB's quantitative data on the impact of V-A theory include only one data point above 1.0 (1958 in Fig. 8). WSB point out that 'in the years 1957–60 the ratio of actual to expected [random] references', from experimental to general theory papers 'was close to 1.0' (p. 319); and they describe this as 'a huge perturbation relative to the years 1952–56' (p. 319), when the value was close to zero. But this summary of the quantitative data omits 1951, which has a value close to 1.0 and above those for 1957 and 1960 when the V-A theory is supposed to have been making experiment extraordinarily dependent on theory.

Moreover, not only are data points below the random level taken as evidence of interdependence for the period immediately following the publication of the V-A theory (1959, 1960), but this interpretation of the quantitative data is quite inconsistent with that carried out elsewhere in the paper. Thus in Fig. 5, WSB deal with citations in the opposite direction, that is, from theory to experiment. In this case a ratio of almost 1.0 (1953) and several close to 1.0 (1962–3) are simply discounted. WSB merely assert that the relatively high level of citation by theory of experiment in 1953 does not represent dependence of theory on experiment. And despite an overall level of citation of experimental papers by theorists which is at least as high as that of theoretical papers by experimentalists, WSB choose only to recognize the dependence of experiment on theory. Thus WSB's quantitative data, rather than furnishing a 'finely calibrated assessment of the state of a research programme' (p. 305), is freely reinterpreted or ignored wherever it appears to conflict with the qualitative intellectual history that they decide to tell. It is by no means clear where this qualitative history of weak interactions comes from. Our guess is that it is the analysts' versions of that class of scientists' folk history in which crucial experiments and theoretical tours de force provide the main interpretative components (Latour and Woolgar, 1979; Fisher, 1980; Gilbert and Mulkay, 1981b).

WSB's overall account of the development of weak interactions stays close to the interpretative conventions which scientists maintain within the formal research literature. Elements of social contingency hardly enter into their version of events; presumably because such elements are almost completely excluded from scientists' discourse in the formal setting. Thus the development of the network and the relationship between its members are presented as unfolding in accordance with, and as a result of, scientists' formulation of an increasingly accurate theory. The abstract accounts of 'theoretical' and 'experimental' actions which scientists employ in their papers provide, for WSB, the appropriate categories for capturing researchers' concrete actions in the lab, the conference hall and at the coffee table. As we will see below, when sociologists focus on participants' accounts produced in contexts other than the research literature, they come to tell a significantly different kind of analysts' story.

Relativism and the social construction of the paranormal

In the preceding section, we examined a study in which an attempt was made to use quantitative techniques to describe and interpret the nature of social action and belief in science and to specify the social processes of scientific progress. In this section we turn to a study at the other end of the methodological spectrum, namely, the qualitative analysis of parapsychology carried out by Collins and Pinch: 'The Construction of the Paranormal: Nothing Unscientific Is Happening' (1979). These authors stress that their study has been undertaken from a relativist position. This relativistic approach to the sociology of scientific knowledge is based on the premise that the epistemological status or 'real existence' of the phenomena being studied by participants is of no interest to the sociologist. They claim that, as sociological analysts, they are not interested in parapsychological phenomena as such, but only in participants' understandings of these supposed phenomena and in the social effectiveness of various versions of these phenomena. Their objective in this study, therefore, is to examine how participants establish among themselves, through their own actions and culturally-based interpretations, the existence/non-existence of parapsychological phenomena.

A second assumption, which is central to their analysis, is that the 'orthodox philosophical view' of the formation of scientific knowledge is incorrect. According to Collins and Pinch (henceforth CP), this orthodox view takes for granted that scientific knowledge claims are accepted/rejected insofar as they satisfy certain socially invariant criteria; for example, definitive experimental demonstration, replicability of experimental results, and so on. From this orthodox perspective, valid scientific knowledge is that which is *constituted* through the application of such universal or *non-contingent* criteria. If the sociologist were to adopt this philosophical position, he would, at least in principle, be able to distinguish correct from incorrect belief about the natural world. Correct belief would be that which had been properly constituted in accordance with philosophically justified procedures. Incorrect belief would be that which had come to be accepted as a result of contingent considerations. Sociological analysis of correct as well as of incorrect belief would still be possible. But the two forms of belief would be treated differently. In other words, the traditional philosophical view of scientific knowledge, as envisaged by CP, implies a marked asymmetry in the sociological analysis of correct and incorrect belief. This asymmetry is clearly incompatible with CP's postulate of relativism. These authors recognize this incompatibility and they clearly reject what they call 'old-fashioned philosophic orthodoxy'. Indeed, their adoption of a relativist position is partly a response to the breakdown of such orthodox thinking about science and to the absence of any clear philosophical criteria which successfully distinguish between scientific and non-scientific beliefs. Nevertheless, despite their rejection of the orthodox philosophical view and despite their commitment to a relativist form of sociological analysis, CP employ a central conceptual distinction which grows directly out of the traditional approach to science.

CP suggest that scientists' actions take place within two main forums: the constitutive forum and the contingent forum. The constitutive forum 'comprises scientific theorising and experiment and corresponding publication and criticism in the learned journals and, perhaps, in the formal conference setting' (pp. 239–40). This forum contains those essentially cognitive elements which have traditionally been supposed to be solely responsible for the constitution of scientific knowledge. The contingent forum, in contrast, contains those social elements which are traditionally 'not supposed to affect the constitution of "objective" knowledge' (p. 240). These elements include the forming and joining of professional organizations, the recruitment of students, fund raising and publicity seeking, informal discussion, gossip, the content of popular and semi-popular journals, and indeed 'everything that scientists do in connection with their work, but which is not found in the constitutive forum' (p. 240).

The aim of CP is to use this traditional conceptual distinction to undermine further the orthodox philosophical and sociological assumptions on which it is based. They do this by trying to show that actions undertaken in the contingent forum actually have a definite impact on those scientific assessments whereby the existence/non-existence of parapsychological phenomena is constituted. Thus they make 'no epistemological distinction between the two forums. That is, for the authors, contingent actions do constitute scientific knowledge, and the constitutive actions are as much a social construct as anything else' (p. 241). The point which the authors are trying to bring home here is that no satisfactory *epistemological* distinction can be made between the two forums or the two kinds of action, because the sociological analyst can show that, in fact, *all* social actions and beliefs are contingent. Consequently, any apparent epistemological differences must be due to participants' ability to produce misleading, exclusively cognitive, accounts of actions which in reality are social and contingent in character.

CP begin their empirical analysis by distinguishing between adherents and opponents of parapsychology. They then examine the actions and beliefs of each party separately, attempting to show that both parties rely on actions in the contingent forum to establish their scientific case and that elements from the contingent forum regularly intrude into the forum of constitutive debate. Their central argument is that parapsychological knowledge claims were defined from the outset by most orthodox scientists as beyond the scope of science proper. Consequently, both contingent and constitutive resources were marshalled in a flexible and selective fashion by the orthodox to rebuff these claims. As the cognitive issues of science are never entirely resolvable by constitutive means alone, the lack of a secure social base within the legitimate research community worked to parapsychologists' disadvantage. Because they were not accepted as genuine scientists, apparent scientific successes on their part could be explained away by their critics as a product of improper scientific action. Gradually parapsychologists came to recognize that their intellectual failure was not due simply to constitutive inadequacy and they came to formulate a programme of action in the contingent forum to obtain social recognition as a legitimate area of scientific inquiry. As they have succeeded with this social strategy, so the existence of paranormal phenomena has come to be accepted as a fact or as a possibility by other scientists.

CP's claim is that, insofar as parapsychologists have come to be socially defined as 'real scientists', so the phenomena that they study have come to be seen as 'really there'.

Qualitative analysis and participants' discourse

This study concentrates on 'the tactics used by parapsychologists in their efforts to gain scientific recognition for their discipline and its findings, and the tactics used by orthodox scientists to deny them this stamp of legitimacy' (p. 237). The whole analysis depends, therefore, on the possibility of making a clear distinction between parapsychologists and orthodox scientists. However, the authors themselves note at one point that a clear distinction is impossible. 'Unfortunately... there are an embarrassing number of orthodox scientists actively experimenting with psi; an embarrassing number who, if not actually engaged in such research, are at least prepared to entertain it; and an embarrassing number of critics of psi experimentation among the ranks of the experimenters themselves' (p. 238).

In what sense is this methodological difficulty *embarrassing* for the authors, instead of being just one more practical research problem? The authors say that it is embarrassing because it prevents them from 'doing really neat quantitative fieldwork' (p. 238). But there is more to it than this. The impossibility of distinguishing clearly between orthodox scientists and parapsychologists is particularly awkward because it runs counter to the central analytical claim in the paper. CP maintain that both parapsychologists and orthodox scientists adopt complementary strategies in the constitutive and the contingent forums. They stress that both parties' constitutive judgments depend on contingent elements. Yet if there are committed parapsychologists who are critical of parapsychological work, and if there are orthodox scientists who take part in parapsychological research, then the consistency of participants' overall strategies seems doubtful. If there is this degree of intellectual, that is, constitutive, variability among those classed as orthodox and among those classed as parapsychologists, the close connection between contingent and constitutive elements, which CP present as uniform for each party, becomes highly questionable. This conclusion leads to two further questions. Where do the analysts obtain their categories of 'parapsychologist' and 'orthodox scientist'? And does their use of these categories affect their analysis?

The term 'parapsychologist' is taken directly from participants, who seem to use it frequently. It is not clear from the data presented by CP exactly *how* participants assign themselves and other actors to this category. But there is little doubt that it is employed flexibly and interpreted variously as participants engage in informal debate. The variability of meaning of the term is, of course, not an issue for participants. If they use the term on different occasions to refer to different sets of actors and to imply different attributes, this may well suit, or be irrelevant to, their practical purposes. But when CP take the term from participants' discourse and proceed to use it in a similarly unreflexive manner, then it becomes an issue of analytical significance. For example, when 'parapsychologists' are described as 'incorporating the complex techniques available to physicists, biologists etc.' (constitutive forum) and also as striving for social metamorphosis in the contingent forum, we are given the impression that the same actors are involved in both forums or, at least, that the actors in the two forums represent the same analytical category. Indeed, the overall analysis depends on this social identity of actors in the two forums. However, given that 'parapsychologist' covers various subcategories, the meaning of CP's claim becomes unclear. Is it 'orthodox-scientists-cum-parapsychologists' who adopt the orthodox constitutive strategy and 'unorthodox-scientists-cum-parapsychologists' who pursue the contingent strategy? The answers to these important questions are hidden from us, and presumably from the analysts, because their terms and their analysis stay too close to the unexplicated discourse of the actors they are investigating.

This is even more obviously true of their use of the concept 'orthodox scientist'. Unlike 'parapsychologist' the term 'orthodox scientist' does not appear in any of the data quoted by CP. This may be partly due to the fact that most of their data comes from the critics of parapsychology who, one would expect, would be unlikely to refer to themselves as 'orthodox'. The reason for this is that the term carries clear pejorative overtones in science. It is a term which is customarily used by scientists to express disapproval and condemnation. The notion of a body of orthodox scientists implies an unwillingness to respond in what might be described as a 'properly open-minded fashion to innovative, but legitimate, knowledge-claims'. It seems likely, therefore, that this concept, although not necessarily this term, is employed particularly by parapsychologists to make sense of their reception by the great mass of unconvinced or actively resistant scientists. (Ironically, CP themselves use the term pejoratively, when they refer to 'old-fashioned philosophic orthodoxy'.)

As with the term 'parapsychologist', the use of participants' notion of 'orthodox scientist' appears to have consequences for CP's analysis. For by far the greater part of their paper (10 out of 14 sections) is devoted to showing that the apparently constitutive arguments of the orthodox scientists are actually in various ways contingent. In other words, much of their analysis is a gloss upon the pejorative implications of scientific orthodoxy. In contrast, the constitutive strategy of the parapsychologists is not undermined in this way. It is treated as if it were constitutive in a more literal sense. Even though CP are committed to the view that *all* apparently constitutive actions are really contingent, they present the constitutive strategy of the parapsychologist at face value. '*It might be thought* that a number of such carefully conducted experiments, competently reported and presented in the constitutive forum, would be sufficient to establish the existence of psi phenomena' (p. 244, italics added). But who would have thought in this way? Certainly not CP, because they already *know* that constitutive formulations depend for their power on contingent actions, and certainly not the orthodox scientists because they do not accept that the experiments in question are scientifically convincing. Thus the only people who might have thought in that way are parapsychologists. It appears clearly at this point, therefore, that CP are, in a disguised fashion, constructing their analysis from the point of view of (some) parapsychologists.

We suggest that CP incorporate into their analysis some of the terminology and interpretative practices of some parapsychologists. In doing so, they depart from two of their own basic analytical commitments. In the first place, they recognize in principle that participants continually construct the meaning of their own and of other actors' actions and beliefs. But they fail to accept the full implications of this for their analysis. Participants establish meanings at least partly through the selection and application of specific terms and concepts to actions and beliefs. By adopting terms uncritically from the discourse through which participants establish such meanings, the analyst is led into treating certain of participants' characterizations of events as 'this is the way things really are' rather than as 'this is the way some actors made things appear to be'. As a result, some actors' accounts come to be treated as less sociologically problematic than others. In this study, the analysts' interpretation comes to reflect the partial perspective of some parapsychologists, rather than remaining independent of any particular 'appearance of reality' produced by specific actors. CP's recognition that *all* actors continually construct the meaning of actions requires them to adopt a form of analysis which consistently remains impartial to variations of discourse among participants.

Secondly, CP's failure to deal with this issue prevents them from maintaining their relativist approach. They define relativism as requiring the analyst to remain uncommitted epistemologically. It should not matter to the analyst which participants are scientifically correct or, in the case of parapsychology, whether the phenomena actually exist. All that matters for the sociologist is that some participants act as if the phenomena existed. However, this kind of epistemological impartiality cannot be separated from a wider *social* impartiality. CP argue that participants' definitions of social phenomena are linked to their definitions of the physical world. '[W]hen scientists "turn their attention to something, then [for participants] that really is something" ' (p. 263). In the view of CP, it is impossible to separate participants' views of the physical world from their views about who is or is not a proper scientist. If this is so, then it seems that the analyst is also required to remain socially neutral if he is to remain epistemologically neutral. As we have seen, CP do not succeed in maintaining this former kind of neutrality. By adopting the perspective and terminology of certain parapsychologists, they are led to side with the latter's knowledge claims.

We must make it clear that we are not claiming here to have identified a motive or intention lying behind these authors' analysis. We are, rather, referring to the way in which their analytical text is organized and to the marked dependence of their text on interpretative work carried out by a specific class of participants. Further support for this view of their text is provided by a note added subsequently to the paper by the authors, in which they comment on the fact that by the date of publication their paper was being (mis)-interpreted by participants on both sides of the controversy as favouring the parapsychologists' case (p. 263).

So far in this assessment, we have shown how a major part of CP's analysis derives from interpretative work carried out by participants. We now intend to show how their analysis is further weakened by a failure to take into consideration certain socially structured variations in scientists' discourse. The difficulties to which we wish to draw attention are clearly evident in the problems encountered in allocating acts to particular forums of action. Acts or judgments are said to occur in the constitutive forum if they are 'seen to be based on universalisable non-contingent premises'. Acts or judgments are said to occur in the contingent forum if 'they do not look as though they are constitutive of scientific knowledge' (p. 240). So acts or judgments are placed in one forum rather than another depending on how they appear to be linked to the assessment of knowledge claims.

CP recognize that any specific act or judgment can be portrayed in various ways. It is for this reason that they profess to be concerned with the *apparent* rather than the *literal* character of scientists' actions. They also recognize that the versions which are given of specific actions will tend to vary systematically in accordance with the social context in which the version is being produced. Thus, 'it is possible to generalise about the type of arguments and actions which may be legitimately expressed, in the normal way, within' (p. 240) the two forums. It follows from this that the versions actors give of an action will vary according to the context within which these versions are produced. In particular, the versions of their acts which scientists give in the constitutive forum, in other words in the formal literature, will always look as though they were legitimately constitutive of scientific knowledge; whilst the versions given *of the same acts* may, in other settings, look much more contingent.

It is impossible, therefore, to categorize actions or debates or controversies in themselves as constitutive or as contingent. For these allocations will simply be the direct result of the kind of participants' discourse that we take into consideration in each case. Yet CP do regularly try to allocate specific actions and even whole controversies in this kind of definitive manner. Thus the controversies involving Barkla and Bohm are said to have taken place 'within the constitutive forum'. But the reason for this allocation is simply that, because both these cases are historical controversies, the main kind of record used by the present-day analyst was the formal research literature. It is clearly misleading of CP to claim that these controversies 'occurred within' the constitutive forum or that they were carried out primarily in terms of the vocabulary of that forum, when the apparently limited scope of these controversies is due to the fact that we simply have no record of any informal discussions, personal allegations and other contingent events which may well have occurred, but which would have been largely or entirely omitted from the constitutive literature.

What is happening once again is that CP are tending to reify variations in participants' discourse. In much the same way that their adoption of parapsychologists' specific categories leads them to focus on revealing the contingent aspects of so-called orthodox scientists' actions and belief, so their access to, or use of, particular areas of participants' formal or informal discourse tends to influence their categorization of acts as constitutive or contingent. In the appendix to their paper, CP provide a list of sources showing how they distinguished between the two forums. Participants' actions appear to have been placed in the contingent forum if the analysts obtained their information either from *New Scientist* or from *Scientific American*. (In the main text, the authors also use *The Nation* in this way.) On the other hand, actions seem to have been allocated to the constitutive forum if the analysts obtained their versions of those actions from more formal research journals, like *Nature*, the *Journal of Personality* and the *International Journal of Neuropsychiatry*. It seems, then, that the analysts' distinction between the two forums simply reflects the different ways in which participants characterize their actions, judgments and beliefs in the different contexts of formal and of informal discourse.

When CP try to specify what the two forums consist of, they refer to both action and discourse. The constitutive forum is said to contain theorizing and experiment (action) and corresponding publications in the learned journals (formal discourse). Similarly the contingent forum includes informal discussion, gossip and the content of popular journals (informal discourse) and the forming of organizations, recruitment of students and everything else that scientists do in connection with their work (action). But how can the analyst characterize actions and thereby allocate them to a specific forum, without recourse to participants' *accounts* of those actions? Does a given set of actions constitute an experiment, an attempt indirectly to raise more research funds, an effort to secure professional credibility, a bid for more students; or is it any or all of these, depending on the context in which the actor is talking or writing about these acts? If the latter is the case, and we suggest that it is, then 'the meaning' of those acts is variable and context-dependent and it is impossible to allocate acts as such to one forum or another. It is only possible to allocate in this way actors' *versions* of their acts, that is, particular segments of their discourse. Unfortunately, however, CP frequently write misleadingly as if they were identifying discrete sets of actions and then showing that one type of act (contingent) directly impinges on another quite different type of act (constitutive).

Given that specific actions can be construed by participants and by analysts in a variety of ways, it is not especially difficult for the analyst to produce a plausible argument showing that contingent and constitutive actions are interrelated in some way. CP only consider actions which they take as having *some* bearing on scientists' professional work. Actions such as creating a university department, attracting students, founding a professional association and joining the American Association for the Advancement of Science (AAAS), are necessarily interpreted by participants as bound up to some extent with the process of knowledge production and with the success of participants' knowledge claims. It is to be expected, therefore, that the analyst will be able to find passages of informal or semi-formal discourse where participants themselves treat these actions as impinging on the evaluation of certain kinds of knowledge claims. On other occasions, however, and especially in formal research papers, participants will treat such 'extraneous' factors as irrelevant. In particular, they will seldom be allowed to appear relevant to the detailed technical evaluation of specific claims. Accordingly, although we find that CP can produce stretches of discourse in which participants appear to take contingent factors into account in their general appraisal of parapsychology, they do not present any instances where such factors can be seen in formal discourse to lead to the acceptance of specific knowledge claims. The reason for this is that participants systematically eliminate reference to such factors as positive grounds for the validation of a knowledge claim in the course of formal discourse (Gilbert and Mulkay, 1980).

One consequence of this is that CP are able to demonstrate only a rather weak, general connection between contingent factors and the constitution of scientific knowledge. This is apparent in the formulations they use to express this connection. Thus they summarize the findings of their previous work as follows: 'Collins has attempted to *show the social component involved in* the process of testing...'; 'Pinch has attempted to *show the social components associated with* the rejection of the work of the physicist, David Bohm...' (p. 237). The present study receives a slightly stronger formulation: '[We] are saying that the constitution of scientific knowledge *can be looked at as a product of* contingent actions...' (p. 262, italics added). The fact that social components are involved in or associated with the production of scientific knowledge is hardly an issue. But the claim that scientific knowledge is *in any strong sense*, a product of 'social' components, is not established by their study of parapsychology. As has been noted elsewhere, the most they can claim to have shown is that parapsychologists' contingent actions *may* have fostered a general climate of opinion in which specific (but undocumented) claims *may* have been judged more favourably (Mulkay, 1979).

The limitations of CP's analysis stem from certain basic analytical errors which we will now try to identify. In the first place, CP take over from participants' discourse a fundamental conceptual distinction which is actually incompatible with their more sociologically informed assumptions. This distinction is that between contingent and constitutive or between social and cognitive. They express their own uneasiness about this distinction, when they point out that, in reality, all acti᷄ ᷄s are contingent (or social), but that participants make certain actions appear non-contingent (purely cognitive). Their analytical aim then becomes that of showing that what appear to be non-contingent actions are influenced by, a product of, or dependent on, contingent actions. But in formulating the problem in this way, they have adopted an interpretative vocabulary which is very close to that of scientists themselves and which embodies the presupposition that there actually are two distinct kinds of actions involved. Accordingly, the only way in which they can identify contingent and constitutive actions is by means of participants' versions of these actions. However, those advancing knowledge claims systematically exclude reference to contingent action from the formal discourse on which the analysts have to draw in showing the intrusion of contingent elements into the constitutive forum. Because the analysts have adopted a basic conceptual distinction about separate types of action from participants, and because they have to use participants' discourse about action in order to identify instances of each type, the analysts are prevented from showing any strong connection between the supposed types of action by the systematic accounting procedures which participants use to construct crucial parts of their discourse as if the two kinds of action were separate (Gilbert and Mulkay, 1980).

The approach adopted by Collins and Pinch to the analysis of sociological data is more sensitive than that of the study discussed in the preceding section to the variability of scientists' discourse and to the ways in which actors construct and reconstruct the meanings of their actions. Their analysis and methodology are, therefore, closer to that which we will specify more clearly below. Nevertheless CP make what we regard as a crucial mistake in failing to develop a coherent form of analysis which is consistent with their own recognition that scientists can make given actions appear in various different guises. Unlike Collins and Pinch or White, Sullivan and Barboni, we contend that the analyst cannot move from the highly variable appearances constructed in the course of scientists' discourse to a specification of the connections between 'real actions', without first understanding how that discourse is flexibly organized to produce divergent versions of action. If this is so, we must turn our attention, at least initially, from the nature of scientific action (and belief) to the systematic procedures by which scientists construct the various versions of their actions (and beliefs) in the course of interaction.

The methodological priority of discourse analysis

In the previous sections, we have seen how two sets of analysts committed to very different methodological and epistemological positions are dependent for their conclusions on participants' discourse. Because this discourse varies systematically in accordance with changes in interpretative context, it is possible for analysts to produce conclusions which are plausibly based upon that discourse, yet which are radically different. However, as we have shown, these conclusions are open to a range of objections, many of which derive from analysts' failure to deal in a satisfactory way with the interpretative work embodied in scientists' discourse.

In the case of WSB, we saw that their analysis is composed of three elements which are taken over from participants' discourse: sometimes they adopt the terminology and the accounts of action and belief explicitly provided by scientists in the texts of the formal literature; at other times they adopt the notions of cognitive interdependence which are taken to be implicit in scientists' patterns of citation; and at certain important junctures they restate what they take to be the general view of the field as expressed in participants' empiricist folk history. The central defect in their analysis is that it is participants rather than analysts who carry out crucial parts of the sociological interpretation. The major contribution made by the analysts is that of selecting out and ordering a limited class of interpretative material taken from the full range of such material actually generated by participants.

Because WSB base their analysis primarily on the discourse characteristic of the formal scientific literature and because they consider only those social actions which participants subsumed under the formal concepts of 'theory' and 'experiment', their interpretation closely resembles the formal scientific literature in eliminating virtually all reference to personal or social contingency. As a result, their version of events inevitably provides a rational reconstruction of scientific development which, although it differs in detail from that of Lakatos, continues to represent science as a self-contained, progressive and internally coherent endeavour. This view of science is given its ultimate validation by reference to scientists' own accumulated wisdom. However, the apparent plausibility of WSB's analysis is achieved only by ignoring certain important aspects of scientific discourse. In particular, WSB undertake no systematic examination of scientists' informal discourse, in the course of which quite different, and often highly variable, accounts of action, belief and scientific development are likely to occur. Furthermore, WSB make no allowance for the fact that scientists' accounts of action, belief and scientific development vary from one social context to another; for instance, from the formal to the informal context. Once these features of scientific discourse are acknowledged, WSB's conclusions come to be seen as essentially a by-product of the analysts' highly selective adoption of one context-dependent form of scientific discourse.

CP's study is a significant advance on that of WSB, in that the former recognize the existence of different interpretative contexts in science as well as the fact that given actions can be variously portrayed in different social settings. In addition, CP make use of a wider range of discursive material in building up their version of events in para-psychology. Nevertheless, despite their recognition of the socially constructed character of scientists' discourse, CP succumb to the temptation of taking over certain features of participants' discourse directly into their own analysis. Although CP accept in principle that all actors continually construct and reconstruct the meaning of their social world through the formulation of divergent accounts, they do not adopt an appropriate form of analysis. Instead of distancing themselves from participants' discourse and treating that discourse as sociologically problematic, CP adopt certain of their participants' terminology and accounts, and they treat many of these accounts, not as socially generated versions of events, but as literal descriptions.

This leads to fundamental analytical inconsistencies. For instance, by adopting parapsychologists' concept of 'orthodox scientist', CP come to organize their analysis from the social and cognitive per-spective employed by some parapsychologists. As a result, they fail to maintain the epistemological neutrality required by their relativist approach and are led to side with, that is, to treat as literally con-stitutive, some of the knowledge claims of the parapsychologists. In a similar fashion, CP take over from participants the distinction between contingent and constitutive, or social and technical, actions (Latour and Woolgar, 1979); even though this distinction is basically incompatible with their sociological assumptions about the variability of scientists' accounts of actions and their central analytical objective of showing that constitutive actions are really contingent.

Consequently, in allocating particular actions and whole controversies to specific social forums, rather than particular accounts of action or particular versions of controversy, CP come to reify the structured variations in scientists' discourse. In this way, they become the prisoners of scientists' interpretative practices. By relying heavily on scientists' informal and contingent accounts, CP are able to show that contingent action occurs which is treated by participants as being bound up with the creation of scientific knowledge. However, because scientists themselves systematically eliminate references to contingent action as positive grounds for the validation of knowledge claims in the formal literature, CP are never able to complete their analysis by revealing a direct connection between contingent factors and the formal constitution of knowledge. Thus CP's analytical dependence on participants' discourse, along with participants' variable yet patterned forms of discourse, together prevent them from being consistently relativist and from providing a strong sociological explanation of scientific belief.

Although we have been highly critical of the studies by WSB and CP, our underlying concern has not been with the inadequacies of these studies as such, but with fundamental and unresolved methodological issues which pervade the sociology of science as well, perhaps, as other areas of sociological inquiry (Potter et al., forthcoming). Because these two studies are very different in terms of their epistemological as well as their methodological commitments, it seems reasonable to suggest that any inadequacies which they have in common are likely to be widespread, at least in the sociology of science. In the most general terms, we can conclude that in both these studies scientists' discourse constitutes the basic analytical resource; that much of the interpretative work carried out by participants and embodied in their discourse is carried over unexamined into the sociologists' analysis; that neither set of analysts has paid sufficient attention to the potential variability of scientists' discourse, nor to the manner in which such discourse is itself socially generated; and that the analysts' failure to investigate the social production of their data leads them into major analytical problems. We suggest, therefore, that a systematic investigation of the social production of scientific discourse is an essential preliminary step in developing a satisfactory sociological analysis of action and belief in science. Until we understand how actors socially construct their accounts of action and how actors constitute the character of their actions primarily through the use of language, we will continue to fail, as WSB and CP have failed, to furnish satisfactory answers to the long-standing questions about the nature of action and belief in science. It is this kind of analysis of scientists' language-use which discourse analysis attempts to provide.

Regularities in scientists' discourse

The central feature distinguishing discourse analysis from previous approaches to the sociology of science is that, in the now familiar phrase, it treats participants' discourse as a topic instead of as a resource. Previous approaches have been designed to use scientists' symbolic products as resources which can be assembled in various ways to tell analysts' stories about 'the way that science is'. Given the diversity of scientists' discourse it is possible, as we have seen, to produce radically different, yet quite plausible, stories by selecting from and reassembling that discourse in different ways. The discourse analyst, however, begins from the assumption that participants' discourse is too variable and too dependent on the context of its production to be amenable to this kind of treatment. In order to produce plausible, coherent stories, analysts are forced into making narrow selections from the full range of discourse available in principle and into treating some of scientists' highly variable accounts as literal descriptions of the events under study. Unless procedures like this are adopted, the analyst is unable to produce a coherent story. Yet to adopt such procedures, to treat participants' discourse in this way, is fundamentally unsociological in that the socially generated character of the discourse itself is denied. Thus the discourse analyst, at least initially, abandons the goal of using scientists' discourse to reveal what science is really like, and concerns himself instead with describing the interpretative methods which can be used, not only by participants but also by traditional analysts, to depict scientific action and belief in various different ways. Instead of taking as his initial question: how can we extract from scientists' variable discourse a definitive analysts' version of action and belief in science?, the discourse analyst concentrates on what appears to be the methodologically prior question: how are scientists' (and analysts') accounts of action and belief socially generated?

Discourse analysis, then, unlike the kind of analysis exemplified above, does not seek to go beyond scientists' accounts in order to describe and explain actions and beliefs as such. It focuses rather on describing how scientists' accounts are organized in ways which portray scientists' actions and beliefs in a variety of specifiable and contextually appropriate ways. Thus, discourse analysis does not answer traditional questions about the nature of scientific action and belief. What it may be able to do instead is to provide closely documented descriptions of the recurrent interpretative practices employed by scientists and embodied in their discourse; to show how these interpretative procedures vary in accordance with variations in social context; and to reveal with increasing clarity how the secondary, analytical literature on science is largely derived from, as well as constrained by, the discursive practices constitutive of scientific culture (Potter and Mulkay, 1982). Let us give some examples.

Several analysts have drawn attention to, and described in varying degrees of detail, the ways in which scientists portray their actions and beliefs differently in the formal literature and in informal discourse (Medawar, 1963; Gusfield, 1976; Latour and Woolgar, 1979; Collins and Pinch, 1979; Gilbert and Mulkay, 1980; Knorr-Cetina, 1981). One helpful way of describing these differences in the organization of scientists' discourse is to refer to scientists' use of two principal interpretative repertoires or, in Halliday's (1978) terms, two linguistic registers. In the formal context, participants rely almost exclusively on what has been called an empiricist repertoire. Stylistically, this means that scientists write in a conventionally impersonal manner. By reducing explicit references to human agency to a minimum, authors construct texts in which the physical world often seems literally to speak and act for itself. When the author is allowed to appear in the text, he is presented either as being forced to undertake experiments, to reach theoretical conclusions, and so on, by the unequivocal demands of the natural phenomena which he is studying or as being rigidly constrained by rules of experimental procedure (Bazerman, 1981a; Gilbert and Mulkay, 1981a).

In less formal contexts, this empiricist repertoire, although still regularly used in the course of various kinds of interpretative work, is supplemented by, and sometimes opposed to a repertoire which emphasizes the part played by social and personal contingencies in scientific action and belief. Once we begin to employ this notion of discursive repertoires and to become aware of the different contextual location of scientists' empiricist and contingent repertoires, we can begin to understand more clearly how it is that those sociological research strategies which focus on the formal literature, like that of WSB above, tend to generate analyses which are themselves empiricist and internalist in form. Similarly, we can begin to appreciate more fully why studies which rely heavily on informal discourse generate analyses in which the construction of scientific knowledge can be more easily depicted as a contingent social process. Because traditional forms of analysis tend to adopt participants' forms of discourse, the nature of their analysis will tend to reflect fairly directly the contextualized interpretative repertoires on which they focus when obtaining their data.

As well as this broad and still rather crude type of study of the contextual location of interpretative repertoires in science, there is now a rapidly growing number of detailed descriptions of particular accounting procedures which scientists regularly employ when carrying out specific kinds of interpretative work. One example is the regular pattern of accounting which occurs when scientists give explanations of theoretical error or incorrect belief. When scientists are engaged in this task, they regularly present correct belief, which is almost without exception taken to be identical with their current views, as arising unproblematically from the experimental evidence; whilst incorrect belief is explained by reference to the distorting effect of personal, social and generally non-scientific factors (Latour and Woolgar, 1979; Mulkay and Gilbert, 1982a). In other words, scientists regularly apply the empiricist and contingent repertoires asymmetrically to account for correct and incorrect belief. In addition, the significance of such criteria of theory choice as testability and simplicity is portrayed very differently when participants are accounting for the adoption of theories taken to be correct and incorrect. Criteria are presented as constituting a clear-cut, impersonal, unavoidable constraint on the choice of correct theories; whilst the same criteria are much more likely to be depicted as socially contingent and malleable when they are cited in connection with incorrect theories (Potter, 1981; Mulkay and Gilbert, 1981).

Like the analysis of scientific repertoires described above, the analysis of asymmetrical accounting not only extends our under-standing of how scientists' discourse is systematically organized, but it also throws new light on the secondary, sociological literature. For it is undoubtedly the case that virtually all of the studies in which relatively strong claims have been advanced about the social contingency of scientific belief have dealt with areas of scientific controversy (Collins, 1981). In such areas we will, of course, find the greatest incidence of scientists' accounting for error and, consequently, the most frequent appearance of contingent elements in scientists' discourse. Thus, even this preliminary analysis of scientists' accounting

procedures enables us to see why controversies have proved so generative an arena of sociological inquiry and why the discourse forthcoming
from less lively fields has proved to be comparatively intractable to
sociological investigation. This means that, contrary to many analysts'
inclinations, it is very doubtful whether one can generalize easily
from studies of controversies to make claims about the nature of
social action in more settled areas. For scientists' discourse, and thus
sociologists' data, is likely to be patterned quite differently in what
sociologists recognize as controversial scientific fields.

These brief examples of discourse analysis must suffice. Many more
can be found in the references given, on topics such as theory choice,
discovery, the structure of formal texts, scientific humour, evaluation
and justification of action and belief, pictorial representation, theory
and practical application, the construction of folk histories, and so on
(Anderson, 1978; Bazerman, 1981a, 1981b; Brannigan, 1981; Callon
et al., 1981; Gilbert and Mulkay, 1981a, 1982b; Latour and Fabbri,
1977; Lynch, 1982; Morrison, 1981; Mulkay and Gilbert, 1982a;
Mullins, 1981; O'Neill, forthcoming; Potter, 1982; Potter and Mulkay,
1981; Roe, 1977; Woolgar, 1976, 1981; Yearley, 1981a, 1981b). The
goal of this form of analysis is more modest than that of previous
approaches to the sociology of science. It does not claim or promise to
provide definitive explanations of how science really operates. It
offers instead the possibility of carefully documented descriptions of
scientists' interpretative practices and repertoires, accompanied by an
attempt to show how these practices and repertoires are linked to
variations in social context. In short, the first step in discourse analysis
is rather like a natural history of social accounting. If it is successful,
it will provide us with a wide-ranging description of the contextually
variable methods which scientists use to construct versions of their
action and belief as well as with a clearer understanding of how the
basic data on which sociologists necessarily rely is socially generated.
It therefore constitutes the only approach which holds out a promise,
by its very nature, of rebuilding the sociological analysis of action and
belief on a firmer methodological basis.

We have emphasized that discourse analysis is, in part, an attempt
to move away from the traditional sociological objective of using
participants' accounts as the basis for definitive analytical versions of
action and belief. It is perhaps necessary to make it clear that discourse
analysis does not replace definitive accounts of action with definitive
readings of participants' texts and utterances. Any form of analysis
which required us to assume that a particular collection of words could

be read in only one way would clearly be misconceived. For example, it is quite possible for someone unfamiliar with scientific culture to 'miss the point of' a scientific joke. In other words, a given utterance can be heard or read either as a joke or as a serious statement, depending on the recipients' interpretative competence. We are all familiar with the experience of making a 'funny remark' which is taken seriously. However, the fact that a 'joke' can be read (heard) in different ways, does not mean that what are widely treated as humorous utterances are not regularly structured in a specific fashion. For instance, it has been shown that texts which scientists themselves characterize as funny or ironic are often designed in ways which display the existence and incompatibility of scientists' empiricist and contingent repertoires and which use the latter repertoire to undermine the primary empiricist repertoire (Mulkay and Gilbert, 1982c). Thus scientists' humour has structural features which are linked to other regular aspects of scientific discourse. But this form of textual organization, although frequently evident in discourse which scientists define as humorous, in no way forces any particular recipient to read any specific text as funny. Accordingly the task of discourse analysis is not to furnish definitive readings of texts, but to identify the recurrent structural features of participants' discourse and to describe how scientists accomplish their own readings.

Although we have maintained that discourse analysis is methodologically prior to those forms of analysis which seek to describe and explain scientific action and belief, we do not urge all sociologists of science immediately to adopt our analytical perspective. In the long run, we hope that advances in the analysis of discourse will provide a more reliable interpretative basis than is at present available for the investigation of action and belief. But until discourse analysis has borne undeniable fruit, it seems more sensible that the sociology of science as a research area should continue to operate on the kind of broad and eclectic front exemplified in this volume. However, even the limited discussion presented in this chapter should make analysts and readers more sensitive to the ways in which sociological conclusions typically grow out of the interpretative work undertaken by participants and, perhaps, more appreciative of the efforts of those, like ourselves, who believe that the best chance of analytical advance lies in the elucidation of the ways in which scientists' procedures of language-use generate the multifaceted social world of science.

References

Anderson, D. C. (1978) 'Some Organizational Features in the Local Production of a Plausible Text', *Philosophy of the Social Sciences*, 8 (1): 113–35.

Bazerman, Charles (1981a) 'What Written Knowledge Does: Three Examples of Academic Discourse', *Philosophy of the Social Sciences*, 11 (3): 361–87.

Bazerman, Charles (1981b) 'Forces and Choices Shaping a Scientific Paper: Arthur H. Compton, Physicist as Writer of Non-Fiction', paper presented at the Sixth Annual Meeting of the Society For Social Studies of Science, Atlanta, November.

Brannigan, Augustine (1981) *The Social Basis of Scientific Discoveries*, Cambridge: Cambridge University Press.

Callon, Michel, Courtial, J. P. and Turner, W. (1981) 'Co-Word Analysis: A New Method For Mapping Science and Technology', mimeo, Université Louis Pasteur, GERSULP, Strasbourg.

Collins, H. M. (1981) 'Stages in the Empirical Programme of Relativism', *Social Studies of Science*, 11 (1): 3–10. Special issue 'Knowledge and Controversy', H. M. Collins (ed.).

Collins, H. M. and Pinch, T. J. (1979) 'The Construction of the Paranormal: Nothing Unscientific Is Happening', pp. 237–70 in R. Wallis (ed.), *On the Margins of Science: The Social Construction of Rejected Knowledge*, Sociological Review Monograph, No. 27, University of Keele.

Edge, David O. and Mulkay, Michael (1976) *Astronomy Transformed*, New York: Wiley.

Fisher, N. (1980) 'Heroes and Hero-Worship: History of Chemistry in the Nineteenth Century', mimeo, University of Aberdeen.

Gilbert, G. Nigel (1976) 'The Transformation of Research Findings into Scientific Knowledge', *Social Studies of Science*, 6: 281–306.

Gilbert, G. Nigel (1977) 'Referencing As Persuasion', *Social Studies of Science* 7: 113–22.

Gilbert, G. Nigel and Mulkay, Michael (1980) 'Contexts of Scientific Discourse: Social Accounting in Experimental Papers', pp. 269–94 in K. D. Knorr et al. (eds), *The Social Process of Scientific Investigation, Sociology of the Sciences Yearbook*, vol. 4, Dordrecht/Boston: Reidel.

Gilbert, G. Nigel and Mulkay, Michael (1981a) 'Warranting Scientific Belief', *Social Studies of Science*, 12 (3): 383–408.

Gilbert, G. Nigel and Mulkay, Michael (1981b) 'Experiments Are the Key: Scientists' and Historians' History-Making', mimeo, Universities of Surrey and York.

Gusfield, Joseph (1976) 'The Literary Rhetoric of Science: Comedy and Pathos in Drinking Driver Research', *American Sociological Review*, 41: 16–34.

Halliday, M. A. K. (1978) *Language As Social Semiotic*, London: Arnold.

Knorr-Cetina, Karin D. (1981) *The Manufacture of Knowledge*, Oxford: Pergamon Press.

Lakatos, I. (1970) 'Falsification and the Methodology of Scientific Research Programmes', in I. Lakatos and A. Musgrave (eds), *Criticism and the Growth of Knowledge*, Cambridge: Cambridge University Press.

Latour, Bruno and Fabbri, P. (1977) 'La Rhetorique du Discours Scientifique', *Actes de la Recherche en Sciences Sociales*, 13: 81–95.

Latour, Bruno and Woolgar, Steve (1979) *Laboratory Life: The Social Construction of Scientific Facts*, London and Beverly Hills: Sage.

Lynch, Michael (1982) *Art and Artifact in Laboratory Science: A Study of Shop Work and Shop Talk in a Research Laboratory*, London: Routledge and Kegan Paul.

Medawar, P. B. (1963) 'Is the Scientific Paper A Fraud?', *The Listener*, 12 September: 377–8.

Morrison, K. L. (1981) 'Some Properties of "Telling-Order Designs" in Didactic Inquiry', *Philosophy of the Social Sciences*, 11 (2): 245–62.

Mulkay, Michael (1974) 'Methodology in the Sociology of Science: Some Reflections on the Study of Radio Astronomy', *Social Science Information*, 13 (2): 107–19.

Mulkay, Michael (1979) *Science and the Sociology of Knowledge*, London: Allen and Unwin.

Mulkay, Michael (1981) 'Action and Belief or Scientific Discourse? A Possible Way of Ending Intellectual Vassalage in Social Studies of Science', *Philosophy of the Social Sciences*, 11 (2): 163–72.

Mulkay, Michael and Gilbert, G. Nigel (1981) 'Putting Philosophy to Work: Karl Popper's Influence on Scientific Practice', *Philosophy of the Social Sciences*, 11 (3): 389–407.

Mulkay, Michael and Gilbert, G. Nigel (1982a) 'Accounting For Error: How Scientists Construct Their Social World When They Account For Correct and Incorrect Belief', *Sociology*, 16: 165–83.

Mulkay, Michael and Gilbert, G. Nigel (1982b) 'What Is the Ultimate Question? Some Remarks in Defence of the Analysis of Scientific Discourse', *Social Studies of Science*, 12 (2): 309–19.

Mulkay, Michael and Gilbert, G. Nigel (1982c) 'Joking Apart: Some Recommendations Concerning the Analysis of Scientific Culture', *Social Studies of Science*, 12 (4): 585–613.

Mullins, Nicholas C. (1981) 'Paper Forms and Groups', paper presented at the Sixth Annual Meeting of the Society For Social Studies of Science, Atlanta, November.

O'Neill, John (forthcoming) *Science Texts: Studies in the Organization of Scientific Discourse*.

Potter, Jonathan (1981) 'Testability in Scientific Discourse', paper presented at the British Sociological Association Annual Conference, Aberystwyth, 6–9 April. 'Testability, Flexibility: Kuhnian Values in Scientists' Discourse Concerning Theory Choice', mimeo, University of York.

Potter, Jonathan (1982) 'Nothing so Practical as a Good Theory: The Problematic Application of Social Psychology', in P. Stringer (ed.), *Confronting Social Issues: Applications of Social Psychology*, vol. 1, London: Academic Press.

Potter, Jonathan and Mulkay, Michael (1981) 'Making Theory Useful: Application Accounts in Social Psychologists' Discourse', mimeo, University of York.

Potter, Jonathan and Mulkay, Michael (1982) 'Scientists' Interview Talk: Interviews as a Technique for Revealing Participants' Interpretative Practices', in M. Brenner, J. Brown and D. Canter (eds), *The Research Interview: Uses and Approaches*, London: Academic Press.

Potter, J., Stringer, P. and Wetherell, M. (forthcoming), *Literature, Social Psychology*, London: Routledge and Kegan Paul.

Roe, Peter (1977) *Scientific Text: Selections From the Linguistic Evidence Presented in a Study of Difficulty in Science Text-books*, Discourse Analysis Monographs No. 4, English Language Research, Birmingham University.

White, Hywel D., Sullivan, Daniel and Barboni, Edward J. (1979) 'The Interdependence of Theory and Experiment in Revolutionary Science: The Case of Parity Violation', *Social Studies of Science*, 9 (3): 303–27.

Woolgar, Steve (1976) 'Writing an Intellectual History of Scientific Development: The Use of Discovery Accounts', *Social Studies of Science*, 6: 395–422.

Woolgar, Steve (1979) 'Changing Perspectives: A Chronicle of Research Development in the Sociology of Science', in J. Farkas (ed.), *Sociology of Science and Research: Papers of the International Sociology of Science Conference Budapest 1977*, Budapest: Akademiai kiado.

Woolgar, Steve (1980) 'Discovery: Logic and Sequence in a Scientific Text', pp. 239–68 in K. D. Knorr et al. (eds), *The Social Process of Scientific Investigation, The Sociology of the Sciences Yearbook*, vol. 4, Dordrecht/Boston: Reidel.

Woolgar, Steve (1981) 'Interests and Explanation in the Social Study of Science', *Social Studies of Science*, 11: 365–94.

Yearley, Steven (1981a) 'Textual Persuasion: The Role of Social Accounting in the Construction of Scientific Arguments', *Philosophy of the Social Sciences*, 11 (3): 409–35.

Yearley, Steven (1981b) 'Contexts of Evaluation: A Sociological Analysis of Scientific Argumentation with Reference to the History of Earth Science', D.Phil. thesis, University of York, England.

8

Temporal Order in Laboratory Work

Michael Lynch
Eric Livingston
Harold Garfinkel
University of California, Los Angeles

Introduction

At the present time a number of ethnomethodological studies of scientific work are underway.[1] Some of these have already resulted in published works, and other publications will be forthcoming. Our purpose in this chapter is to introduce these studies to readers of science studies literatures, and to briefly discuss some themes the studies can be used to illuminate. For the purposes of coherent exposition, our discussion will be organized around a complex of themes which concern temporal order in laboratory work. This treatment does not define a programmatic basis for ethnomethodological studies of work in the sciences. Instead, these studies of scientists' work are motivated by the attempt to rediscover the problem of social order in and as the real-world detail of scientific praxis. Each author of the studies in this collection has worked out distinctive sets of issues for treating this domain of inquiry. Each study, rather than seeking closure on some set of 'issues relevant to the current literature of science studies' has attempted, through the use of empirical materials, to open for investigation scientists' work as a naturally organized ordinary activity. The reader is reminded that this chapter serves as an introduction to those studies, and the reader is urged to consult the individual studies in order to find the ways in which the production of social order in scientific activity is given unique and detailed treatment.

Ethnomethodological studies of work

The studies discussed in this chapter are part of a larger collection of ethnomethodological studies of work.[2] A number of programmatic initiatives set these studies apart from other treatments of the problem of social order, while at the same time they preserve the topic of social order for a radically different mode of investigation. These initiatives are discussed elsewhere and will only be given cursory treatment here. In brief, the overriding preoccupation in ethnomethodological studies is with the detailed and observable practices which make up the incarnate production of ordinary social facts, for example, order of service in a queue,[3] sequential order in conversation,[4] and the order of skilfully embodied improvised conduct.[5] The specific studies discussed here address natural science work as incarnate practices of doing laboratory experiments in introductory chemistry (cf. Schrecker, 1980), achieving the 'followability' of a mathematical proof (Livingston, 1978, 1982), reading 'state of the art' research materials (Morrison, 1980, 1981), producing an orderly series of observatory runs which compose the interior course of a discovery (Garfinkel et al., 1981), and assembling displays of electron-microscopic photographs (Lynch, 1979, 1982a).

In each of the studies there is a unique preoccupation with local production and with the worldly observability of reasoning. This means that reasoning is displayed in the midst of orders of intersubjectively accountable details: the order of spoken utterances by different parties in conversation, the compositional order of manipulated materials at the laboratory bench, or the transitive order of written materials on a page of text. Ethnomethodological studies attempt to elucidate these structures in reference to their use as worldly domains of 'consciousness'; as mnemonics, temporal 'states' of reasoned projects, and as observable courses of directed bodily movement. One is confronted with streams of embodied action simultaneously identified with 'material' arrangements and rearrangements accomplished by one or more parties to the respective discipline. This provides an entirely different basis for analytically elucidating reasoning practices than would be the case when reasoning is conceived as a stream of consciousness in exclusively 'private experience'.[6]

Ethnomethodological studies commonly employ audiotaped and videotaped records of activities as their data, though there is no insistence in principle that such data are prerequisite for adequate analysis. On a more fundamental level, ethnomethodological studies are directed to the empirical analysis of competence systems which are autocthonous[7] to such distinctive material surfaces as written texts (Morrison, 1980, 1981), montages of microscopic photographs (Lynch, 1979, 1982a), written mathematical proofs (Livingston, 1978, 1982), and the arrangement of chemistry apparatus on the surface of a lab table (Schrecker, 1980). It is these produced-and-analyzed displays which make up the 'data' for ethnomethodological studies, though in some instances audio- and videotaping assists in making such displays investigatable for the purpose of recovering the locally productive origins of such displays.

A key aim of such analyses is to describe these competencies as demonstrable courses of inquiry with distinctive materials at hand, whether those materials are conversational utterances, embodied places in a queue, or flasks and beakers being handled by an experimenter. Painstaking attention to the detailed production of such exhibits then enables the analysis to specify their constitutional properties as orderly structures.

It may seem puzzling that investigators would see fit to approach scientific activities in such a fashion. Why investigate disciplines which already account extensively for their own methodic and replicable character? Science is replete with detailed instructions on how to use its various methods: students are instructed not only on the 'things' of biology and physics, etc., but also on the rigorous monitoring of their work of experimentally and observationally disclosing those 'things'. However, as has been shown in ethnomethodological studies, something more is involved in actually engaging in a practice than can be formulated in even the most detailed of instructions. However carefully one attempts to follow, say, a manual of lab procedures, much more will need to be taken account of than is anticipated in the instructions. It is this ubiquitous 'something more' that delimits a field of investigatable phenomena which is not thematized in formal accounts of scientific methods. Scientists have to come to terms with the singularity of their situations of inquiry, and in doing so they are thrown again and again into circumstances which require practices that are vaguely, if at all, specified in methodological guidelines and other formulations about how science is done *in general*. To mention this is not to make an issue about idiosyncratic origins in science, but to note instead that despite the absence of specific accounts of scientific methods, when scientists are at work they evidently *are not* at a loss over what to do. They find their ways through singular troubles, vernacularly organized discussions, and embodied routines of inquiry, and they do so as an unremarkable competency with 'the facts of daily life'. In other words, much of what evidently makes up the orderliness, and ordinariness, of scientific activities *is not worth talking about* in the idiom of 'scientific method'. Paradoxically, that is what supplies the motive for ethnomethodological studies; that there is no motive for generic methods accounts to make an issue of the ordinary practices through which scientists produce the evidently scientific character of their day's work.

Ethnomethodology is, therefore, a *foundational* discipline. Unlike other attempts to recover the foundations of science in cognitive beliefs, tacit assumptions, communally held thematic prejudices, or unstated agreements, ethnomethodological studies attempt to discover and to demonstrate the ways in which various scientific practices compose themselves through vernacular conversations and the ordinariness of embodied disciplinary activities.[8] It is still an open question for ethnomethodology as to how the genetic origins of science are demonstrable. The problem implicates an historical development although not one specified through chronologically linked 'events'. Instead the historicized[9] domain that is consulted in ethnomethodological studies consists of the origins of scientific activity in embodied work and vernacular 'shop talk'. Unlike the phenomenologists' conception of genetic origins, where origins are traced through the activities of a transcendental consciousness,[10] ethnomethodological studies consult locally observable sequences of conduct that make up the details of a discipline's daily work.

Ethnomethodological studies are foundational inquiries and thereby are inexorably addressed to temporal phenomena. Foundations of scientific objects, events, or demonstrations are exhibited in the temporal 'building', and 'building-up' of those phenomena in actual courses of activity. The remainder of this chapter will concern the issue of genetic origins discussed as the temporal accountability of laboratory practices.

The temporal accountability of
laboratory practices

Some of the ways in which scientific activities can be analytically collected around the theme of temporality are suggested in the following topics:

(1) canonical descriptions of lab methods and actual courses of action;

(2) the retrospective-prospective assembly of scientific methods on the basis of results in hand;

(3) the 'scientific object' as an icon of laboratory temporality;

(4) transitivity.

Each of these topics is given brief treatment in the discussion below. Considerations of length preclude our use of the kinds of empirical demonstration which identify ethnomethodological studies. Studies which do provide demonstrations of these and many other matters will be mentioned in the discussion, though they should be read in their original form in order for readers to appreciate what this chapter is talking about.

Canonical descriptions of lab work
and actual courses of action

It has frequently been noted by practising scientists as well as by sociologists of science that doing technical work in science entails a kind of craft, or embodied expertise, which is not incorporated into the mode of methods reporting that is characteristic of scientific literatures.[11] There may be many reasons for this. One, perhaps, has to do with the essential impossibility of encapsulating the innumerable and singular situations of day-to-day inquiry within a generic account of methods instruction and methods reporting.[12] This fundamental difference between the sensibility of reportage and the sensibilities of actual inquiry is encountered in the day's work. This difference has long been interesting to professional sociologists. It is of course a standing issue for laboratory practitioners in their attempts to follow methods instructions and to construe their activities for the purposes of written report. In addition, and aside from any discrepancy between 'actual' scientific practice and the description of practice in written reports, 'written inquiry'[13] in science can be approached as a distinctive practical terrain with autocthonous analytical features, that is, as the organizational grounds of apparent scientific structures.

The problem of applying or modifying the formal resources of a discipline (and these resources include such matters as laboratory equipment, in addition to the many forms of written instruction and indexing used in laboratory research) requires an unremitting course of 'ordinary discoveries' which work out efficacious ways to proceed in day-to-day lab activities. When monitored in continuous temporal succession, scientific projects show innumerable false-starts, improvised repairs, and situated inquiries on 'what's going on here?' Practitioners of histology, for example, employ idiosyncratic methods which are sometimes said, in the laboratory vernacular, to contain 'superstitious' features of sequential or instrumental design.[14] According to some practicing scientists, these features exist inevitably because of practitioners' use of an empirical mode of reasoning which assigns functional necessity to details of a course of practical action on the basis of results of the action on prior occasions. Sometimes modifications in procedure turn up features, previously thought to be functionally necessary, that were irrelevant to the achievement of 'good results'. In addition, some formalized lab techniques are said to be 'capricious' due to unaccountable departures from 'good' results on different occasions when the 'same' technique is used. On the other hand, when scientists write up methods reports they use established formats of written procedure which render methods into a generic, subject-free syntax. The economy of such a format precludes mention of the innumerable singular crises and ordinary discoveries in the day-to-day work, as well as the unformulated work of producing and deciding the equivalency between successive runs of a technical operation.[15]

The difference between formalized instructions and reports about methods and the observable events in any situated production of a methodic routine is not raised in ethnomethodological studies in order to provoke ironic interest. Instead, it is used in those studies as initial grounds for directing attention to the features of scientific shop work which are achieved in situ, and which resist generic accountability in methods reports. By the same token, it allows for the study of scientific writing as a distinctive phase of the work rather than as descriptive data about actual lab activities. Three analytic relevancies of scientific writing which are given original treatment in ethnomethodological studies are discussed below.

(i)   Written instructions and situated procedures
In a study of the embodied work of doing didactic experiments in chemistry, Schrecker (1980: 2–3) states:

To do the experiment accurately, the students were given a laboratory manual with an assignment sheet for each experiment. This informed the students about the basic chemical reasoning of the respective experiment and about its experimental performance. These written instructions were of utmost importance for the students since they served as guidelines on how to do the work at the bench. This instructional material served as a pedagogical device for the students to actually perform the experiment and to produce the desired results. But these written instructions were simply not adequately descriptive of the work of doing an experiment since they omitted the embodied engagement of the students with the lab-table equipment. And since the students did not yet know these embodied practices, it was up to their discovering work to find them. Their discovering work had to turn the written instructions into a course of practices at the bench, and to turn these instructions into an adequate description of their work by circumstantially inspecting them and by practically achieving what they were talking about.

Friedrich Schrecker, a graduate student from the University of Frankfurt, spent the academic year 1979–80 visiting UCLA for the purpose of attending seminars and work tutorials in ethnomethodology and conversational analysis. His study of laboratory work in an undergraduate chemistry lab was done as an assigned problem in Harold Garfinkel's seminar in Methods of Ethnomethodological Research. The seminar explicated such issues as the 'Heideggerian relevance' of blindness, paraplegia, stroke and other handicaps as research strategy with which to disclose as technical work the locally achieved ordinariness of common tasks; the production properties of local phenomena; together with a radical reformulation for the natural sciences of themes from gestalt theories of perception so that instead of a theme – figure-ground relations, for example – being treated as a perceptual function it was treated as a developingly available practical achievement, construed as technical details of the work of local order production in developing and embodied situations of inquiries. Arrangements were made for Schrecker to assist a partially paralyzed student with his lab exercises for an undergraduate chemistry course in 'quantitative analysis'. (See below pp. 225–9.) Videotapes of two complete lab assignments were made with the assistance of Richard Fauman, an advanced graduate student in ethnomethodology, and these were analyzed by Schrecker with directions from, and in collaboration with, Harold Garfinkel and Michael Lynch. The initiatives and themes of Schrecker's study were obtained from Garfinkel's seminar, but because of the brilliance and assiduousness with which the work was carried out, the analysis was gratifyingly collaborative. References in this chapter, therefore, to Schrecker's study should be understood as references to Schrecker's involvement in a collaboration with Garfinkel and Lynch.

Schrecker (1980: 3–4) uses four thematic headings, adapted from Garfinkel's lectures on the properties of locally produced laboratory events, to address the work of turning lab instructions into an actual chemical experiment. These are outlined under the following headings: (1) that the practices were *embodied*, (2) that they were *circumstantially contingent* and 'found only in and as a course of locally situated work', (3) that they produced the experiment 'in the spatiality of the arrangement of the lab-table's display', and (4) that they were done *unwittingly*. Through the use of videotaped analysis in conjunction with an unusual circumstance for elucidating the embodied features of lab work (this will be elaborated later in this chapter under the heading of 'The Cartesian setting', see p. 225), Schrecker's study addressed the above list of features with an unprecedented orientation to the observable events of bench-work.

Schrecker mentions numerous problems which were encountered in attempts to translate the step-by-step instructions in the lab manual to a course of embodied procedures. Many of these concerned sequential issues. Where the manual specified a linear sequence of discrete steps, the embodied enactment of those steps enabled, indeed necessitated, that several steps be done simultaneously. 'Doing more than one thing at a time' entailed students' working-out of arrangements where they could interrupt a coherent sequence of steps while moving to actions in another sequence. Students had to find out for themselves where in the course of any sequence such interruptions were practicable, and where latency periods provided 'time' for alternative activities. While the formal instructions were indispensable for the students, their adequacy was not accomplished by reading a page of writing, and idly wondering about its meaning. Instead, the sense of what the instructions *instructed* was found by turning to the lab bench and bodily engaging a complex of equipment to *perform* chemistry's events.

(ii) Constituting inquiries in anticipation of formal presentation
It is not only the case that scientific activities are 'written up' into research reports at the end of projects. The eventuality of the published report pervades the detailed organization of inquiries all along their course. The congruence between the anticipatory 'design' of research and its eventuation in a written report circulated to colleagues and rivals in the discipline is not a matter of observing a priori plans of

action or rules of experimental design (cf. Garfinkel et al., 1981: 135). One way in which the constraints of formal demonstration pervade the situated production of research is treated in Wieder's (1980) study of chimpanzee researchers and their animals.

Wieder conducted an observational study of experimental research on the 'intelligence' of 'higher' animals. In a preliminary analysis, based on themes on the achievement of intersubjectivity found in the writings of the constitutive phenomenologists, Wieder describes a pervasive chasm between, on the one hand, the way in which 'chimpers' (persons who work intimately with chimpanzees in research settings) assume access to and make use of chimp 'consciousness' and 'intelligence' in their everyday interactions with their animal colleagues, and, on the other hand, the highly constrained ways in which those researchers construe 'intelligent behavior' for the purposes of experimental demonstration. Wieder characterizes the reportable programme of chimp research as being constrained by a programme of 'behavioristic operationalism' (p. 85), a pervasive format of experimental design and report which limits what can be shown and said about the phenomenon of animal intelligence to 'physical' observables described in spatio-temporal terms and without reference to the consciousness of the experimental subject. Behaviouristic operationalism is not synonymous with a deliberately chosen theoretical framework, such as any of the extant versions of behaviourism in experimental psychology. Instead, Wieder describes it as a 'methodogenic ontology' which is built into the established tradition of rigorous observation, report, and experimental design in animal research.

> Although certain students of the 'higher animals' do not subscribe to behavior-istic operationalism, even they find that it operates as a constraint on their thought and conduct. As a blind to everyday practical experience, it is a continuous source of paradox and incongruity. Researchers who are sensitive to the intersubjective life-world that is inhabited by themselves and their subjects employ the implementing practices of behavioristic operationalism as restraints upon what can be done rather than positive directives. The impact of these practices, then, is reflected more in the presence and relevance of phenomena that cannot be acknowledged or investigated than it is in forms of behaviorizing that are altogether discontinuous with life-worldly experiences. (p. 92)

Wieder goes on to outline some of the unacknowledged practices of interspecies communication. What is interesting, for our purposes, is that these practices are not merely the unreported underlife of the lab,

but are the very methods through which behaviouristic experiments are
operationalized in a different sense than in behaviouristic operationalism:

> Throughout the course of an experiment, the chimpanzee is monitored for its
> production of the observables that are the topic of the experiment, and the
> chimpanzee is also constantly monitored for the direction of its gaze, what it
> is paying attention to, lapses in attention, and the like. All of this is evident
> through the bodily orientation of the chimpanzee – one sees what the chim-
> panzee sees in that fashion. Although the content of these perceptions falls
> outside the tightly circumscribed methodogenic ontology, they are employed
> by chimpers in choosing their next move toward the chimpanzee and, at a
> higher level, in designing or redesigning the experiment.
>
> Actions toward the chimpanzee are likely to have no place in the standard
> report of the experiment, though the chimper experiences them as motivating
> the chimpanzee to engage in the experiment in the first place. (p. 97)

The 'hiatus between lived actions and behavioristically-operationalis-
tically-mapped actions' which Wieder (p. 77) describes, results in a
'double-life' for animal researchers as they attempt to come to terms
with the incongruity between the ways their results are reported and
the commonplace modes of inquiry and understanding that operate in
a day-to-day research situation.

A related incongruity appeared in the laboratory work of neuro-
scientists studied by Lynch (1979, 1982a, b). Lab members used a
vernacular distinction between 'lookers' and 'users' to formulate a
difference between electron micrographs used as illustrations in research reports and public lectures and micrographs used for generating
analytic data which were presented only in summary statistical form
in published writings. A different aesthetic accompanied decisions that
a micrograph was 'good enough' for the purposes of analysis despite
evident artifactual features, than in decisions in which photographs
were selected as illustrations for publication. In the latter case lab
members oriented not only to the adequacy of the photograph as
an illustration of the 'things' written about in the publication, they
oriented as well to the photograph's display of the quality of the lab's
technical mastery of electron microscopy. Any appreciable visibility
of artifact, even if it was irrelevant to the photographer's depiction of
cells, was treated as grounds for rejection in such cases.

It was not only the case, however, that reportability formats
operated as constraints on day-to-day inquiries. In some instances, the
hiatus between reportably demonstrable 'facts' and locally accepted
'facts' was deliberately disattended for the purposes of sustaining a

programme of discovering research. In the neuroscience laboratory studied by Lynch (1979) an array of projects was mobilized for the purposes of discovering the biochemical 'mechanism' responsible for the 'proliferation response' of microglia cells. The 'proliferation response' was observed to be a widespread meiotic division of microglia cells in a neural region where the incoming axons had just previously been destroyed through an experimental lesion in the animal brain. This 'response' was used in lab researches as an index of a more extended series of events which eventuated in the structural replacement of destroyed neuronal synapses with axon terminals from 'intact' neurons; a process designated as 'axon sprouting'. There was some possibility that the 'proliferation response' and the other events in the 'axon sprouting' sequence were triggered by a diffusable chemical compound originating within the brain tissues. The *in vitro* isolation of that compound and the *in vivo* demonstration of its effects promised to be a discovery of major proportions. The lab's systematic pursuit of that discovery entailed that its projects incorporated several publicly controversial features, which for local purposes had to be accepted as 'facts', as part of the system of constituents which were utilized on the way to the discovery. For instance, the very existence of microglia as a distinctive cell type was questioned in the neuroanatomical literature.[16] Furthermore, that the 'proliferation response' originated through meiotic division within the brain, rather than from an influx of microglia cells from the blood stream and crossing the blood-brain barrier, was also a matter of some controversy in the field at large.

It was not as though the 'fact' of microglia and the 'fact' of the 'endogenous' origins of the microglia response were accepted on faith by lab members. Rather, from their point of view, these matters had been addressed and 'proven' in their own researches, though those 'proofs' had not as yet been conclusive for the sake of resolving the extant literary controversies. The 'public' (in this case, a handful of neuroscience labs world-wide) was said to be 'slow' to catch up to the understandings about microglia that lab members used as proximal aspects of their local system of demonstrations.

The lab's researchers were aiming at a big discovery: the isolation of a diffusable compound which could be demonstrably linked to regenerative changes in the brain. In contrast, settling the controversy over microglia had no such big promise. It mattered little whether the lab's work could 'set straight' a community of neuroanatomists. Indeed, the lab director was contemptuous of such an aim, and spoke as though he could not care less about what some neuroanatomists thought.

It was as if an edifice was built on a foundation of controversial convictions which could not, for the time being, be supported through universal agreement in the relevant research communities. These 'convictions' were not global presuppositions or tacit subscriptions in a consensual community of scientists; they were locally demonstrated resolutions of what, for other labs, were explicit topics of interest and dispute. Demonstrating the facticity of microglia was a subsidiary topic; it did not provide anything like a theme against which the results of the inquiry would be assessed. Instead, the inquiry pursued the big discovery, where its eventual demonstration would perhaps implicate the validity of its subsidiary constituents (or, perhaps, lead to a disregarding of those constituents in light of the achieved facticity that the experiment 'works' and that the resultant extractable chemical factor can be applied under numerous other circumstances — in different brain systems, for different animal species, under medical circumstances, etc.). As it turned out, the pursuit of the chemical agent became 'bogged-down' during Lynch's field study, though not because of the specifically controversial matters mentioned here.

(iii) Embedded pedagogies in written materials
A manifest feature of introductory texts, lab manuals, math problems, and other didactic materials is that they provide 'problems' to be worked on by readers in a search for an 'answer'. The correct answer is implicated in the problem, while at the same time the formulation of the problem conceals or 'withholds' (Morrison, 1981: 249) the answer from the student until the student technically derives the answer from the initial materials supplied in the problem. This structure of inquiry embedded in the design of textual formats is described by Morrison as a sequential phenomenon. Morrison cites studies of question-answer sequences in conversation by Schegloff (1968) and by Sacks, Schegloff and Jefferson (1974) in outlining a class of such sequences in written materials where 'what is offered as the knowable (the answer) has the peculiar feature that its outcome/correctness is prefigured in advance of an interrogatory' (Morrison, 1981: 248). In other words, rather than asking a question to a recipient in order to elicit an answer that supplies what the asker marks as absent or unknown to the asked (as in the question, 'what time is it?'), a 'devised formatted question' (p. 248) intends, not the answer per se, but an answer to be assessed in reference to what the asker already has available.

In a devised question, though the asker apparently asks a question, it is just as apparent that he already has an answer in hand, such that *what* is asked in a devised format is derivable from the answer first. What interests us about these sorts of formattable sequences is that they seem to exhibit instances in which an asker apparently has an answer in hand to the question he asks, where if this is so for a certain class of materials, we might then have instances of a class of questions in which, apparently, what the asker is after is not an answer *per se* (since he already has it), but instead something like a knowledge assessment. (p. 249)

Paradoxically, in a 'devised question format' the asker of a question presents the recipient of that question with a situation where the answer is both absent and yet derivable from the initial materials of the question. This places the recipient/reader in a position of having to disclose what the text hides in the devices of its question, while at the same time exposing the activity of answering to assessment vis-à-vis the correspondence of the answerer's answer to the withheld answer 'contained' in the question. This closed situation of inquiry is distinct from the ordinary situation of discovering research where the search for an 'answer' to a 'question' can arise within an open horizon of inquiry. The characteristic formatting of 'written inquiry', however, bears the burden of recorded description and pedagogy in science: and by the same token, according to Morrison, provides embodiment for the traditional sense of affiliated science topics found in extant authoritative discussions of 'scientific facts', 'scientific inquiry', 'demonstrability', and 'objective knowledge'.

An implication of Morrison's study is that scientific texts, whether explicitly didactic or otherwise, require of readers that they work out what the text is saying, and further that this working out can occur not simply as a matter of thoughtful interpretation, but as visible actions on a distinct 'textual surface'. A number of ethnomethodologically 'researchable' sites can be collected around this general phenomenon (again, not a documentary 'proof' of the conjecture involved but as initial points of departure for detailed inquiry). For instance, the sheet of lab instructions used by Schrecker in his lab work required of students that they locate the text's instructions, and, accordingly, the answers and practical reasoning conveyed by the text's specifications, by turning away from the text and initiating embodied activities on the distinctive surface of the lab bench. Similarly, in his research on mathematicians' work Livingston (1978) points to the scratch-pad and blackboard work which composes a course of mathematical reasoning that works through a math problem. The point that he makes is that the extractable course of that work, in and as the material details of it, is, in fact, the solution or proof, and that the discovery of that materially exhibited course of reasoning – presented as the 'solution' – forgets the contingencies of its organizational achievement. Although, presumably the statement of the problem tells all that a student needs to work out an answer, an examinable sequence of real-time activities with a beginning and end, and with a course of writing, scratching-outs, repairs, etc., surpasses the formal and disengaged 'problem' and its 'solution' and is hidden within the finalized form of that structure.[17]

The key point of this very brief review of issues on canonical description and actual courses of action is not that scientists actually do different than they publicly say. To leave it at that would be to settle for an ironic trivialization of the matter. The point instead is that the practices which in actual situations of inquiry compose the incarnate working out of what a statement of the formal problem foreshadows, as well as the working up of research into reportable results, are hidden within the analyzable specifics of formal scientific expressions. Such expressions are 'docile records'[18] which are the disengaged products of real-time courses of action. Such 'docile records' nicely lend themselves to analytic manipulations which treat them separately from their actual generative circumstances, but the 'ideal' and generic sensibility of such records hides the situated inquiries which composed their original production and which compose any subsequent reactivation of their 'sense'. Ethnomethodological studies then attempt to open up for empirical study the visible ways in which such transcendental accounts of scientific activities have their origins in human praxis.

The retrospective-prospective assembly of scientific methods on the basis of results in hand

Schrecker (1980: 59) comments on the situated realization that something had gone wrong, or could potentially go wrong in the unfolding experiment, a recurrent facet of lab sequences, which he calls 'going back in time'.

> Only when the hands actually started working on the equipment did these circumstantial contingencies arise which were not previously anticipated. Only when the hands went for the bunsen burner did they discover the danger of knocking over the equipment. Only when the buret had been fixed at its holder did the beakers underneath it get in the way. One change in the display motivated another unforeseen and unimagined activity. This practical

work was done unwittingly: not through plans projected in the head, but instead through the engagement of the hands in a terrain of chemical equipment.

Within such unforeseen circumstances the question then arose of just what to do to repair the projectable order of the experiment. How to sustain the experiment in the face of such contingent realizations was, of course, not specified in the lab instructions in most instances. In the above instance of trouble, Schrecker managed rapidly to effect a repair. The trouble consisted of his discovery, while setting up the bunsen burner for the next step of the experiment, that the glassware from a prior step now 'stood in the way of' his embodied movements across the lab-table surface. He then had to 'back up' in the sequence. He had to suspend the work he had just begun and turn to the prior sequence in order to clear away the residue of that sequence.

Circumstantial contingencies, and the 'backward' inquiries they motivated, were not always so trivial. For instance, toward the end of the lab period, Schrecker and his lab partner often were faced with the following sort of dilemma:

> The boundaries between an inaccuracy and a mistake were not clear-cut. We had to discover whether an inaccuracy was tolerable or whether we had to do a procedure again. We had to agree interactionally on what it was that we were looking at. To see something as a 'mistake' had its consequence, in that it meant we had to provide for some sort of a repair procedure. Would the remaining time allow us to repair it? Or worse, would it allow us to do an extensive sequence all over again? Or should we go on and hope for the best? When we did not recognize an inaccuracy as a mistake it became just one of many possible inaccuracies, and in the final assessment of inaccurate results we would never be able to exactly find out what had led to the inexact number. (pp. 81–2)

When faced with 'something-having-gone-wrong' the two lab partners acted as local historians. Potentially vast arrays of prior activities in any sequence were implicatable as possible error sources. Questions were asked, such as, 'was the glassware cleaned sufficiently to prevent unwanted reactions with the chemicals subsequently placed in it?'; 'was it consequential now that a "blob" of reagent was added instead of an exactly counted series of drops during an earlier titration sequence?'; or, 'was an error source hidden in the midst of apparently adequate actions?' Depending on what was diagnosed in a situation of apparent error, more or less global consequences ensued for the sequential prospects of the experiment. In some cases a repair entailed going back to a just-prior step while retaining the local achievement of the experiment up until that point. In one case, an experiment was found to be globally contaminated by an error noticed late in the game, and an entire day's work was wasted and had to be repeated 'from scratch' during the next lab period.

Studies of discovering work in science suggest that the ways in which time can be found to have been 'wasted' are compounded by the fact that, unlike student lab experiments, a 'correct value' is not yet unequivocally available as a standard for deciding if an experiment was performed adequately. Given the hiddenness of 'error sources' in the innumerable contingent events of an experiment, a positive or negative result for any given run presents the problem of determining whether to accept that result as a basis for further inference and action.[19] Furthermore, innumerable ambiguities accompany the incarnate work of attending just when a positive or negative result is indeed at hand. That, for instance, a notable 'jump' on an oscilloscope screen is 'anything at all' depends in part upon the further course of inquiry: it can turn out to be evidence for a positive finding or as 'nothing but' an artifact. Accordingly, the 'what-was-seen' at any given point in an experiment is an historicized construct based upon 'what it turned out to be' in the end. Even more fundamentally, the very 'seeing' of anything at all, whether it later is treated as fact or artifact, 'noise', or nothing worth bothering about, is itself embedded in a local history of technical activities.

As may be inferred from the above, ethnomethodological studies treat the temporality of practices as competently initiated and sustained through members' access to and use of 'circumstantial' features of their current situations of inquiry. Furthermore, what can count in any given case as actual or possible events to be taken seriously in projecting further work is bound within members' technical mastery of the specific equipmental assemblies and prior embodied actions which make up their active research engagement. Accordingly, it would be premature to move to a generic theory of scientific contingencies and their impact on specific inquiries of all kinds, since it remains to be discovered for any given case of inquiry how 'reasoning' begins with a unique set of disciplinary materials.

The object as an icon of laboratory temporality

A research policy from early ethnomethodological studies which has been taken up in ethnographic studies of the sciences is that accounts of scientific activities, that is, 'inscriptions',[20] factual statements, documentary records, and published reports, become disengaged from the actual course of scientific activity that produced them. The ethnomethodological studies of work discussed here have gone beyond the earlier emphasis on the production of accounts of order (or of a sense of social structure) and have proceeded to examine the embodied production of social objects. The implicit bifurcation incorporated in a focus on accounts versus objects has been replaced by an insistence on the irreducibility of the embodied production of an object to an account of that work, and an elucidation of Merleau-Ponty's theme of the 'intertwining' (1968: 130–55) in terms of the inspectable details of social objects in and as the ordinary day's work. This insistence is exemplified in a study by Garfinkel, Lynch and Livingston (1981) which addresses a discovery in astronomy by tracing a geneology of the discovered object (in this case the optical discovery of Pulsar NP 0532) through the temporal and embodied details of a sequence of observatory runs. The difference in saying that the astronomers discover an object rather than an account is elaborated as follows:

> Different understandings of the IGP as Cocke and Disney's discovery need to be sorted out. A first and incorrect understanding takes the Independent Galilean Pulsar to be an *account*. The IGP can be construed as an achieved account of their night's work, an account that rendered their work in the astronomically adequate terms of the IGP, and is found in their published paper. But taking the IGP as an account can be irreparably distracting. It needs to be remembered that Cocke and Disney don't discover an *account* of the pulsar; they discover an astronomically demonstrable pulsar. Correctly understood, the IGP is an *object*, and a cultural object, not a 'physical' or 'natural' object. In the entirety of its technical astronomical properties, IGP is a cultural object. (pp. 141–2, fn. 28)[21]

By calling the IGP a 'cultural object', reference is made to the discovery's genetic origins within the embodied situation of work. This calls attention to the way in which it is made to appear again and again, and in an increasingly definite way, over the course of a night's work at the observatory.

In the case of the discovery of the optical pulsar, a tape recording of several successive runs at the observatory was made available for analysis. Preliminary research by Garfinkel, Lynch and Livingston in consultation with two of the original discoverers and other astronomers suggested that the work of attaching the pulsar to nature[22] was a situated preoccupation at the time of the discovery. Furthermore, analysis of the sequence of spontaneous remarks by the discoverers on the tape, when informed by astronomers' instructions on how to hear those utterances in terms of the phenomena and instruments peculiar to their discipline, enabled the issue of 'attaching to nature' to be documented by the temporal development of observations and runs recorded on the tape. Embodied efforts by the discovers to 'check' prior runs for possible equipmental sources of artifact acted concretely to disengage the as yet unsubstantiated 'pulse' from selected features of the instrumental complex. The object became progressively 'attached' to nature simultaneously with these embodied efforts to 'detach' it from locally explicated features of the instrumental 'grasp' of that object. Over the course of several successive runs the object became transformed from an 'IT' looking for its adequate reference,[23] to 'a relatively finished object'. This transformation was apparent in the way in which the discoverers collaboratively addressed the object at hand as it developed over the course of their night's work (cf. Garfinkel et al., 1981: Appendix 5, pp. 154–8).

To summarize in a few sentences what the work of 'attaching the object to nature' consists of as an actual technical accomplishment would be to cover over an immense and highly interesting phenomenon. It would be a disservice to the studies reviewed here to suggest that they have in any final way settled the issue. For present purposes, however, it will be sufficient to claim that those studies have set off on a unique approach to the issue of the geneology of the object by tracing the 'Galilean Objects' of science back to their origins in the embodied inquiries that make up ordinary technical activities in science. This does not entail the use of Transcendental Ego to stand for the constitutive 'pole' of the object, since for ethnomethodological studies a far more concrete and visible 'region' of activities is available for detailed study: the ordinary ways in which, for instance, astronomers find themselves and each other at the work of doing astronomy. The problem then becomes one of addressing the *transitivity* of such communally organized activities to the objects of the respective disciplines.

Transitivity

The term 'transitivity' is used to unify two distinct though interpenetrating senses of the word: one sense expresses the work of sequential transition, and the other the transparency of instrumentation in the face of a contingently-achieved naturally analyzable field, which we gloss as 'getting through to the object'. The investigatable ties between the temporal embodiment of scientific work and the stable objects of scientific inquiry provide a fundamental topic for ethnomethodological studies of scientific work. Livingston's research on mathematicians' work – partially reported in his dissertation on the work of proving Godel's theorem (1982) – indicates that it is the embodied presence of two mathematicians at work at the blackboard that allows those mathematicians to find, in each other's board writings and talk, the real thing that the collaborators could be proposing to one another. Compatible emphasis is also found in Morrison's (1981) investigation of 'telling-order designs' in written inquiries. It is far beyond the scope of this chapter to follow out the rich implications of the various treatments that the different studies give. Instead, what will be provided is an illustrative sketch of how two particular ethnomethodological studies treat the issue of transitivity.

Ethnomethodological inquiries confront the following observation: effective practices render themselves visible as their stable, disengaged products, along with their analyzable features, that is, as their 'contents'. In order to attend to the existence of the practices, and to the matter of how those practices achieve evident 'contents', one needs to turn away from a naturalistic fascination with the 'sensible' order of ordinary things. Ethnomethodological studies, beginning with Garfinkel's (1967) early studies have used a variety of methods for breaking the hold of naturalistic sensibility by orienting to 'troubled' instances of activity as an initial condition for revealing order-productive practices. Two of the approaches used in ethnomethodological studies of scientific work are discussed below.

(i)   The broken instrument
Research artifacts occupy a strategic place in a study of research practices in neurobiology (Lynch, 1979: ch. 4). In neuroscience research, artifacts include varieties of visible features of electron micrographic displays, for example, which are referenced to 'constructive' origins. It has been argued by research scientists as well as social constructivists that virtually everything that makes up the observable data of electron microscopy is artifactual in origin, since the visibility of cellular details rests upon the artifices of staining, thin sectioning, and embedding of dead tissue. However, in commonplace research usage, 'artifact' has a particular reference to aspects of a visible field that are

demonstrably disjunct from, for instance, visibly normal intracellular formations. In this more limited sense, artifacts include such phenomena as blotches of stain, degraded membrane separations, plastic deformations, òr 'noise' on an oscilloscope screen attributable to the effects of nearby machinery.

The argument given in support of an 'archaeology' of research artifacts is that the phenomena which researchers call artifacts in their data provide positive cases of an orientation away from a 'naturalization' of the stable products of scientific work and towards an articulation of the dependency of visible results upon 'unwitting' features of actual methods. This argument adapts the Heideggerian (1962) metaphor of the 'broken hammer' to the situated analysis of scientific work. For Heidegger, the broken hammer demonstrates the ontological difference between the instrument's mere presence as an object and its readiness for human activity. In being useless for activity it is thematized as a degraded thing which implicates the peculiar ontological sense of the instrument's 'readiness-to-hand' as its normative identity.

In laboratory work, occasions where research artifacts were noticed revealed vernacularly accountable[24] 'ties' between a sequence of practical actions in the lab and concretely visible features of an electron microscopic field of neuronal organelles. In cases where artifacts were at issue (which turned out to be quite frequent in day-to-day research) displays of biological objects were articulated as historical records of an indefinite order of practical actions and research circumstances.

The accountability of artifacts in laboratory activities provided an endogenous locale for 'members' archaeology' which was used in Lynch's study as an initial basis for treating biological objects as icons whose formal characteristics revealed indefinite horizons of human work and 'hidden' human error. These spontaneously occurring 'archaeologies' of research artifacts facilitated an approach to 'constructive' activities in science which was founded on an empirically researchable basis in the activities and descriptions of scientists themselves. This contrasts with any adoption of 'social constructivism' as an overall programme for describing the telos of science in general. The issues and arguments that identify 'constructivism' are thus transformed into technical and researchable features of actual researchers' practices, and no longer involve an imposition of 'constructivism' upon science as a theoretically postulated descriptive philosophy; a philosophy that remains endlessly embedded in academic arguments about science with no attention being paid to the endogenously produced variants of argument and practice that constitute the technical development of ordinary scientific inquiry. Like any other philosophy of science, 'constructivism' then stands as an occasional relevancy in actual situations of inquiry (although one with a particular appeal for sociologists' investigations) with productive and analyzable relations within the praxis of science.

(ii) The Cartesian situation – metaphorically speaking
In Schrecker's study (1980), a methodological set-up was used for the purpose of perspicuously identifying the mutual dependence of chemical reasoning and embodied action. Schrecker volunteered his services to aid a handicapped student in his laboratory work for an undergraduate chemistry course. He then received the student's permission to use his experimental work as a research topic. There resulted a division of labour and responsibility between Schrecker, who was largely ignorant of the field of chemistry – and ignorant as well of the specific lab assignments he bodily assisted – and Gordon, the chemistry student, who because of a spinal injury was paralyzed from the neck down with very limited use of his hands. Gordon depended upon Schrecker to bodily perform the work at the bench for weekly lab experiments assigned to students in the course on 'Quantitative Analysis'.

The isolation of Schrecker's handiwork from its theoretical basis in chemistry necessitated that Gordon and he make explicit for one another how the experiment was progressing as a witnessable production of chemistry. Gordon provided instructions for Schrecker on what to do next, while at the same time he relied upon Schrecker's developing work to show him what 'next' meant in terms of where they stood in the course of the experiment's events. He depended on Schrecker's embodied competence with lab equipment to visibly display events in the experiment, and the two of them collaborated in assuring the local recognizability and understanding of these events as events of chemistry.

This 'Cartesian' situation is not usable as a 'model' of shop work, in the literal sense of being a 'communication' between isolated spheres of theory and practice. Instead it provided an actual setting that was peculiarly encumbered by the necessity to interactionally exhibit and describe the 'how to do it' of an experiment while the experiment developed from beginning to end. The extensive interchanges between Gordon and Schrecker in the course of this experiment, along with the evident ways in which the remarks were fitted to features of the unfolding bench-work and the many troubles which arose during the experiment, were later exploited in Schrecker's analysis to specify features of the experiment's temporal organization. One continuous laboratory experiment of three hours was video-taped and was later analyzed. With the tape, and because of the way the disrupted unity of the experiment's work exhibited the embodied work *in vacuo*, previously undiscovered relevancies for gestalt versions of action were detected and inspectable.[25] Schrecker's embodied work with the material surfaces of the equipment at hand constituted developingly ordered spatial arrangements of that equipment on the lab table, and the observability of those transient productions was made coherent in inspectable detail. Several familiar themes from gestalt theories of perception were used to call attention to these orderly productions with the equipment.

Working at the lab bench, Schrecker unwittingly arranged the surface of the lab table into a field of gestalt contextures.[26] (The word 'unwittingly' is used here since these orderly features were only dis-covered subsequent to the completion of the experiment when the videotape was examined.) These contextures were discovered, not as principles of gestalt coherence, but as coherences between disparate items of equipment placed on the table which became visible when one took account of their ties to the sequential organization of the experiment being performed.[27] Moreover, these ties *were* the unfolding temporal order of the experiment itself. The experiment visibly de-veloped in and as the arrangements of the materials and their relative placements within a field in front of, and in easy reach of, Schrecker's body. For instance, his bodily work of 'setting up' equipment for a next step of an experiment, and his 'clearing away' of items used in prior sequences, was analyzable with the theme of Figure-Ground to formulate the embodied work of constituting the 'clearing' and its interior arrangements.

The thematic field of the table, when viewed from above, exhibited orderly developments in the sequential placements of flasks, tubes, bunsen burner, and vials of identified and unidentified chemicals, in various juxtapositions and within easy reach of Schrecker's embodied movements. These various materials were *not* haphazardly arranged within the manipulatory space, but were assembled groupings ordered around present, past, and future uses of existing items in the unfolding experiment. As the experiment progressed, the space of the bench became differentiated. Items were placed in reference to other items as ordered elements in a sequence of embodied activities.

'Groupings' were not necessarily reflexive to positional relations of togetherness, but were oriented to relations of togetherness intrinsic to projected movements and events in the experiment. For instance, a complex of items was placed together in preparation for the experimental step of 'titration', and a different complex was prepared for 'heating chemicals', etc. These complexes were assembled in readiness for Schrecker's actions with them in a foreseeable future. In some cases, seeing how the equipment on the table formed a practical constellation entailed that the analyst be familiar with the habitual events and ordinary apparatus of 'doing chemistry'. Such a manner of seeing gestalt orderings was informed by, while being informative of, a chemist's way of analyzing human actions and equipment. This situated 'theory of action' made up the undergraduate pedagogy and discipline of chemistry.

Gestalt figures were ordered with regard to the body at the bench; its reach and its motility from one place on the surface to another. Accordingly, items relevant[28] to any upcoming step in the experiment were placed within easy bodily access, and irrelevant items were put aside. A figure was thereby constructed in the assembly of any array of materials close to hand in preparation for activities using those items. At the same time a 'ground' was composed by removing from the space most conveniently at hand those items that had passed out of use, and which had no immediate prospect for use. This 'ground' was further differentiated into regions of differing practical relevance: a 'dump' of used-up and no longer 'interesting' items, a region 'just out of reach' and 'out of the way of' the active movements at the bench where soon-to-be-relevant items were placed, and habitual places for materials used over and over again in different operations. Schrecker's embodied movements not only operated within the constraints of this ecology of equipment, they moved the equipment around in orderly ways and progressively constituted and reconstituted that 'terrain'.

Schrecker's handling of equipment was not merely an athletic accompaniment of chemical reasoning, it was part and parcel of chemical reasoning (in the same way that playing a musical instrument is not an athletic accompaniment of music but the existence-in-the-production of everything that music could be). 'Reasoning' did not occur exclusively on one side of the artificial 'Cartesian' division between Gordon's immobilized knowledge of chemistry and Schrecker's 'unknowing' bodily competence with the equipment.[29] Both Gordon and Schrecker oriented to the developing display of equipment as a place where chemistry was happening. Insofar as the developments in that visible place were inevitably tied to Schrecker's movements in the field, and his movements had to make visible the events of chemistry for Gordon's (and the lab instructor's) assessment, he was recognizably doing chemistry, whether he knew it or not. Of course, from Schrecker's side it was no easy matter to analytically extricate the chemistry from the visible course of his bodily activities. This proved, in fact, to be a concrete source of trouble in his attempts to do experimental actions.

To take a simple case of such a trouble, Schrecker mentions the difficulties he had in 'washing glassware' in preparation for an up-coming sequence of tasks in the experiment. Washing became a difficult procedure for him which sometimes necessitated an inquiry to Gordon on just how clean different items needed to be. The difficulty lay in his being unable to foresee what the equipment was to be used for. How clean, for instance, a beaker needed to be depended upon the sensitivity of the chemical it would soon house to contamination by the beaker's previous contents. These included the residues of washing itself. For potentially reactive agents, more thorough cleaning and drying were called for than in cases where a quick and dirty rinse was adequate for the task at hand. Similarly, the selection of size for flasks and beakers to be used in upcoming phases of an experiment depended upon volumes and proportions of chemicals to be employed.

These, of course, are misleadingly simple cases which require no more than a rudimentary competence with chemical experimentation to appreciate. In many other more detailed ways, the visible arrangements at the lab bench articulated the relevance of precautionary measures and concrete 'anticipations' concerning what the experiment would, or might, involve in a near future.

In addition, some of the errors which evidently occurred during the experiment were directly traced to Schrecker's incomplete access to the chemical analyzability of his sequences of conduct:

> The highlight of confusion came at the very end of the day and it was then that I lost control over my hands and started knocking over equipment. We had messed up the iron-solution and had started to repeat the preparation of this solution. Time was running short: there were about 25 minutes left. The time pressure created a hectic atmosphere. While hooking up the hose of the bunsen burner at the gas-faucet I almost knocked the Erlenmeyer flask down from the burn-ring. It was waiting there, ready to be heated up again. I knocked it off with my left arm but I caught it in its fall with my right hand. I was starting to lose control over the ways my hands were going.... I finished adding the stannous chloride, put the iron-solution into a waterbath, brought over the mercury chloride from the hood, ready to add it to the solution 'all at once' this time, when Gordon suddenly interrupted this sequence

of activities. It was 'all of a sudden' only for me, not for Gordon. He was prepared for this sequential change: while I had been adding the stannous chloride, he had already made the calculations of how much of the dichromate we would have to weigh out. This horizon of what the next step would be was in no way visible to me. I had not imagined a sequential change and was completely shocked by it. It was then that my hands 'went the wrong way' again and knocked over the graduated cylinder of mercury chloride. *My hands were engaged in a territory whose spatial arrangement did not adequately exhibit the sequential organization any longer:* the graduated cylinder was sitting in the foreground of the table since I had brought it over from the hood, but after Gordon had introduced the sudden sequential change it became an obstacle to what the hands were going for in the new sequence. I was in the wrong place since I did not work on it any longer. At that point I knocked it over. (1980: 39−40, italics in original)

The placework articulated on the table surface was in a literal sense a repository of chemical reasoning which had consequences for the projectable course of what had to be done next. This is to say, among other things, that the unfolding of the experiment increasingly took on the appearance of an orderliness in the constituted array of equipment. In Schrecker's words, the display of equipment on the table was, 'a practical account of the present state of the experiment' (p. 64).[30] What to do next, how to do it, where to do it, and when, was found in an environment of objects which 'held their places' for any next action, which, in turn, rearranged those places. The arrangements, and their orderly reflexivity to the experiment's unique 'lesson', acted as mnemonics, or as records of 'activities-so-far' in a project of action. Furthermore, all of these relevancies − whether as spatio-temporal arrangements or as arrangements keyed to a specific system of knowledge − were chained to the bodily presence of the experimenter, who operated the items of equipment and generated their orderly relations.

Conclusion

This chapter has alluded to the detailed findings of several ethnomethodological studies organized around the topic of temporal order. An overall view of temporality was not provided in the collection of studies discussed here except to the extent that each of the studies exhibited temporal issues in the substantive details of the specific practices they investigated. A theory of temporal organization was not abstracted from the objects, courses of action, or equipmental arrangements described in the studies, and this was a deliberate omission.

Temporal issues were, instead, addressed in a more immanent 'region' than in general theorizing about science: the region of inquiry opened up via an engagement with scientific activities, in their midst. Warrant for this can be provided by referring to what 'anyone' who wishes to do science must begin with.

Notes

Michael Lynch, having been invited to prepare a chapter for inclusion in this volume, wrote a draft that was delivered at the Annual Meetings of the Society for Social Studies of Science, Atlanta, Georgia, November 1981. Because of the collaborative nature of the work and because the issues addressed in the chapter cannot be disengaged from our work histories, joint authorship was necessary.

While the joint authors assisted in the exposition, and while that exposition relies on our joint studies and on the studies and seminars of Harold Garfinkel, it does not reflect a common understanding of ethnomethodology. Instead, the authors urge that ·the chapter be read as a docent's tour, and thereby as a bowdlerization done in the interest of not swamping the reader with the technical refinements that would be required were it the chapter's task to make ethnomethodological studies available to the research practitioner as the constraints of a current situation of inquiry. Their collaboration therefore does not constitute an endorsement of the chapter as an adequate introduction to ethnomethodological studies. For this, readers are referred to *A Manual for the Study of Naturally Organized Ordinary Activities* edited by Harold Garfinkel (1982a, b, c).

1. For purposes of this discussion, 'ethnomethodological studies of scientific work' will mean work in the natural sciences and will include studies cited in this chapter authored by Burns, Garfinkel, Livingston, Lynch, Morrison, Schrecker and Wieder. These studies evolved in reference to one another and, of course, in reference to a larger community of ethnomethodological studies in the United States, Canada and Europe. Studies by these authors have been published together in *A Manual for the Study of Naturally Organized Ordinary Activities* edited by Harold Garfinkel (1982a, b, c, d). The issues discussed in this chapter are topics with common origins and communal development in these collections. The intention of this chapter is to introduce these studies to readers in the science studies community, but not to furnish a novel theory of scientific work aside from what can be appropriated from a reading of the original works.

A number of recent ethnographies and analytic studies of natural scientific activities in one way or another take up topics affiliated to literatures in 'ethnomethodology'. These works include recent contributions by Latour and Woolgar

(1979), Knorr (1980), Mulkay and Gilbert (1982), Law (1982), Traweek (1981), McKegney (1981), and Zenzen and Restivo (1980). We considered it inappropriate within the limited project of this chapter to argue the similarities and differences between the studies cited in this chapter and other ethnomethodological studies of natural scientific work, and various treatments of scientific communication, scientific construction, and social history of science. That task has been taken up elsewhere and by the above authors. All have taken their turn as ethnomethodology's expositors. The value of such writings for the tasks of teaching colleagues is problematic and they need not detain us. It is our experience that an adequate appreciation of the fundamental differences between ethnomethodological studies and social studies of science requires a research practitioner's autonomously critical grasp of differences, where his grasp is motivated by practitioners' insistence that the differences that count do so because of their relevance to the research community's interests in news.

2. In addition to the ethnomethodological studies of work specifically concerned with practices in the natural sciences, a larger group of studies make up its corpus of studies. In addition to the studies of science reviewed in this chapter, these include studies by Melinda Baccus (1976, 1981), Stacy Burns (1978a, 1978b, 1978c, 1981), David Sudnow (1978, 1980), Trent Eglin (1974), Richard Fauman (1980), Harold Garfinkel and Stacy Burns (1979), Kenneth Liberman (1980, 1982), Eric Livingston (1976), Melvin Pollner (1970), Christopher Pack (1975a, 1975b), and Britt Robillard et al. (1980, 1981). Many of these studies appear in Garfinkel (1982a). Still another and much larger collection of ethnomethodological studies is relevant to the thematic initiatives of the above corpus; and of course, a massive collection in conversational analysis instituted by Harvey Sacks and Emanuel Schegloff and their co-workers is unavoidably relevant. Reason to treat these collections as a coherent community of studies is found in their distinctive emphasis upon, empirical approach to, and essential technical relevance for the radically situated origins of order in the embodied shop talk and shop practices of the professions and sciences.

3. Various topics of order elucidated in and as locally-produced order phenomena of queues are presented in Garfinkel (1982a).

4. A large corpus of studies by Harvey Sacks, Emanuel Schegloff, Gail Jefferson, Anita Pomerantz, and many others, have explicated detailed and generic features of interactional and local order production in conversation. Several collections of these studies are available, including Schenkein (1978) and Psathas (1979).

5. David Sudnow's studies of the embodied work of jazz piano playing (1978) and typing without notes (1980) provide illuminating cases.

6. Our focus upon the irreducible embodiment of the activities exhibiting worldly 'reasoning' has a programmatic origin in the writings of Merleau-Ponty (1962, 1968) and Heidegger (1962, 1967). We are heavily indebted to Merleau-Ponty's daemonic discussions of the 'intertwining' (1968) and Heidegger's masterful exposition of the question of 'the Thing' (1967). It has remained for ethnomethodological studies to use the incipient topicality of these expressions to discover and work out the locally produced phenomena of order in and as the ordinary society in identifying features of empirically situated activities. This task has been more than a matter of 'applying theory to facts' since it has necessitated that the tradition of philosophizing, which gave Heidegger and Merleau-Ponty

a continual point of departure and return, be abandoned in a search for the witnessable varieties of practical actions which animate topics of order as non-literary accomplishments. For instance, whereas the relation between object and appearance is recognizable as a traditional topic for academic thought and argument, it is given a distinctive situation of inquiry when treated as a phenomenon in an embodiedly and instrumentally enacted series of observatory runs (Garfinkel et al., 1981). There it becomes a topic that no longer has its adequate origins in generic theories of perception and/or methods of a unified science. Instead, it becomes a lively matter addressed over the course of the astronomers' night's work, and not as a topic of idle 'interest' but as the task at hand.

7. Gurwitsch (1964) speaks of 'autochthonous' properties of a 'gestalt contexture', meaning the identifying properties of a figure with origins in the figure's ensemble presentation of its constituent features. These 'autocthonous' features are not reducible to any a priori definition of figural elements, but arise within the composition of the figure's accomplished unity. In using the term here we are not referring to the stable significations in a textual figure but to the mutually identifying details in a productive activity which compose and identify the material or textual products of a discipline. Rather than starting with a gestalt figure in the attempt to demonstrate principles of gestalt contexture, ethnomethodological studies examine how a naturally analyzable product comes to be produced such that it exhibits a discipline's work in its witnessable features. The discipline's identifying details are thus 'autochthonous' to a particular material and equipmental ensemble as their produced and oriented-to analyzability. They are not characteristics of, for instance, 'the scientist' or 'scientific practice' which are extraneous to the scenic details of shop work.

8. By 'disciplinary' is not meant that embodied action in science proceeds in a way governed by compliance to the ideals of a science. Instead, the word refers to the demonstrability of a scientific discipline in the embodied practices of shop work, that the practices are discipline specific, and, moreover, that they show the discipline's contents in their temporal production.

9. Carr (1974) and Derrida (1978) discuss the distinctive treatment of historicity developed in Husserl's intentional history of Galileo's achievement of the mathematization of nature (1970). Their arguments offer a resource for ethnomethodological studies since they point up the phenomena of genetic origins in the historicity of praxis in the sciences. But because they do so with 'in-principle' arguments and descriptive characterizations, it remains for ethnomethodological researches to critically examine how the phenomenon of historicity is delineated in concurrently observable instances of science's distinctive and identifying practices. As is elaborated upon in the studies reviewed in this chapter, ethnomethodological studies do not orient to existing scientific practices as historically determined in such a way as to pose questions on the origin, say, of 'science' from 'proto-science' or of 'rational' from 'common-sense' methods of reasoning and practice, or to answer such questions with studies of seventeenth-century developments. Although it would be pointless to claim that the concurrently examinable genesis of 'objects-in-the-Galilean-mode' (Garfinkel et al., 1981) recapitulates a sequence of events in a chronologically established tradition in science, it seems clear that 'sciencing' originates in, and from out of, 'ordinary' occasions of human practice — embodied action, vernacular shop talk, and day-to-day labours of essentially situated inquiries.

10. This applies particularly to Husserl's writings. Despite Husserl's programme of the *Crisis* to discover the primordiality of the *Lebenswelt*, Husserl nevertheless retains the transcendental standpoint as a condition for his philosophizing. Heidegger and Merleau-Ponty, each in a distinctive way, abandon Husserl's transcendental philosophy. Heidegger develops an ontology of 'Dasein' – of Being-in-the-World – while Merleau-Ponty thematizes the body as the irreducibly lived work 'in-and-as the World'. Neither writer, however, initiates inquiries that start with and bring under empirical examination recurrent settings of actual lived activity. Instead, imagined and recollected 'experience' bears the burden of exemplification for projects of generic theorizing.

11. Among the many discussions of this issue are: Holton (1978), Kuhn (1970, 'Postscript'), Medawar (1969), Knorr and Knorr (1978), Gilbert (1976), Gusfield (1976), Woolgar (1976), and Latour and Woolgar (1979).

12. The problem is not merely a matter of reducing action to a finite descriptive account, since, as Feyerabend argues (1975), there is an essential openness in scientific practice that is betrayed by the very notion of scientific method when method is construed as a rationally secured foundation for action which relieves situated praxis of its burden of finding a way through an unscheduled future while making a convincing case for what is 'somehow' extracted from that future.

13. The term 'written inquiry' is used by Kenneth Morrison and John O'Neill to identify the phenomenon that preoccupies their continuing studies.

14. The phenomenon of 'superstitious' features in lab work is discussed at length in Lynch (1979: ch. 4).

15. This problem of producing the equivalency of Runs in a series is treated in Garfinkel et al. (1981: 139–40).

16. For some electron microscopists 'microglia' were a 'doubtful' cell type. In a study of glial cells (a group of brain cell types characterized by mobility, and functional activities other than neuro-transmission of electro-chemical impulses) in the cat cerebellum, Eager and Eager (1966: 553) claim that 'cells identifiable as microglia were never observed'. The authors suggest that what had been called 'microglia' might be indistinguishable on anatomical grounds from oligodendricytes or 'reactive astrocytes' (two other classifications of glial cell types). A general text on neuroanatomical ultrastructures (Peters et al., 1970: 126–7) describes microglia as an 'uncertain' cell type and gives a number of anatomical pros and cons for classifying microglia as a distinct cell type. The controversy on microglia was still unsettled in 1976 when the fieldwork reported in Lynch (1979) was completed.

17. Holton (1975: 329) makes a distinction between the 'time trajectory' of science presented in published discourse ('public' science) versus the trajectory occurring in the course of actual research activities ('private' science).

18. Docile records are discussed at length in Burns (1978c), and in Garfinkel and Burns (1979).

19. See Holton's discussion of Millikan's unformulated procedures for selecting results in a series of experimental runs of the oil drop experiment (1978).

20. Latour and Woolgar (1979) develop a theory of literary inscription in their ethnography of laboratory activities.

21. The reference to 'IGP' is to the Independent Galilean Pulsar which renders the work of astronomical discovery, by John Cocke, Michael Disney and Don

Taylor at Steward Observatory, Arizona, into an independent, astronomically accessible and measurable, and natural locus of properties.

22. The phrase 'attaching the pulsar to nature' is adapted from Kuhn's (1970) discussion of 'symbolic generalizations' where he stated:

> One widely shared example is Newton's Second Law of Motion, generally written as f=ma. The sociologist, say, or the linguist who discovers that the corresponding expression is unproblematically uttered and received by the members of a given community will not, without additional investigation, have learned a great deal about what either the expression or the terms in it mean, about how the scientists of the community attach the expression to nature. (p. 188)

In order to underscore the way in which Kuhn's insight is appropriated in Garfinkel, Lynch and Livingston's analysis, one should begin by replacing 'symbolic generalizations' with 'the IGP'. The radical difference is that the IGP is not a statement about the object, but an ensemble of instrumentally demonstrable 'properties' ('properties' understood in the sense of achieved-identifications, achieved-measures, and achieved-stabilities over the course of a succession of equipmental runs at the observatory) which provide for everything an object can be as an astronomically analyzable matter.

23. The use here of the term 'reference' is not meant to imply any of the semiotic versions of reference but instead is to be so read in the active voice as to borrow its meaning from the conversational work of referring that was discovered and elucidated by Harvey Sacks and Emanuel Schegloff.

24. For the notion of a 'vernacular' culture in the local situation of lab research we are indebted to an early discussion by Senior (1958).

25. A review of the themes of gestalt theories of perception will be found in Kohler (1929) and Koffka (1935). For a criticism of gestalt theory and an examination of gestalt themes as gestalt phenomena from the standpoint of transcendental phenomenology, see Gurwitsch (1964).

26. It was Gurwitsch's seminal achievement to have done original and authoritative studies of gestalt contexture. Limited to the phenomenology of geometrically diagramed perceptual figures, his studies make no reference to the embodied origins of the constitutive relations that are 'found' in and as the visible order of any contexture.

27. The version of gestalt themes which Schrecker used to articulate his materials was worked out in lectures and unpublished writings by Garfinkel to which Schrecker was given access.

28. The terms 'relevant' and 'irrelevant' used in this passage are to be understood in the sense used by Gurwitsch (1964) in his concept of the gestalt figure as an ensemble of functional significations. A gestalt contexture is identified as an ensemble of relevances.

29. Merleau-Ponty (1964: 15) quotes the painter, Cezanne as having said, '...the painter is not an imbecile', to which Schrag (1980: 104) adds, 'The painter does not strip the aesthetical from the working of thought but rather points to the origin of thought. He achieves rationality by thinking with the end of his brush.'

30. Daniel LaCoe (1977) elaborates upon this theme in his descriptive analysis of the work of repairing a leaking bathroom fixture.

References

Baccus, Melinda (1976) 'Sociological Indication and the Visibility Criterion of Real World Social Theorizing', Department of Sociology, UCLA. Appears in Garfinkel (1982c).

Baccus, Melinda (1981) 'Multipiece Truck Wheel Accidents and their Regulation', unpublished paper, Department of Sociology, UCLA.

Bellman, Beryl L. (1981) 'The Language of Secrecy', unpublished monograph, Department of Sociology, University of California, San Diego.

Burns, Stacy (1978a) 'A Comparison of Geertzian and Ethnomethodological Methods for the Analysis of the Production of Member-Relevant Objects', in Garfinkel (1982c).

Burns, Stacy (1978b) 'A Comparison of March-Olson and Ethnomethodology on the 'Circumstantial' Analysis of Decision-Making Work', in Garfinkel (1982c).

Burns, Stacy (1978c) 'The Lived-Orderliness of Lecturing', unpublished paper, Department of Sociology, UCLA.

Burns, Stacy (1981) 'Becoming a Lawyer at Yale Law School', unpublished paper, Yale Law School, New Haven.

Carr, David (1974) *Phenomenology and the Problem of History*, Evanston: Northwestern University Press.

Derrida, Jacques (1978) *Edmund Husserl's Origin of Geometry: An Introduction*, Stony Brook: Nicholas Hays.

Eager, R. and Eager, P. (1966) 'Glial Responses to Degenerating Cerebeller Cortico-Nuclear Pathways in the Cat', *Science*, 153 (29) (January).

Eglin, Trent (1974) 'Introduction to a Hermeneutics of the Occult: Alchemy', in E. Tiryakian (ed.), *On the Margin of the Visible: Sociology, the Esoteric, and the Occult*, New York: Wiley.

Fauman, Richard (1980) 'Filmmakers' Work: On the Production and Analysis of Audio-Visual Documents for the Social Sciences', Department of Sociology, UCLA. Appears in Garfinkel (1982b).

Feyerabend, Paul (1975) *Against Method*, London: New Left Books.

Garfinkel, Harold (1967) *Studies in Ethnomethodology*, Englewood Cliffs: Prentice-Hall.

Garfinkel, Harold (1982a) *A Manual for the Study of Naturally Organized Ordinary Activities*, 3 volumes including vol. I *Introduction for Novices*, London: Routledge and Kegan Paul.

Garfinkel, Harold (ed.) (1982b) *Ethnomethodological Studies of Work in the Discovering Sciences*, vol. II in Garfinkel (1982a).

Garfinkel, Harold (ed.) (1982c) *Ethnomethodological Studies of Work*, vol. III in Garfinkel (1982a).

Garfinkel, Harold (1982d) 'Recurrent Themes in Ethnomethodological Studies of Work', introduction to Garfinkel (1982b).

Garfinkel, Harold, Lynch, Michael and Livingston, Eric (1981) 'The Work of a Discovering Science Construed with Materials from the Optically Discovered Pulsar', *Philosophy of the Social Sciences*, 11 (2): 131–58.

Garfinkel, Harold and Burns, Stacy (1979) 'Lecturing's Work of Talking Introductory Sociology', Department of Sociology, UCLA. Appears in Garfinkel (1982c).

Gilbert, G. Nigel (1976) 'The Transformation of Research Findings into Scientific Knowledge', *Social Studies of Science*, 6: 281–306.

Gurwitsch, Aron (1964) *The Field of Consciousness*, Pittsburgh: Duquesne University Press.

Gusfield, Joseph (1976) 'The Literary Rhetoric of Science: Comedy and Pathos in Drinking Driver Research,' *American Sociological Review*, 41 (February): 16–34.

Heidegger, Martin (1962) *Being and Time* (trans. John Macquarrie and Edward Robinson), New York: Harper and Row.

Heidegger, Martin (1967) *What is a Thing?* Chicago: Henry Regnery.

Holton, Gerald (1975) 'On the Role of the Themata in Scientific Thought', *Science*, 188: 328–34.

Holton, Gerald (1978) *The Scientific Imagination: Case Studies*, Cambridge: Cambridge University Press.

Husserl, Edmund (1970) *The Crisis of European Sciences and Transcendental Phenomenology* (trans. David Carr), Evanston: Northwestern University Press.

Knorr, Karin and Knorr, Dietrich (1978) 'From Scenes to Scripts: On the Relationship Between Laboratory Research and Published Paper in Science', *Research Memorandum*, 132, Institute for Advanced Studies, Vienna, Austria.

Knorr-Cetina, Karin (1981) *The Manufacture of Knowledge*, Oxford: Pergamon Press.

Koffka, Kurt (1935) *Principles of Gestalt Psychology*, New York: Harcourt Brace.

Kohler, Wolfgang (1929) *Gestalt Psychology*, New York: Liveright.

Kuhn, Thomas (1970) *The Structure of Scientific Revolutions*, second enlarged edition, Chicago: University of Chicago Press.

LaCoe, Daniel (1977) 'Do it Yourself Work Around the House', unpublished paper, Department of Sociology, UCLA.

Latour, Bruno, and Woolgar, Steve (1979) *Laboratory Life: The Social Construction of Scientific Facts*, London and Beverly Hills: Sage.

Law, John (1982) 'Putting Facts Together: A Study of Scientific Persuasion', *Social Studies of Science*, 12 (4): 535–58.

Liberman, Kenneth (1980) 'Understanding Interaction in Central Australia: An Ethnomethodological Study of Australian Aboriginal People', doctoral dissertation, Department of Sociology, University of California, San Diego.

Liberman, Kenneth (1982) 'The Economy of Central Australian Aboriginal Expression: An Inspection from the Vantage of Merleau-Ponty and Derrida,' *Semiotica*, in press.

Livingston, Eric (1976) 'An Ethnomethodological Approach to the Study of the Arts', Department of Sociology, UCLA. Appears in Garfinkel (1982c).

Livingston, Eric (1978) 'Mathematicians' Work', paper presented in the session on Ethnomethodology: Studies of Work, Ninth World Congress of Sociology, Uppsala, Sweden. Appears in Garfinkel (1982b).

Livingston, Eric (1982) 'An Ethnomethodological Investigation of the Foundations of Mathematics', doctoral dissertation, Department of Sociology, UCLA (in preparation).

Lynch, Michael (1979) 'Art and Artifact in Laboratory Science: A Study of Shop Work and Shop Talk in a Research Laboratory', doctoral dissertation, School of Social Sciences, University of California, Irvine.

Lynch, Michael (1982a) *Art and Artefacts in Laboratory Science*, London: Routledge and Kegan Paul.

Lynch, Michael (1982b) 'Technical Work and Critical Inquiry: Investigations in a Scientific Laboratory', *Social Studies of Science*, 12 (4): 499–534.

McKegney, Doug (1981) 'Temporal Change and the Formalization Spiral in Scientific Inquiry', paper presented at the conference on Communication in Scientific Research, Simon Fraser University, 1–2 September.

Medawar, Peter (1969) *Induction and Intuition in Scientific Thought*, Philadelphia: American Philosophical Society.

Merleau-Ponty, Maurice (1962) *Phenomenology of Perception* (trans. Colin Smith), New York: Humanities Press.

Merleau-Ponty, Maurice (1968) *The Visible and the Invisible* (trans. Alphonso Lingis), Evanston: Northwestern University Press.

Morrison, Kenneth (1976) 'Readers' Work: Devices for Achieving Pedagogic Events in Textual Materials for Readers as Novices to Sociology', doctoral dissertation, Department of Sociology, York University, Toronto.

Morrison, Kenneth (1980) 'Some Researchable Recurrences in Science and Social Science Inquiry', York University, Toronto. Appears in Garfinkel (1982b).

Morrison, Kenneth (1981) 'Some Properties of "Telling Order Designs" in Didactic Inquiry', *Philosophy of the Social Sciences*, 11 (2): 245–62.

Mulkay, Michael and Gilbert, G. Nigel (1982) 'Accounting for Error: How Scientists Construct their Social World when they Account for Correct or Incorrect Belief', *Sociology*, 16: 165–83.

Pack, Christopher (1975a) 'Features of Signs Encountered in Designing a Notional System for Transcribing Lectures', Department of Sociology, UCLA. Appears in Garfinkel (1982c).

Pack, Christopher (1975b) 'Towards a Phenomenology of Transcription', Department of Sociology, UCLA. Appears in Garfinkel (1982c).

Peters, Alan, Palay, Sanford L. and Webster, Henry De F. (1970) *The Fine Structure of the Nervous System*, New York: Harper and Row.

Pollner, Melvin (1970) 'Notes on Self-Explicating Settings', Department of Sociology, UCLA. Appears in Garfinkel (1982c).

Psathas, George (ed.) (1979) *Everyday Language: Studies in Ethnomethodology*, New York: Wiley.

Robillard, Albert R. (1980) 'Applied Behavioral Analysis', unpublished paper, Department of Human Development, Michigan State University.

Robillard, Albert R. and Pack, Christopher (1980) 'The Clinical Encounter: The Organization of Doctor-Patient Interaction', unpublished paper, Department of Human Development, Michigan State University.

Robillard, Albert R., White, Geoffry M. and Maretzki, Thomas W. (1981) 'Between Doctor and Patient: Informed Consent in Conversational Interaction', unpublished paper, Department of Psychiatry, University of Hawaii.

Sacks, Harvey (1964–75) 'Unpublished Lectures', UCLA and UC, Irvine.

Sacks, Harvey, Schegloff, Emanuel and Jefferson, Gail (1974) 'A Simplest Systematics for the Organization of Turn-Taking in Conversation', *Language*, 50 (4): 696–735.

Schegloff, Emanuel (1968) 'Sequencing in Conversational Openings', *American Anthropologist*, 70: 1075–95.

Schenkein, Jim (ed.) (1978) *Studies in the Organization of Conversational Interaction*, New York: Academic Press.

Schrag, Calvin (1980) *Radical Reflection and the Origin of the Human Sciences*, West Lafayette, Ind.: Purdue University Press.

Schrecker, Friedrich (1980) 'Doing a Chemical Experiment: The Practices of Chemistry Students in a Student Laboratory in Quantitative Analysis', Department of Sociology, UCLA. Appears in Garfinkel (1982b).

Senior, James K. (1958) 'The Vernacular of the Laboratory', *Philosophy of Science*, 25 (2): 163–8.

Sudnow, David (1978) *Ways of the Hand*, Cambridge, Mass.: Harvard University Press.

Sudnow, David (1980) *Between Two Keyboards*, New York: Alfred Knopf.

Traweek, Sharon (1981) 'Culture and the Organization of the Particle Physics Communities in Japan and the United States', paper presented at the conference on Communications in Scientific Research, Simon Fraser University, 1–2 September.

Wieder, D. Lawrence (1980) 'Behavioristic Operationalism and the Life-World: Chimpanzees and the Chimpanzee Researchers in Face-to-Face Interaction', *Sociological Inquiry*, 50 (3/4): 75–103.

Woolgar, Steve (1976) 'Writing an Intellectual History of Scientific Development: The Use of Discovery Accounts', *Social Studies of Science*, 6: 395–422.

Zenzen, Michael and Restivo, Sal (1980) 'The Mysterious Morphology of Immiscible Liquids: A Study of Scientific Practice', *Social Science Information*, 21 (3): 447–73.

9

Irony in the Social Study of Science

Steve Woolgar
Brunel University, UK

> Woe to him who cannot tolerate the fact that irony seeks to balance the accounts. (Kierkegaard, 1965: 340)

Introduction

Numerous recent case studies of a range of aspects of science have taken their cue from the realization that the social study of science need not be inhibited by traditional conceptions of scientific method. In particular, the detailed content of science is now said to be amenable to social study. In realization of this, a large proportion of the 'new style' social studies of science have espoused an analytical perspective which falls under the general rubric of a relativist, constructivist approach (see Knorr-Cetina, this volume). Considerable advances have been achieved by this perspective, especially when compared to the legacy of an earlier epoch. But now that it has been demonstrated that the constructivist perspective can indeed be applied to science, it is time to ask 'What Next?' It is perhaps especially timely to ask whether social studies of science are now in danger of becoming bogged down by constructivism. Will the repeated application of the constructivist formula prevent us from yielding the full potential of our acquaintance with the details of scientific practice?

This chapter presumes the need for an assessment of future developments in the social study of science. As a first step in that direction, the argument below aims to illuminate some of the basic assumptions and strategies of the present constructivist perspective. In particular, a preliminary attempt is made to understand the character of sociological irony and its importance in sustaining the constructivist position. Although the use of irony is a widely noted feature of sociology in general, its pervasion of the constructivist social study of science has gone unexamined. This is particularly remarkable since ironies done with respect to science have a special poignancy; it is these ironies which enable the constructivist sociologist to advance knowledge claims about knowledge claims.

The chapter begins by articulating a key general problem of methodology and by suggesting that analytical perspectives in the social study of science can be usefully understood as differential responses to this problem. By making comparisons with substantive areas other than science, the use of irony is considered as the particular response of the constructivist perspective. Finally, we address the possibility that a change in our conception of irony might radically reshape our thinking and lead to an alternative perspective on the study of science.

The Problem

Much of the argument below comprises an examination of the response by recent social studies of science to a problem which refuses to go away. The problem can be generally formulated in terms of methodological adequacy: what grounds provide the warrant for the relationship between the objects of study and statements made about those objects? In principle, this problem is equally applicable to the work of social science and natural science. For example, in the work of a solid state physicist it might appear as a concern for the correspondence between the inscription of a pen chart recorder and the current state of atomic alignment in a sample of metal alloy. For the sociologist, the problem is classically associated with the relationship between a chosen social indicator and the corresponding social reality. Among historians, we can identify a concern for what about a historical situation is revealed by particular items of documentary evidence.

A vast number of similar examples could be given, suggesting that the problem pervades every aspect of research practice. It is a problem which 'refuses to go away' in the sense that although it can be 'dealt with' or 'managed' on any specific occasion, the general form of the difficulty remains and threatens to re-emerge at each next instance of interpretation. The problem is a general and irresolvable problem of epistemology, which requires artful management whenever it makes its appearance, lest it entirely disrupt research practice. One management strategy is to transform the problem into a merely technical difficulty. For example, the problematic relationship between the shape of the trace and changes in atomic alignment are attended to in terms of those factors (the speed of the trace, the setting of the gain amplifier, the polarity of the electrical connections and so on) which might have biased the pen recording. The basic assumption here is that the removal of such factors will eventually (if only after much effort) restore the rightful connection between trace and atomic alignment. But the general form of the Problem still lurks: on what grounds can we establish a connection between any of these 'biasing' factors and the behaviour of the trace? In practice, such considerations are usually relegated to the background by attaching primary significance to practical resolution of the initial difficulty. Thus, the Problem does make its presence known, but it is managed by transforming it into a resolvable and limited matter of technical adequacy. Sometimes this way of managing the Problem is accompanied by statements to the effect that preoccupation with such technical matters is an over-indulgence which detracts from the research goals at hand. A second management strategy entirely denies the relevance of the Problem for the practical matters at hand. For example, the Problem is perceived as a concern for epistemological questions which should remain within the confines of philosophical discussion. On these occasions, practitioners flatly refuse to accept any link between the Problem and their immediate concerns.

The Problem 'refuses to go away' by virtue of its curiously ambivalent relation with research practice. The difficulty of ever establishing *ultimate* grounds for proposed interpretations and explanations is generally acknowledged, and yet research practitioners continue to do interpretation and explanation. Students who are new to sociology quickly spot this same difficulty, and yet they are taught that sociology is a discipline which proceeds 'in spite of known problems' (Atkinson, 1981: 203). The acquisition of craft skills is a widely recognized feature of apprenticeships in professional research. At one level, we should perhaps recognize that the acquisition of craft skills also involves learning how to manage a problem which is irresolvable.

In the social study of science the ambivalent relation of the Problem to research practice is particularly marked. This is because the many recent contributions to the social study of science espouse a perspective of sociological constructivism and epistemological relativism. This either implicitly or explicitly makes problematic the warrant claimed by natural scientists for the relationship between scientific statements and the objects of scientific study; in other words, the Problem, as outlined above, is invoked with respect to the work of science. At the same time, as we shall see below, the relevance of the Problem for the work of the social study of science is either denied or transformed. This kind of social study of science thus flirts with relativism by playing up its relevance for scientific work and yet repressing it in the course of its own constructivist explanation. In the next section we examine in detail how this is achieved.

Playing with relativism

The generality of the Problem can be appreciated by expressing it in terms taken from early work in ethnomethodology (Garfinkel, 1967: ch. 3). Every act of interpretation and explanation can be cast in terms of a perceived relationship between 'surface documents' and associated 'underlying realities'. The term 'document' refers to any of a wide range of entities: words, utterances, conversational extracts, signs, gestures, objects, events and so on. The document is, in short, whatever is taken as the surface appearance of an entity. The term 'underlying reality' can similarly refer to a wide range of entities which might be taken to, for example, 'lie behind' the surface document. Examples of such underlying realities are the meaning of the words, what the object actually is, what the action really consisted of, the motives, intentions, desires, interests of actors and so on. In each case, the underlying reality is the actual character of the thing whose appearance is made available in the surface document.

In ethnomethodology, and in particular in Garfinkel's early writings, a prime focus for analysis is members' use of the documentary method whereby they effect connections between surface documents and under-lying realities. The paradox on which ethnomethodology is based is that members routinely treat such connections as good enough for the practical purposes at hand, even though in principle there are a series of severely damaging methodological and epistemological arguments which undermine the possibility of ever making such connections. The Problem can thus be understood in terms of the relationship between surface statements (which for convenience I shall refer to as 'accounts') and objects in the world; how is it that researchers deal in practice with what at an epistemological level is an irresolvable difficulty?

Let me distinguish between three positions on the relation between accounts and objects and events in the real world[1] (see Figure 1). The first position on accounts stems from the notion that (at least some)

FIGURE 1
Three positions on the relationship between accounts and reality

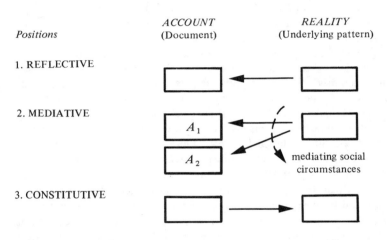

Positions	*ACCOUNT* (Document)	*REALITY* (Underlying pattern)
1. REFLECTIVE		
2. MEDIATIVE	A_1 / A_2	mediating social circumstances
3. CONSTITUTIVE		

real-world entities enjoy an existence independent of their description; in this view, what a thing is is somehow different from, and resides outside of, its description. In this view the description of an item becomes an ancillary to the reality of the item itself. In other words, the account is an appendage, a more or less accurate attempt to capture, report upon or otherwise re-present the thing itself. Whatever is said tends to be said *about* a thing, the implication being that the entity itself will continue to retain its essential character regardless of individuals' attempts to describe or characterize it.

We can call this first position the *reflective* view of accounts. The accounts produced are taken as a direct reflection of the character of the thing being described. Overwhelmingly, this position is the rhetorical butt of nearly all social studies of science. It is, for example, referred to as the passive, contemplative apprehension of reality (Barnes, 1977), the window-pane theory of knowledge generation (Gusfield, 1976) and so on. It is most generally characterized as a position which locates the origin of knowledge (accounts) in the character of the natural world.

It is tempting to call this position naïve. Certainly, this seems to be the implication of arguments for the preferred alternative position (the mediative position). And yet it is important to remember that elements of this first position appear in all our attempts to make sense of the world; in other words, we constantly proceed in practice by assuming the reflective mode to be good enough, and our sociological inquiry is no exception to this. We should therefore be cautious in adopting any denigratory tone of reference to the reflective mode.

The second position on accounts can be called the *mediative* position: the idea here is that accounts are not straightforward representations of external realities. The position holds that there is nothing inherent in the character of real-world objects which uniquely determine accounts of those objects. In the case of scientific accounts, theories and descriptions of the world, experimental results and interpretations of phenomena, all are *underdetermined* by the facts of the natural world. This means that nature can give rise to alternative accounts of the world; in Figure 1 at least two accounts, A_1 and A_2, can result from the corresponding reality.[2] Hence, the accounts can be thought of as products of the social, cultural and historical circumstances which *intervene between* reality and the produced account. Consequently, it is argued, a proper understanding of the generation of scientific knowledge can be gained by turning attention to these social circumstances. I use 'social circumstances' here as a generic term; specific variants of 'social circumstances' appear in the social study of science as social factors, contingencies, social and cognitive interests, the prevailing socio-historical context, relationships between participating scientists, the social structure of which they are a part, and so on. The main aspect of this position is that any or all of these social circumstances *mediate* in the production of knowledge accounts. These accounts are to be understood as actively constructed accounts, rather than passively received reflections of an external world, and they are to be understood in terms of the social circumstances which shape their construction. Hence, it is the mediative position which forms the basis for the *constructivist* social study of science in particular and constructivism in general (see below, p. 248); accounts are to be viewed as the end product of a process of construction.

This second position can be formulated as an argument that scientific knowledge originates in the social world *rather than* the natural world. This way of expressing it enables us to identify some important ambiguities in the second position; specifically, these ambiguities stem from the significance attached to the phrase 'rather than'. To what extent is the social world regarded as a *full* substitute for the natural world in knowledge determination? The evidence is admittedly equivocal, but adherents to the second position tend to hedge their bets on this issue. Notwithstanding calls for a *thoroughgoing* sociological study of the content of science, the recommendation of a strong programme in the sociology of scientific knowledge, the castigation of Mannheim for limiting the scope of the sociology of knowledge and the explicit espousal of a relativist perspective, many practitioners in the social study of science make statements suggesting a wish to retain some role for the independent existence of objects in the real world. Thus, in some places, it is said that accounts are products *both* of reality *and* of prevalent social circumstances (Barnes, 1974). This also seems to be the implication of the statement that 'there is...nothing in the physical world which uniquely determines the conclusions of [the scientific] community. *It is of course self-evident that the external world exerts constraints on the conclusions of science*' (Mulkay, 1979: 61, my italics). Consider also the conclusion of a recent piece 'that empirical facts *by themselves* do not determine the fate of knowledge claims' (Harvey, 1981: 95, my italics). Even where practitioners of the social study of science allude to the possibility that the external world has *nothing* to do with scientific knowledge, this is tempered by its juxtaposition with the more reasonable line. For example: 'the natural world has a *small or non-existent* role in the construction of scientific knowledge' (Collins, 1981a: 3, my italics). We might speculate that such statements and the ambivalence which they embody are more an indication of the programmatic purposes of their authors than a reflection of a coherent epistemological position. These statements are occasioned pronouncements, post hoc reconstructions of practice, the ambivalence of which can be read as differences in emphasis. Not surprisingly, such perceived differences in emphasis have formed the basis for some minor disputes between adherents to the second position (e.g. Barnes, 1974; Collins and Cox, 1976; Law, 1977; Collins and Cox, 1977).

Both reflective and mediative positions contrast with a third position, that accounts are *constitutive* of reality. In this view there is no a priori distinction between accounts and reality; it is not that accounts reflect reality, nor that they are the mediated products of actors' attempts to characterize an actual reality while under the influence (so to speak) of their social milieu. Instead, the accounts *are* the reality; there is no reality beyond the constructs we imply when we talk of 'reality' (Garfinkel, 1952: 351). The important difference of this third position is that there is no commitment, implicit or otherwise, to the independent existence of any reality. As denoted by the direction of the lowest arrow in Figure 1 (Constitutive Position), the reality is created in virtue of the accounting done by actors. This position rarely appears in programmatic pronouncements in the social study of science; when it does, it is perceived as absurd. This is of course a reflection of the fact that we live our lives in a non-absurd ('realistic') way. We presume a reality independent of our accounting procedures, even though it is not possible to demonstrate this independence; each of our attempts to 'tell' reality inevitably involves the use of accounting procedures.

It is precisely this which makes so dramatic the study of scientific discovery. While the constitutive position denies a reality independent of the accounts produced, the act of discovery is commonly regarded as an occasion when an independently existing reality (or aspect of reality) is revealed for what it has always been. The splitting and inversion model of the discovery process (Latour and Woolgar, 1979: 176ff.) argues that an initial use of accounting procedures to *constitute* a new reality is subsequently regarded as no more than an attempt to report upon or *reflect* what was there all along. In this model, the constitutive position is juxtaposed with the reflective position and the discovery process is characterized as a transformation between the two, in the course of which the direction of the perceived connection between account and underlying reality is reversed (see Figure 1). A discovery can also be thought of as a move which has successfully negotiated the second mediative position. The metaphor of discovery, that which uncovers, can be understood as a reference to the *removal* of those interceding factors which adherents to the mediative position wish to reintroduce into descriptions of science. In this view, the removal of various intervening factors (such as lack of technical expertise, social and cognitive biases of practitioners, the absence of the right equipment and so on) enables us to detect (that is, produce an account of) an object and takes us out of our current state of ignorance (wherein we have only null accounts). The reversal of the connection between account and object also entails the removal from the scheme of any constitutive activity on the part of the discoverer. The splitting and inversion model of discovery may be usefully extended to strategies of causal explanation, wherein new causes are 'discovered' (Woolgar, 1981a), and to the practical character of perception and interpretation in general (Woolgar, 1981c).

The important point of this example is that analytical treatment of the discovery process in terms of splitting and inversion depends upon the *juxtaposition* of the three different positions on accounts. It is not so much that the authors explicitly align themselves to any of the positions; instead, the positions are used to characterize the practice of others. In a similar way, the mediative position depends on its characterization of both reflective and constitutive positions and on its declared stance in relation to both. The reflective and constitutive positions appear only very rarely in their pure form in explicit programmatic pronouncements. It is difficult, for example, to imagine a scientist seriously making any general claim for the universally unmediated connection between his findings and the real world, even though on some particular occasion he might want to portray specific achievements in this way.[3] The reflective and constitutive positions are consequently more like 'ideal types' than accurate depictions of research practice; they are resources drawn upon by practitioners to characterize their own and others' activities. It follows that arguments for ways of doing the social study of science depend heavily, if not entirely, on the deployment of these resources. In attempting to understand the basis for the mediative position, it is therefore important to look closely at the way in which positions are ascribed, and at the claimed relationships between positions.

Central to the mediative position is the use of the principle of underdetermination. This takes the form of the assertion that at least two alternative accounts can result from the same fact of nature. Note here that it is not necessary to specify the fact of nature which is being accounted. For example, in the work of Collins and Pinch (Collins, 1975; Collins and Pinch, 1979, 1982) the concentration on scientific controversy provides the sociologist with a set of 'ready-made' alternative accounts; controversy between scientists is portrayed as a struggle between members of different communities to establish one of two interpretations of the same experimental results. Other authors provide for two alternative accounts by contrasting their own account with that already available. For example, Knorr (Knorr and Knorr, 1982; Knorr-Cetina, 1981: ch. 5) contrasts the public and private faces of science by juxtaposing the writings of formal scientific papers with her own description of what occurs in the laboratory.

Establishing a contrast between alternative accounts is a crucial preliminary to constructivist analysis. Once established, this contrast is 'explained' in terms of prevailing social circumstances.[4] Schematically, we can think of these social circumstances as a means of *deflecting* the direction of the connection between an underlying reality and a particular account (see Figure 1). It is due to the influence of social circumstances that account A_2 results instead of account A_1; and it is by virtue of the difference between accounts A_1 and A_2 that the sociologist justifies his investigation of these social circumstances. Clearly then, it is important to look at the way this contrast is achieved. To what extent is the contrast critical of the achievements of science? How far does the mediative position entail an epistemological perspective distinct from that of either reflective or constitutive positions? Under what circumstances could similar contrasts be legitimately established with respect to the constructivist position itself?

Unfortunately, it is characteristic of the mediative position that no consistent answers to any of these questions are possible. Instead, the mediative position maintains a remarkable ambivalence with respect to these and similar issues. In the next section, a look at some features of constructivist sociology in substantive areas other than science shows the importance of irony as a device for maintaining this ambivalence.

Irony

As a figure of speech, irony has enjoyed extensive discussion in literary criticism. Indeed, the range of perspectives brought to bear on the notion of irony and the number of diverse instances subsumed under its rubric, have led to a situation where, as Booth (1974) comments, irony has come to stand for so many different things that we are in danger of losing it all together. In its blandest formulation irony denotes a figure of speech in which the intended meaning is the opposite of that expressed. But it is also clear that irony refers to actions whose consequences or outcomes tend to the opposite of what was anticipated. Given that irony has to do with issues of meaning, intention and the characterization of actions, and given the frequent observation that much of sociology is ironic, it is perhaps surprising that irony has enjoyed relatively little detailed attention in the social sciences (but see Brown, 1977: ch. 5; Gusfield, 1980, 1981: ch. 8). In the specific field of the social study of science, there has only been passing reference to the notion of irony; the one exception being an article by Weinstein (1982) whose discussion of irony concentrates on ways of understanding the unanticipated outcomes of technological innovation.

In what follows I suggest that the mediative position in constructivist social study of science sustains itself by the use of a kind of irony which is recognizable in constructivist sociology in general. It is instructive, therefore, to begin by examining the operation of this kind of irony in areas other than the social study of science.

To do irony is to say of something that appears one way, that it is in fact something other than it appears. In terms of the earlier schema, to ironicize an account produced by an actor is to say that his account is not an accurate account of reality; although the underlying reality appears as account A_1, the ironicist would wish to argue that the reality is in fact better accounted for by A_2.

It is helpful to begin with a relatively straightforward example: the case of official statistics. This arose when sociological studies of suicide took issue with the relationship between the number of suicides recorded and the actual number of suicides (see especially Douglas, 1967). One major argument was that it is inappropriate to rely upon statistics generated for purposes quite different than those of the sociologist. The official institutions and agencies responsible for compiling statistics would, it was argued, have arrived at different accounts (numbers) of the same reality (suicides) but for the particular social circumstances in which their production was done. Now this observation could be understood as an accusation of bias, or at least, the highlighting of a source of technical error whereby the accuracy of official statistics might have been improved once one was more aware of the affect of various social factors on their compilation. This indeed seems to be how some sociologists responded (e.g. Hindess, 1973). On the whole, however, sociologists were not content to let the irony go at that; the assertion that the official statistics could have turned out differently was used as the justification for an investigation of the factors that supposedly affect the end result. Thus, the argument of the ironicist is that official statistics tell you more about the social circumstances of the constructing agency than about the extent of the phenomena they purport to measure: official statistics are to be treated as constructed rather than as reflecting the actual state of affairs. This opens the way for an investigation of the scenes which gave rise to the statistics.

Note here the recurrence of the phrase 'rather than', indicating the same ambivalence with respect to the underlying reality as in the case of scientific accounts. To say that official statistics tell you *more about* the social circumstances of their construction than about the phenomenon they claim to measure, is to imply a minimal, residual, but none the less finite, role for reality. In this view, the actual number of suicides do have *some* influence on the statistics. In other formulations, the irony leads to a complete absence of reality in the determination of the constructed account. For example, to say that official statistics tell

you about the circumstances of their production *but not* about the
reality they purport to describe, leans more towards the constitutive
view of accounts (the third position above) and away from any commitment to an independently existing objective reality (the actual number
of suicides).

Of course, suicide statistics are just one of a large family of official
statistics (birth rates, death rates, numbers of unemployed, crime rates,
divorce rates and so on) to which the same kind of irony has been
employed. Much more generally, these issues arise in many substantive
areas in recent sociology. In the sociology of deviance, for example, the
categorization of individuals as deviant is ironicized by invoking the
possibility of their categorization in entirely different ways. The
possibility of alternative categorizations leads to the claim that categorization cannot arise solely (or, at all) from the actual character of the
deviant. Much sociological study of deviance uses this as the basis for
postulating a range of interceding factors (social circumstances) which
give rise to the deviant categorization. In some discussions of social
problems the same analytical perspective proceeds by ironicizing the
definition of a social problem: for example, the definition of homosexuality as an abnormal sex relation is taken as a reflection of the
categorization system in use rather than of the actual character of
homosexuality (Spector and Kitsuse, 1977); alcoholism is said to be
the end result of a series of social definitions rather than a reflection of
the actual nature of certain social behaviour (Gusfield, 1981); and it is
claimed that child abuse has only been 'discovered' by virtue of the
concerted efforts of a small section of the medical profession (Pfohl,
1977); and so on. Sociological studies of the media have taken issue
with the production of news in much the same terms (e.g. Cohen and
Young, 1973; Glasgow Media Group, 1977; Fishman, 1978). The news
is ironicized in order to argue that its content arises by virtue of a
complex of various social and organizational factors rather than as a
reflection of what actually happened.

This kind of irony is widespread in constructivist sociology, providing the sociologist with analytical purchase in the discussion of a range
of different substantive areas. To the extent that recent perspectives in
the social study of science depend on the same kind of irony, we can
see they are merely following an established analytical tradition.

Let us look more closely at the component moves of constructivist
irony. A first, preliminary move is the selection of an account to be
ironicized. This is clearly important because the selection has to be
seen to be relevant to the sociologist's general topic. If, for example,

it is to be a contribution to the sociology of science, the selection must at least entail the implicit claim that the account is relevant to the way science operates or the way the scientist sees his world. In the use of a scientist's interview responses, for example, the minimal claim of the ironicist is that these specific materials bear some relation to the scientist's behaviour *qua* scientist. A second move is to assert that accounts quite different to the first are possible. Given the appearance, the number of divorces recorded, the account of his work produced by a scientist, the description of the scientific method advocated by a philosopher, the categorization of the deviant resulting from police procedures, the sociologist claims that each can be supplanted by another version. There are various ways of achieving this assertion of alternatives. Commonly, there is appeal to general principles of cultural and historical relativism; since the perception of realities varies between cultures or over time, it is argued that the present account, the subject of immediate attention, is equally amenable to variation. As already noted, the sociological study of controversy often uses ready-made alternative accounts. Opposing sides to a scientific dispute themselves provide the alternatives; the sociologist does irony merely by pointing to the discrepant versions of participants.

The third move is crucial to sociological irony. The accounts are not only supposed to be different, they are taken as alternative versions of the *same* reality. This is important in the sense that it would clearly be vacuous to argue for the juxtaposition of accounts which avowedly described or arose from distinct realities. The sociologist thus has to base his irony on the assumption that the production of accounts relates to the same reality. In addition, he must assume that this reality remains unchanged between the advocacy of separate accounts, and that advocates of different accounts are assumed to be talking about the same thing. A clear example of these assumptions occurs in a recent influential text on social problems (Spector and Kitsuse, 1977). The authors note that during the 1930s the official definition of marijuana (account A_1) included the notion that it was both dangerous and addictive. During the 1960s, however, marijuana was removed from the addiction classification (account A_2). The irony is then completed and made to speak to the presence of a range of investigable sociological factors:

there is nothing in the nature of marijuana itself to explain this definitional change. *The nature of marijuana remained constant throughout the interval* and, therefore, an explanation of the variation must come from another source. In fact, it's 'nature' cannot adequately explain either the definition of marijuana as an addictive or nonaddictive substance. The explanation of the definition must be sought in the conceptions held by various groups, the notion of addiction they applied, the type of evidence they used to support their views, the political strategies and tactics they used to gain acceptance of their definitions, and the support given to them by governmental agencies for institutionalising those definitions. (Spector and Kitsuse, 1977: 43, my italics)

Here then is an unusually explicit example of a recurrent refrain in the social study of science: there is nothing in nature itself which gives rise to accounts of nature because the unchanging character of nature gives rise to discrepant accounts. This example makes clear that the proclaimed relativism of the ironicist conceals a profound commitment to epistemological realism. Beneath the differences in accounts there *is* an (actual) unchanging reality trying to get out. More generally, of course, this same point applies to all instances where cultural or historical relativism are invoked. Alleged variations in interpretation between cultures or across historical situations are premised on the notion that these are interpretations of the same (unchanging) thing. The apparent relativism of social studies of reality disjuncture belies their practical commitment to realism.

The least subtle sociological ironies are content to equate the presumed actual character of the underlying reality with their own account. In these cases ironic contrast occurs between what some actors (are alleged to) construct and what the sociologist 'shows' to be the case. Examples of these least subtle perspectives are found in the general call of several introductory sociology texts to show that things are really other than is thought by the layman. The sociologist's account is advocated as a preferred version to that of everyday life because it entails an investigation of the social factors which give rise to the erroneous version. In the sociology of science, this least subtle tendency is manifested in attempts to contrast what scientists say with what they (actually) do; what scientists write about their work with what (actually) goes on in the laboratory and so on. In each case, the tell-tale sign is the appearance (in my formulation) of the word 'actually'.

Troubles

Taken individually, the moves of the ironicist pose some awkward questions. In the first place, it is not clear how the ironicist would wish to substantiate the relevance of the particular account he selects for ironic treatment. To what extent are we entitled to take the scientist's account as a pertinent reflection of the way he sees the world? Or, to put it slightly differently, what is the point of taking issue with, for example, interview responses or scientific papers or memoirs? If we take seriously the notion that each is an occasioned account, then it is clearly no news to argue that alternative accounts are possible. It appears that for the irony to have any force, the ironicist must assume a relevant connection between the particular documents he ironicizes (say, scientists' interview responses) and the reality he wishes to speak about (what scientists 'actually' do). The assumption of this connection here entails the ironicist's implicit use of the reflective position as a prerequisite to his espousal of the mediative position. Secondly, the assertion that different accounts are possible presupposes the ascendancy of the analyst's criterion of difference. To what extent must the difference between accounts claimed by the analyst coincide with the scientists' own views? In the absence of any clear correspondence between analyst's and scientist's perception of similarity and difference, it is quite possible that the analyst finds a difference where the scientist sees none.[5] Thirdly, even assuming we allow the possibility of an 'actual' difference between accounts, what are the grounds for assuming these relate to the same reality? What, in the example cited above, entitles Spector and Kitsuse to assume that the nature of marijuana is fixed? This kind of assumption stands curiously at odds with the appeal to the constitutive position that social problems are the way they are defined, or in earlier terms, the notion that realities are entirely equivalent to the way they are accounted.

We could ask on what grounds the ironicist assumes his alternative account (A_2) to be better than the account (A_1) he is ironicizing; to what extent is the mediative position critical of the reflective position? In many cases the ironicist steers clear of explicit claims about the superiority of the alternative account. But the mere fact that he points to the possibility of another account can be taken to suggest that there is something inadequate about the original. The humble sociologist may claim that he is merely outlining another way of looking at the same reality, and that he intends no discredit to the original account. Thus, with respect to the mediative position in general, there have been a number of declarations of neutrality. For example, Bloor's (1976) call for a strong programme in the sociology of scientific knowledge explicitly avows impartiality with respect to the truth of the knowledge claims to be analyzed. But such declarations were clearly disingenuous. For the analyst's proposition will be read for its purpose and function rather than as 'just another', 'neutral' description of the same reality. Notwithstanding the declared intentions of the sociologist, the proferred alternative account will be heard as a comment on the adequacy of the original account. This is well illustrated by Gusfield (1981: ch. 8), who reports that his constructivist analysis of the definition of the drinking-driving problem was interpreted by some as a denial of the experiential reality of alcohol problems, alcohol addiction and drinking-driving. He indicates that this has to do with the fact that his ironic stance 'carries with it a tone of skeptical disbelief in the "reality" of the problem' (Gusfield, 1981: 189), but suggests that this is necessary to the development of alternative views on the problem. Gusfield is clear that his irony is motivated by a political interest in making more alternative views of the same situation available. One might better understand the ironicizing of science if it was frequently accompanied by similar explicit statements of political intent to demystify; instead, much ironicizing of science is frequently accompanied by statements of respect for its achievements and declarations of impartiality.

The question of whether or not constructivist irony is critical of extant accounts is closely linked to whether or not the ironical perspective can be applied to itself. If in principle alternative accounts can arise from the scientist's confrontation with the object of his inquiry, does it follow that alternative accounts are equally available as a result of the sociologist's work? The question is important because if the answer is 'yes' we are faced with the problem of not knowing how to evaluate the sociologist's account; it would, after all, be only one of a number of alternatives. If constructivist irony is not to be limited to instances of scientific practice, the sociologist's own account can equally well be ironicized. That is, we could 'highlight' or 'discover' that the sociologist's account is not as straightforward as it seems, that it results from a process of social construction guided by the author's social and cognitive interests, in circumstances reflecting the author's place in a social hierarchy, with a view to certain political ends and so on.

It is generally recognized that if constructivist irony is critical, *and* it can be turned back on itself, then we are in a situation of infinite regress; the sociologist's own account stands in danger of being undermined as soon as he ironicizes any other account. The proponents of the mediative position respond to this possibility in a variety of ways. Authors like Bloor (1976) acknowledge and even encourage the possibility that constructivist irony can be turned back on itself (the 'reflexivity' tenet), but seek to avoid the infinite regress by declarations that irony is not intended as critical (the 'impartiality' tenet). As I have argued above, the latter declaration is a programmatic stance which fails to take notice of the ways in which irony is heard in practice. Gusfield, on the other hand, acknowledges the critical character of irony, as evidenced by its reception in practice, but heads off the possibility that it applies to his own work by suggesting he occupies an epistemologically privileged position: 'The ironicist sets himself above his subjects by claiming a higher level of insight and awareness' (Gusfield, 1981: 190). Other authors claim that it simply does not follow that the reflexive and critical character of constructivist irony undermines the sociologist's own work (see e.g. Collins and Cox, 1976).

The ironicist exploits both the claimed difference between accounts and the ironic edge which places him 'above' and 'beyond' the account to be explained. But in order to specify ('show') the character of the mediating social circumstances, the constructivist falls back to the reflective position. In constructivist analysis, evidence is advanced as an indicator of prevailing social circumstances. For example, the biographies, diaries and letters of a particular scientist are said to 'reveal' his social and cognitive interests. In other words, such accounts are said to arise as a result of underlying interests. Clearly, the constructivist's adoption of the reflective mode in the course of his own explanatory practice is itself amenable to irony; we could point out that the constructivist's own account is but one of several alternatives, and that one needs to appreciate the prevailing social circumstances (his implicit political aims in 'knocking' the achievements of science; his position in an academic hierarchy and so on) which lead him to his particular analysis.

The fact that in practice the ironicist does not address these kinds of questions to his own accounts, even though he casts considerable doubt on those of his subjects, is symptomatic of a deep tension in the constructivist perspective. In claiming to show that things are other than they appear (are defined, are accounted for), the ironicist has to strike a delicate balance between the constitutive and reflective positions.

The ironicist struggles for balance on a particularly greasy pole. If he moves too far in one direction, he could slide disastrously towards total relativism, at which point his colleagues might say that he had fallen from the pole altogether. But rhetorically he needs at least occasionally to outstretch an arm in that direction. His solution at these times is to increase the grip of his other arm, anchoring himself more firmly than ever in the reflective end of the pole. At the same time, he cannot afford to be seen to be espousing the reflective line too closely. Consequently, there are moments when he distances himself from the pitfalls of 'naïve positivism' by releasing his hold just long enough to wag an admonishing finger at the philosophy of science. But the acute observer will see that while doing this, the ironicist's other arm is hanging on to relativism for dear life! The art of successful irony is to change arms in such a way that the ironicist appears secure. But whereas to the casual observer, the ironicist may never appear in danger of slipping, practitioners themselves sometimes like to characterize each other in terms of their relative positions on the pole. Thus one can draw attention to any one of the latest arm movements as evidence of imminent slippage. Such portrayals of distance from either end of the pole are displays of where practitioners differentially decide to stop doubting (Blum, 1971).

In his impressive appraisal of labelling theory, Pollner (1974) shows that Becker's (1963) notion of labelling depends upon two quite distinct versions of the relationship between the *designated* character of deviant action and the actual character of that action. The first version presumes absolutist proclivities on the part of the common-sense actor; the second version advances a relativistic model whereby the properties of the act are seemingly created by community response. In the first version the deviance of the act is treated as existing independently of a community's response; in the second version, deviance is created and sustained by a community's response to an act as deviant. These two versions correspond respectively to what I have called the reflective and constitutive positions on accounts. As Pollner shows, these two positions represent distinctive epistemological models and 'indiscriminate intercourse between the two spawns an internally contradictory theoretical formulation' (Pollner, 1974: 33). The ironicist's task is to manage the tension arising from adopting a position which includes elements of both reflective and constitutive positions.

As has been noted by Anderson and Sharrock (1982) this tension is manifested in other ways. The ironic stance of constructivist sociology entails an implicit accusation of error or blindness on the part of those who (only) operate in the reflective mode. Such an accusation stands uneasily in relation to sociology's tendency towards anti-elitist humanism; what, for example, are the hierarchical implications of the idea that the sociologist knows best (Anderson and Sharrock, 1982: 6)? Similarly, there are awkwardnesses associated with the ironicist's claim to attach paramount importance to the way the world is seen by the subject, while simultaneously claiming the world to be different by virtue of the sociologist's stance 'outside' or 'above' the experience of the subject. This particular tension is sometimes addressed by the declaration that although the sociologist's account of science should *begin with* an appreciation of actors' perspectives, it should ultimately take the form of a deterministic explanation involving interests and other factors which are not part of the actors' first-hand experience.

That the balance of the ironicist is delicate is evidenced by the observation that even a small shift in position can engender strong reactions. For example, displays of position which advocate a more relativistic approach than before are typically characterized in one of two ways, each representing an attempt to force the protagonist to an unacceptable position. On the one hand, it is said of any call for increased relativism that its consequences are absurd because they lead to nihilism and/or subjective anarchy. On the other hand, the same call for increased relativism can be characterized as no more than a technical criticism. Thus, the invocation of relativism with respect to sociological work can be understood as a comment on the adequacy of the sociologist's operation of the reflective mode; the call for a relativistic approach is thus heard as advice to look further and more carefully at factors which might be biasing the research process. In this way, various strategies of characterization make out any attempt at movement as either absurd in its radical implications, or merely helpful in its conservative interpretation. A good recent example is the response by social studies of science to the arguments of ethnomethodology. One can subject the writings of Garfinkel (1967) to either a reformist or radical characterization (Woolgar, 1981b). The former enables the sociologist to interpret ethnomethodology as an injunction to greater methodological caution, while the latter is perceived as having absurd consequences. By concentrating primarily on the reformist characterization one can 'make ethnomethodology safe'. Once defused, ethnomethodology can be enrolled for purposes of ironicizing the practices of scientists. This kind of de-radicalization of any proposed shift along the continuum between reflective and constitutive modes speaks to the substantial tension of ironic balance.

Irony as instrument and irony as project[6]

I have described the form of irony characteristic both of constructivist sociology in general and of recent social studies of science. It is a form of irony which facilitates a delicate balancing act by those who wish to flirt with a relativist epistemology. However, this is just one of many different kinds of irony (Frye, 1957; Kierkegaard, 1965; Booth, 1974; Brown, 1977). In this final section, I briefly consider the prospects for substituting another kind of irony for that employed by the constructivist social study of science.

The irony I have discussed can be termed *instrumental* irony. It acts as a tool for preconceived analytical purposes; the irony itself is not the point of the sociologist's endeavour, merely the means by which the presence of social circumstances can be asserted as investigable phenomena. Accordingly, the reader of constructivist sociology of science is not encouraged to dwell on the irony, far less to question how ironic effect is achieved, but instead to focus on those features of the social situation which 'make available' the irony. This kind of irony is an instrument whereby alternative accounts are contrasted but where the business of accounting and contrasting is passed over. Irony in this sense is not only a methodological convenience (Anderson and Sharrock, 1982: 18), it is a way of doing sociological analysis without attending to the difficult problems involved in description and explanation. In the social study of science, the emphasis on explaining claimed differences between accounts in terms of antecedent social circumstances presumes the problem of descriptions to be solved.

Instrumental irony is remarkably joyless.[7] I suggest this arises in part because constructivism conceives of irony as a tool for use by *anyone*. Unlike Kierkegaard's notion of irony, there is no question of relative sensitivities to instrumental irony, and certainly no question of gradual perception by the reader whereby his sense of appreciation of accounting is heightened; those wishing to work the explanatory formula of constructivism need only take irony as a device for the job. This instrumental facet of constructivist irony is neatly captured in Booth's (1974) discussion of *stable* irony. For Booth, a main feature of stable irony is that its occurrence is presumed *fixed* in the sense that 'the reader is not...invited to undermine it with further demolitions and reconstructions' (Booth, 1974: 6). This is particularly pertinent to our present case: the reader is asked not to undermine the sociologist's irony but to take it as the (fixed) starting point for sociological explanation. Booth also notes that stable ironies are *finite* in application in the sense that the reconstructed meanings (that is, the alternative accounts provided by the sociologist) are local and limited to the particular occasion chosen for analysis. This fits well with the notion that constructivist sociology focuses selectively on particular instances of scientific accounting and presumes these to be peculiarly amenable to irony (by contrast, for example, with his own account). Here, in another guise, we see the denial of the universality of the fundamental features of discourse pointed out by Garfinkel (1967); indexicality, for example, is only invoked with respect to those accounts to be ironicized (Woolgar, 1981b).

Brown's (1977) enthusiastic endorsement of irony in sociological theory turns out to be a manifesto for instrumental irony. His main argument is that irony in sociology is not merely an ornament of style, but a means for 'paradigm innovation' and even a 'logic of discovery'. He speaks of 'dramatic irony' as the main vehicle for the presentation of opposites and contrasts between images, characteristics, frameworks and events, and goes on to suggest that dramatic irony can be found in successful sociological theory because, as in a play, theory comprises the 'representation and formalisation of antagonistic ambiguity'. Yet we can see that Brown's 'dramatic irony' has marked similarities with Booth's 'stable irony'. The events or situations through which dramatic irony operates are strictly bounded. They take place within a text or during a set duration of a play. More importantly, the operation of dramatic irony depends crucially on an assumed stable relationship between play and audience. In particular, dramatic irony 'requires that the audience simultaneously perceive a multiplicity of perspectives' (Brown, 1977: 176). The audience (readers of sociological theory) is provided with foreknowledge whereby 'all action becomes infused with deeper meanings, with possibilities opposite to the intentions of the actors. And *we* are more aware of this than are the actors themselves' (Brown, 1977: 177, italics in original). The business of sociological theory, according to Brown, is to convey foreknowledge to the audience so that described actions can be seen to be other than they appear.

Instrumentalist irony assumes a fixed relationship between ironicist and audience. The ironicist assumes a measure of competence on the part of his audience whereby they can share the victimization of the actors. The subjects of sociological description are the victims of irony because they lack the foreknowledge of the sociologist and his audience. To be an accredited member of the audience, one has to match the expectations of stable irony that one neither undermines the ironicist's own account nor looks beyond the specific instances and occasions for which the irony is claimed to apply. Instrumental irony thus appeals to a sense of community: in order to partake in the irony the reader is assumed to operate as a competent member of the community who can recognize this kind of irony.

What happens if we attempt to modify the features of stable irony? In particular, what consequences follow from withdrawing the assumption that members of a fixed and recognizable community of fellow practitioners have equal access to irony? It is then that we begin to develop an appreciation of irony as *project*.

For Kierkegaard, one essential feature of irony is that the ironicist does *not* want to be universally understood (Capel, 1965: 32). Irony is recognizable by some but not by others. But more than this, the irony of which Kierkegaard writes has the quality of *bringing* a reader to awareness. Thus, Kierkegaard's irony is essentially *dynamic*; it acts in such a way that the reader moves from failing to realize the irony to seeing its possibility. More concretely, dynamic irony has the effect of making the reader take more seriously the deep flexibility of accounting procedures. Not only does he come to realize the variety of different ways in which descriptions can be received; he also comes to see the sense in which one can never know for sure.

By contrast with stable irony, dynamic irony asks the reader constantly to recognize the fragility of the ironicist's own account, how it can be undermined, and how this principle is not only applicable to the specific instance advanced by the ironicist. The joy of irony as project is in the constant change in what the reader sees, not in how any one change might be used for sociological ends.

Finally, as a brief example of what might be involved in dynamic irony, let us consider Garfinkel's well-known proclamation:

> Ethnomethodological studies are not directed to formulating or arguing correctives. They are useless when they are done as ironies. (Garfinkel, 1967: viii)

I suggest we can make (at least) three different readings of this remark. Firstly, we can take it 'straight', or as non-ironic, in which case it stands as an injunction not to engage in irony at all. The implication is that ethnomethodological studies of the kind that Garfinkel would like to see do not have an argumentative or antagonistic stance vis-à-vis other versions of the world; in particular, perhaps, the work he advocates does not aim merely to supply an alternative version of the world. The pertinent ethnomethodological slogan (attributed to Harvey Sacks) is that the world is already sufficiently full of constructions without our merely adding to them. From this point of view, constructivist sociology favours a version of irony whereby it engages in construction in order to supply the world with yet another construction.

We can also read this remark itself as ironic, both in the instrumental and dynamic senses. Hence, a second reading of the remark is in terms of *stable* irony. In this reading the message is opposite to what it appears to say. In other words, we should take it as an indication that ironies can indeed be useful, and that we should look to their strengths as a means of doing social study. The difficulty with this interpretation is that unlike constructivist irony, Garfinkel does not make explicit his preferred alternatives; this remark does not advance the availability of alternative accounts as the means for revealing the social circumstances wherein a first version has been constructed. Garfinkel's remark thus lacks the hallmark of instrumental irony whereby he would proceed to an analysis of the social contingencies of ethnomethodological work. A third reading of the extract is that it exemplifies dynamic irony. By contrast with instrumental irony it does not ask the reader to see something different than is said and to take this as the basis for sociological analysis: instead, it involves the reader in a kind of Russell paradox. If ironies are useless and this is one such irony, then this irony is also useless; in which case, no notice need be taken of it; in which case ironies may after all have some use; and this in turn contradicts the initial notion that ironies are useless; and so on. From this perspective, the reader is encouraged actively to undermine the preferred interpretation and to experience some of the deeper implications of continued undermining. The irony in this reading is not bounded by the text, nor fixed as a specific occasion for sociological work, but highlights for the reader the infinite interpretative possibilities of the text. It is dynamic irony in the sense that while not all readers might react this way, the extract has the potential to encourage a reader to move to a level of interpretation of which they were previously unaware.

Conclusion

I began by suggesting that much recent work in the sociology of science adopts a *mediative* position with respect to a fundamental methodological problem ('The Problem') of the relationship between accounts and their corresponding realities. This mediative position forms the basis for sociological analysis of science from a constructivist perspective. A brief consideration of studies in other areas of sociology shows that the constructivist sociology of science shares the basic assumptions of constructivist sociology in general.

This last observation should provide a warning against the over-enthusiastic adoption of currently available analytical schemes. Undoubtedly, we have successfully demonstrated that constructivist sociology is as applicable to the study of science as to any other substantive area. But the danger of continuing with this formula too long is precisely that we will lose any benefit to be gained from the study of the *specific* area of science. My point is *not*, of course, that we should embark on social study of science with a priori assumptions about the superiority of its methods and achievements. But, by the same token, we need to be wary of the reductionist tendencies evident in treating science in the same way as deviant behaviour, official statistics, social problems and so on. In each case, the constructivist perspective essentially derives from analyst's concerns rather than being informed by the particular phenomenon under study. This persuades me that we should now aim beyond the continual ironicizing and sociologizing of science involved in using preconceived analytical perspectives; we should ask how our study of science might inform our notion of understanding in general and how it might influence and shape our analytical perspectives. Perhaps it is now time to try and make science talk to sociology rather than the other way round.

The constructivist perspective embodies a number of theoretical tensions stemming from its attempt to embrace a relativistic epistemology with respect to selected aspects of science while exhibiting a fairly inflexible commitment to epistemological realism in its own work. An examination of the constructivist perspective shows its dependence on stable, instrumental irony; it is by virtue of this kind of irony that the constructivist sociologist 'manages' the tensions of his perspective and maintains an uneasy balance between reflective and constitutive positions while retaining elements of both in his practice.

The main focus of this chapter has been the ways in which constructivism evades or conceals the Problem with which I began. (I have been less concerned to speculate why this might be than to note how it is done.) The fact that such evasion occurs in constructivism in general is of relatively little consequence here; the political aims of the proponents of constructivism might mean that attention to the fundamentals of argument and persuasion is a less pressing concern than the demonstration that, for example, different versions of the 'same' deviant act might be 'explained' by reference to the social circumstances of their production. When applied to the social study of science, however, it seems to me that constructivism does us a grave disservice. For unless we are to be guided solely by some political motive for the 'demystification' of science, constructivism can only be a distraction from any attempt to come to terms with the fundamentals of knowledge production. Necessarily my argument is negative in the sense that while expressing deep reservations about the constructivist perspective on the social study of science, it does not advance an alternative. Indeed, at present there seems to be no ready-made alternative. (My argument is not a covert attempt to promote any of the versions of ethnomethodological practice currently on offer, even though these do have their origins in an articulation of the Problem which is missing from most discussions in conventional social sciences.) My suggestion, instead, is that we first require a reappraisal of the Problem. By contrast to the way irony is used in constructivism, the idea of irony as project is proposed as a way in which we might at least re-establish, if not celebrate, the Problem. This may be a useful preliminary to the development of a social study of science which lives up to its full responsibilities.

Notes

1. The argument here is a development of the scheme advanced in Woolgar (1981b) to address misunderstandings in Barnes's (1981) and MacKenzie's (1981) response to my critique of the widespread use of interests as an explanatory resource in the social study of science (Woolgar, 1981a).

2. Another way of expressing the same argument is to assert that any one account may have arisen from either of (at least) two underlying realities (or aspects of reality).

3. For example, the language of a particular grant proposal may be well suited to the portrayal of scientific practice *as if* it had proceeded along lines consonant with the reflective position.

4. Lynch (1982) similarly argues that the sociologist inserts a disengaged analytical framework in order to 'make out' the antecedent circumstances and their effect on the technical work of science. The mediative position I identify with constructivist sociology corresponds in general terms to what Lynch calls 'critical inquiry'. 'Critical inquiry' is done not only by sociologists but, with more immediate and consequential implications for the practical research activities, by laboratory scientists.

5. My own attempt to confront a leading scientist with 'discrepancies' in his account of the discovery of pulsars was met with the comment that any scientist

worth his salt could *see* that *in fact* the accounts were quite consistent. Clearly, ideas of 'discrepancy' and 'consistency' are no less amenable to treatment as social constructs than the accounts themselves.

6. My thanks to Doug McLauchlan for first bringing this distinction to my attention.

7. It is clearly not instrumental irony to which Kierkegaard alludes when he comments 'he who does not understand irony and has no ear for its whisperings lacks *eo ipso* what might be called the absolute beginning of personal life' (Kierkegaard, 1965: 339). Brown (1977) uses this quote as the epigraph to his chapter on irony.

References

Anderson, D. C. and Sharrock, W. W. (1982) 'Irony as a Methodological Convenience: A Sketch of Four Sociological Variations', in Wright (1982).

Atkinson, J. M. (1981) 'Ethnomethodological Approaches to Socio-Legal Studies', in Podgórecki and Whelan (1981).

Barnes, B. (1974) *Scientific Knowledge and Sociological Theory*, London: Routledge and Kegan Paul.

Barnes, B. (1977) *Interests and the Growth of Knowledge*, London: Routledge and Kegan Paul.

Barnes, B. (1981) 'On the "Hows" and "Whys" of Cultural Change', *Social Studies of Science*, 11: 481–98.

Becker, H. S. (1963) *Outsiders*, New York: Free Press.

Bloor, D. (1976) *Knowledge and Social Imagery*, London: Routledge and Kegan Paul.

Blum, A. F. (1971) 'Theorizing', pp. 301–19 in Douglas (1971).

Booth, W. C. (1974) *A Rhetoric of Irony*, Chicago: University of Chicago Press.

Brown, R. H. (1977) *A Poetic for Sociology*, Cambridge: Cambridge University Press.

Capel, L. M. (1965) 'Historical Introduction', pp. 7–41 in Kierkegaard (1965).

Cohen, S. and Young, J. (1973) *The Manufacture of News*, London: Constable.

Collins, H. M. (1975) 'The Seven Sexes: A Study in the Sociology of a Phenomenon, or the Replication of Experiments in Physics', *Sociology*, 9: 205–24.

Collins, H. M. (1981a) 'Stages in the Empirical Programme of Relativism', pp. 3–10 in Collins (1981b).

Collins, H. M. (ed.) (1981b) 'Knowledge and Controversy: Studies of Modern Natural Science', special issue of *Social Studies of Science*, 11 (1).

Collins, H. M. and Cox, G. (1976) 'Recovering Relativity: Did Prophecy Fail?' *Social Studies of Science*, 6: 423–44.

Collins, H. M. and Cox, G. (1977) 'Relativity Revisited: Mrs. Keech – A Suitable Case for Special Treatment?' *Social Studies of Science*, 7: 372–81.

Collins, H. M. and Pinch, T. J. (1979) 'The Construction of the Paranormal: Nothing Unscientific is Happening', pp. 237–70 in Wallis (1979).

Collins, H. M. and Pinch, T. J. (1982) *Frames of Meaning: The Social Construction of Extraordinary Science*, London: Routledge and Kegan Paul.

Douglas, J. D. (1967) *The Social Meaning of Suicide*, Princeton: Princeton University Press.

Douglas, J. D. (ed.) (1971) *Understanding Everyday Life*, London: Routledge and Kegan Paul.

Fishman, M. (1978) 'Crime Waves as Ideology', *Social Problems*, 25: 531–43.

Frye, N. (1957) *Anatomy of Criticism: Four Essays*, Princeton: Princeton University Press.

Garfinkel, H. (1952) 'The Perception of the Other: A Study in Social Order', unpublished PhD dissertation, Harvard University.

Garfinkel, H. (1967) *Studies in Ethnomethodology*, New Jersey: Prentice-Hall.

The Glasgow Media Group (1977) *Bad News*, London: Routledge and Kegan Paul.

Gusfield, J. (1976) 'The Literary Rhetoric of Science', *American Sociological Review*, 41 (1): 16–34.

Gusfield, J. (1980) 'Foreword' in P. Conrad and J. W. Schneider, *Deviance and Medicalisation: From Badness to Sickness*, St Louis, Mo.: Mosby.

Gusfield, J. R. (1981) *The Culture of Public Problems*, Chicago: Chicago University Press.

Harvey, B. (1981) 'Plausibility and the Evaluation of Knowledge: A Case-Study of Experimental Quantum Mechanics', pp. 95–130 in Collins (1981b).

Hindess, B. (1973) *The Use of Official Statistics in Sociology*, London: Macmillan.

Kierkegaard, S. (1965) *The Concept of Irony* (trans. by L. M. Capel), Bloomington: Indiana University Press.

Knorr-Cetina, K. D. (1981) *The Manufacture of Knowledge: Toward a Constructivist and Contextual Theory of Science*, Oxford: Pergamon.

Knorr, K. D. and Knorr, D. W. (1982) 'From Scenes to Scripts: On the Relationship between Laboratory Research and Published Papers in Science', in Woolgar (1982).

Latour, B. and Woolgar, S. (1979) *Laboratory Life: The Social Construction of Scientific Facts*, London and Beverly Hills: Sage.

Law, J. (1977) 'Prophecy Failed (for the Actors)!: A Note on "Recovering Relativity"', *Social Studies of Science*, 7: 367–72.

Lynch, M. (1982) 'Technical Work and Critical Inquiry: Investigations in a Scientific Laboratory', in Woolgar (1982).

MacKenzie, D. (1981) 'Interests, Positivism and History', *Social Studies of Science*, 11: 498–504.

Mulkay, M. J. (1979) *Science and the Sociology of Knowledge*, London: George Allen and Unwin.

Pfohl, S. J. (1977) 'The "Discovery" of Child Abuse', *Social Problems*, 23: 310–24.

Podgórecki, A. and Whelan, C. J. (eds) (1981) *Sociological Approaches to Law*, London: Croom Helm.

Pollner, M. (1974) 'Sociological and Common-Sense Models of the Labelling Process', pp. 27–40 in Turner (1974).

Spector, M. and Kitsuse, J. I. (1977) *Constructing Social Problems*, Menlo Park, California: Cummings.

Turner, R. (ed.) (1974) *Ethnomethodology*, Harmondsworth: Penguin.

Wallis, R. (ed.) (1979) 'On the Margins of Science: The Social Construction of Rejected Knowledge', *Sociological Review Monograph*, 27.

Weinstein, J. (1982) 'Irony and Technology: A Qualitative Technique for Applied Social Science', *Social Science Quarterly*, in press.

Woolgar, S. (1981a) 'Interests and Explanation in the Social Study of Science', *Social Studies of Science*, 11: 365–94.

Woolgar, S. (1981b) 'Critique and Criticism: Two Readings of Ethnomethodology', *Social Studies of Science*, 11: 504–14.

Woolgar, S. (1981c) 'Documents in Researcher Interaction: Some Ways of Making Out What is Happening in Experimental Science', paper presented to conference on Communication in Science, Simon Fraser University, 1–2 September.

Woolgar, S. (ed.) (1982) 'Laboratory Studies', theme section in *Social Studies of Science*, 12 (4): 481–558.

Wright, E. L. (ed.) (1982) *Poetics*, Brighton: Harvester.

Subject Index

Notes on Contributors

Barry Barnes is Reader at the Science Studies Unit, University of Edinburgh. He has published widely on sociological theory and the sociology of scientific knowledge. His most recent books include *Interests and the Growth of Knowledge* (1977) and *Natural Order* (ed. with S. Shapin, 1979), as well as articles in *Philosophy of the Social Sciences* and *Social Studies of Science*.

Daryl Chubin is Associate Professor in the Technology and Science Policy Program and School of Social Sciences at Georgia Institute of Technology. He is co-author of *The Cancer Mission: Social Contexts of Biomedical Research* (1980) and author of *Research Circles, 1972–1981* (forthcoming), as well as many articles in the sociology of science.

H. M. Collins is senior lecturer in Sociology at the University of Bath and Convenor of the British Sociological Association's Sociology of Science Study Group. His publications include *Frames of Meaning: The Social Construction of Extraordinary Science* (1982), and as editor, a special issue of *Social Studies of Science* on Knowledge and Controversy (1981).

Harold Garfinkel is Professor of Sociology at the University of California, Los Angeles. He is author of *Studies in Ethnomethodology* (1967) and has recently launched a series of ethnomethodological studies of scientific work in *A Manual for the Study of Naturally Organized Ordinary Activities* (1982).

Karin D. Knorr-Cetina is Professor of Sociology at Wesleyan University. Her most recent publications include *The Manufacture of Knowledge* (1981), *The Social Process of Scientific Investigation* (ed. with R. Krohn and R. Whitley, 1980), and *Advances in Social Theory and Methodology* (ed. with A. Cicourel, 1981), as well as articles in *Theory and Society*, *Knowledge*, and *Social Studies of Science*.

Bruno Latour is currently at the Centre de Sociologie de l'Innovation at the École des Mines in Paris, where he does research in the sociology of science. He is author of *Laboratory Life: The Social Construction of Scientific Facts* (with S. Woolgar, 1979), as well as of a series of articles on this subject in *Fundamenta Scientiae* and the *Sociology of the Sciences Yearbook* (1980). He is also an editor of the science and technics bulletin, *Pandore*.

Eric Livingston is a graduate student in the Department of Sociology at the University of California, Los Angeles. He is currently completing his dissertation on 'An Ethnomethodological Investigation of the Foundations of Mathematics'. He has collaborated with Harold Garfinkel and Michael Lynch on the paper 'The Work of Discovering Science Construed with Materials from the Optically Discovered Pulsar', *Philosophy of the Social Sciences* (1981).

Michael Lynch is currently an adjunct assistant professor in Sociology at the University of California, Los Angeles. He took his PhD in the School of Social Sciences, University of California, Irvine, was a Visiting Post-doctoral Fellow at the Centre of Criminology, University of Toronto (1978–9), and an NIMH Post-doctoral Fellow in community mental health evaluation, UCLA (1979–81). His PhD dissertation has been published as *Art and Artefacts in Laboratory Science* (1982).

Michael Mulkay is Professor of Sociology at the University of York. He has written on sociological theory, art and aesthetics, and widely on the sociology of science. His most recent publications include *Science and the Sociology of Knowledge* (1979) and 'The Sociology of Science in East and West', *Current Sociology* (with V. Milić, 1980).

Jonathan Potter is working on the analysis of social psychologist's discourse at the University of York. He has published a number of articles and is joint author (with M. Wetherell and P. Stringer) of *Social Texts and Contexts: Literature and Social Psychology* (forthcoming).

Sal Restivo is Associate Professor of Sociology at Rensselaer Polytechnic Institute. His most recent publications include 'Mathematics and the Limits of the Sociology of Knowledge', *Social Science Information* (1981) and 'Parallels and Paradoxes in Modern Physics and Eastern Mysticism, Part II', *Social Studies of Science* (1982).

Steve Woolgar took his MA and PhD at Cambridge University. He is currently lecturer in Sociology and Social Anthropology at Brunel University. He is co-author of *Laboratory Life: The Social Construction of Scientific Facts* (1979) and has edited a theme section of *Social Studies of Science* on Laboratory Studies (1982).

Steven Yearley is currently Elizabeth Wordsworth Junior Research Fellow at St Hugh's College, Oxford. He read natural sciences and social and political sciences at Cambridge University and submitted his doctoral dissertation on the sociological analysis of scientific argumentation to the University of York. He has published in *Philosophy of the Social Sciences*.